Celtic Plant Magic

A Workbook for Alchemical Sex Rituals

JON G. HUGHES

Destiny Books
Rochester, Vermont

Destiny Books
One Park Street
Rochester, Vermont 05767
www.InnerTraditions.com

Destiny Books is a division of Inner Traditions International

Library of Congress Cataloging-in-Publication Data

Hughes, Jon G., 1951-
Celtic plant magic : a workbook for alchemical sex rituals / Jon G. Hughes.
p. cm.
Includes index.
ISBN 0-89281-924-3
1. Magic. 2. Plants. 3. Magic, Celtic. I. Title.
BF1623.P5 H84 2002
133'.258—dc21
2002013454

Printed and bound in the United States at Capital City Press

10 9 8 7 6 5 4 3 2 1

This book was typeset in Cheltenham with Optima as the display typeface

Text design and layout by Mary Anne Hurhula

Decorative border and illustrations on pages 72, 100, 109, 143, 149, and 151 by Damien Switzer

To my family—

Yve, my wife, my constant companion and supporter.

Peter, whose music and love have been

with me all my life.

Liz, for her patience and endurance.

Sophie, in whom we all invest our future.

Contents

Part 3

The Druidic Workshop

Part 4

Workings and Rituals

Introduction

In planning the research for this book, I began with the intention of comparing the plant-based preparations, rituals, and magic of the Welsh Druidic tradition with those of the broader and infinitely more documented spiritual traditions practiced all over the world. Before I had progressed very far, I came in contact with the works of ancient and modern alchemists. The part of their work that has been maintained for millennia involves the use of materials from the plant kingdom. This immediately drew my interest. Likewise, my fascination was spurred by the alchemical search for immortality and the involvement with sexual ritual, as both have their place in the Druidic tradition.

For many, the very word *alchemy* conjures up images of fiery furnaces engaged in the age-old quest to make gold from less valuable ores and metals. Hoping to find a common thread between the Druidic tradition and alchemy, I researched the books and experiments of the Lesser Circulation. The Lesser Circulation deals with the herbal processes of alchemy, as opposed to the much better known Greater Circulation, which relates to the mineral (metallic) realm and its reputation for converting base metals into gold. The latter has no equivalent in the Druidic tradition. Both the Lesser and Greater Circulations also exist as metaphors for the creation of a pure, elevated spirit from the basic, unrefined spirit contained within us all.

Alchemy, to a large extent, involves a range of brutal, intensely forceful processes in its efforts to elevate the substances it employs to ever greater levels of purity. As I continued to explore the tenets of alchemy, I grew more and more convinced that although these harsh methods may have a place in the extraction of ores and

the amalgamation of metals, they are wholly inappropriate for the plant kingdom. It also was obvious that they bore little resemblance to the Druidic tradition of gentleness and nurturing taught to me throughout my lifetime as a practicing Druid.

In my quest for a greater understanding of the more subtle aspects of alchemy, I began to see a correspondence between alchemy and the Druidic tradition that at first had eluded me. It was in part based on their practices and partly in the deep, underlying philosophy enshrined in both traditions. My mind became attuned to both conventions and I was able to reconcile the harsher practices of alchemy with the gentler, more sympathetic practices I had been taught within the Druidic tradition.

Although there is to my knowledge no significant convergence of alchemy and Druidic practices—their histories differ greatly, and, as we shall see, their methods differ dramatically—there is an underlying accord between the two disciplines and an intriguing harmony between the two philosophies. The result of my realization of this harmonization is an exploration of the use of plant extracts and compounds, derived predominantly from trees and flowers as opposed to herbal extracts, and their use within the Druidic tradition as remedies, elixirs, and magical potions. The following chapters explore the three progressive steps involved in plant magic: the identification and harvesting of appropriate materials, their careful and meticulous preparation, and their ritual application and benefits. As it is my area of expertise, I have focused on the ancient Druidic practice of sex magic to demonstrate the potency of these arcane compounds and rituals.

Writing this book has been a journey of discovery and revelation. By seeking a greater understanding of alchemy and the Druidic tradition, and by questioning my own conditioned understanding, I have arrived at a new point in my relationship with my own belief system. I sincerely hope that in reading this book and becoming involved in some of the practices it reveals, you will achieve a fuller understanding of the world in which we live and the suppressed potential within each one of us.

The Use of Welsh Language

Much of what is contained in these pages has been handed down through an oral tradition and little, if any, of it has appeared in print before. In fact, the whole of the body of Druidic lore has been maintained solely by an oral tradition. Although this creates an atmosphere of secrecy and mystery, the most profound blanket of secrecy has been laid upon the craft of the Druid not by the selective system of "recruiting" initiate Druidic priests or priestesses or the personal "one-to-one" training methodology but by the fact that this oral tradition is maintained exclusively through the use of the Welsh language.

The vast majority of people who read this book will have little, if any, working knowledge of either the modern or the ancient version of Welsh, and while some practitioners like to include elements of arcane or unknown languages in their rituals to create atmosphere and mystique. I believe that understanding takes precedence.

In the process of researching the alchemical aspects of this book, I was confounded on many occasions by the use of ancient languages long since fallen from popular use. Fortunately for me, many of the commentators on these ancient texts have provided translations for most of this strange and unfamiliar language. As the history of alchemy spans such a great period and covers such a wide geographical area, it is inevitable that it has been recorded in a vast range of ancient and modern languages.

I have, therefore, deliberately refrained from using the modern or ancient forms of Welsh in the main text of this book. You will find occasional Welsh words, along

4

The Use of Welsh Language

with some Irish words, where there are no English equivalents, or where it is necessary to give alternative meanings, as in the names of flowers and trees, for example. I have also included a number of Latin, Greek, and Hebrew words when it may assist the reader to find similar references in other publications.

While it is true that the Welsh language in particular has an enchanting musical sound and that its individual words and phrases have a very powerful and deep meaning, I also believe that these may be translated into English without any serious loss of subtlety—certainly with no more loss of meaning than the ancient form being translated into modern, vernacular Welsh.

One of the greatest dangers I have found among my pupils is that when they come up against words that are not part of their everyday vocabulary, and they are unsure of their true meaning, they attempt to build a concept around the word, when the true purpose of the original word was to explain a concept that may have escaped them.

It is imperative that all the members of your Gathering understand completely what is being said and done during your rituals and also throughout their training. The explanation and understanding of the complicated philosophies and methodologies involved is difficult enough without confusing them with unnecessarily obscure language.

A Cautionary Note

The contents of Celtic plant magic are based on practical experience and traditional Celtic plant lore. The foundation of both of these elements is the ability to confidently identify the plants to be used and a thorough understanding of the properties and potential affects of the plants that are being employed.

In the days of the ancient Druids there were no alternatives to these magical treatments but nowadays the situation is reversed and Celtic plant magic is the "alternative" or complementary therapy to mainstream scientific medicine.

Scientific advances have given us a much deeper knowledge of the causes of many of the illnesses that impinge upon our everyday lives. By understanding the cause, science has, in many cases, enabled us to develop a cure. This does not conflict with the theory of Druidic plant lore because, as you will see as you read this book, the Druids readily assimilated any new knowledge into their practices and would have welcomed modern science with open arms.

Druidic plant lore, however, is based upon a much simpler understanding of the cosmos and the people who inhabit it, an understanding that has both scientific and spiritual aspects in an equal balance.

In reading this book you may decide to use some of the treatments on yourself or others, but please do not do so without first consulting your physician and asking his or her guidance. Never attempt to diagnose or treat illnesses without first seeking medical advice. Since I, as the author, have no direct control over how any reader may apply the treatments outlined in this book, or any way of assessing the individual reader's ability or understanding of its contents, neither I nor the publishers are able to accept responsibility for any results arising from following the information and instructions contained in this book.

Part 1

Alchemy: Its Relationship to the Druidic Tradition

Initial Research

The notion of using plants in some form or another as remedies and medicines has been with us for millennia. Almost every known ancient civilization had its own form of curative and preventive medicine based on the use of plant compounds and extracts.

Many of these medical traditions became extremely sophisticated, and a clear trail of development may be seen from some of these ancient traditions to today's scientific approach to both mainstream and alternative or complementary medicines. We shall see as we progress that much of today's wisdom has been derived from the knowledge, skills, and craftsmanship of these ancient herbalists and their use of the products given to them by nature.

The Druidic tradition, too, is rich in its knowledge and use of plants as remedies and medicines, but in this case it extends this knowledge to the use of plants in the preparation of potions, elixirs, and tinctures employed specifically in rituals and magic workings. Unlike many of the other ancient traditions, Druidic lore retains all of the old, arcane knowledge and focuses as much on the spiritual and mystical elements of the use of plants as it does on the chemical and medicinal aspects.

History suggests that in many traditions much of this spiritual aspect and the inseparable mystical practices associated with it have been abandoned in favor of the purely chemical or "scientific" benefits of selected medicinal plant species.

The fact that many of the drugs in current use are plant derivatives and that many more continue to be discovered as medical science progresses can only be applauded. But I find it a constant source of disappointment that Western medical science refuses

to accept or even investigate the possibilities of the benefits the spiritual and mystical aspects of these ancient traditions may have to offer.

As we shall see, many other traditions have a far more open-minded viewpoint. Many of the Eastern practices in particular accept both the physical and spiritual benefits of the plant kingdom in a more holistic approach to curing and preventing illness. Only in relatively recent times has our Western society even begun to acknowledge that there are other ways to address our physical and mental ailments and needs, but even so, few of us are prepared to embrace what may be considered "unscientific" alternative practices.

Throughout its existence, one of the most durable and invaluable aspects of the Druidic tradition has been its ability to adapt to the needs of the people it serves. If we add to this its willingness to accept and assimilate new ideas without abandoning its essential traditions or its vast store of knowledge, we can begin to understand why this arcane tradition has survived unscathed for so many years.

It was with this in mind that I decided, before setting down what I consider to be the most important elements of the use of plants within the Druidic tradition, that I would explore as many other traditions as possible. My aim was to see which, if any, would validate the knowledge given me of the oral Druidic tradition. In doing this, I would also discover if I could expand or develop the tradition I knew and understood by incorporating complementary elements from other practices and customs. The result of this research has been extraordinary, and the journey has been as rewarding as the destination.

I began my research by looking at the various ways in which many of the world's oldest cultures used the products of the plant kingdom within their societies. This initial research led me to many of the oldest civilizations known to us today. It involved accounts from most continents, from aboriginal Australia to the far north of Europe; from Africa to the Orient; from the oldest civilizations of the Americas to those of Greece, Egypt, and ancient Rome; and from the ancient traditions of the Jews.

My research took me from the dawn of history, through the rise and fall of some of the greatest civilizations known to humanity, right up to the present day. It ended in my workshop here in Ireland with months of detailed experimentation and a wealth of knowledge that has come together to form the core of this book.

10

Alchemy: Its Relationship to the Druidic Tradition

As I explored these various traditions, one word more than any other kept jumping from the pages of the books and articles I read. This word eventually opened up a new understanding for me and placed my entire forty years' experience of Druidic practice in a new light. It made me reconsider my original plans for this book and gave me a focus that I hope will be as illuminating to you as it has been for me.

And the word that made such an impact on my plans and inspired a whole new area of involvement for me? *Alchemy!*

Alchemy and Ancient Herbal Traditions

The Druidic tradition that I have become so familiar with over the years is abundant in its knowledge of the plant kingdom. This is only what one would expect from a tradition that has its origins within paganism and natural magic. Such an ancient natural lore would, of course, be rich in its understanding and application of the bounties of nature, using all of the resources available from the natural landscape within which it evolved.

I was soon to discover that Druidism was not unique in the way it utilized the natural resources at its disposal and that alchemy shared many of its ideas, materials, and beliefs with the Druidic traditions of Wales, Ireland, and northern France. However, there appears to have been no direct historical link between the Druidic tradition and the development or practice of alchemy. It is, in fact, unlikely that any of the Celtic nations would have had significant contact with alchemy prior to its introduction into Europe through Islamic Spain during the Middle Ages.

Even so, as I continued to research the diversity of ancient herbal traditions, the practices of alchemy surfaced time and time again. Not only that, but I also began to observe an increasing similarity between the practices of alchemy, which are very different from what I had originally understood, and the Druidic tradition I had known for the greater part of my life. The more detail my research uncovered, the more the similarities grew. As my insight into alchemy developed, the more eager I became to learn more.

What was it, then, that I found so appealing and motivating? These traditions had developed on the opposite side of the globe, within totally unconnected societies, yet they looked to the plant kingdom for their raw materials and involved practical and mystical elements in their workings just as I had been taught. The fundamentals are very, very similar and there is much to be gained from comparison and the combination of both traditions.

There are, of course, also many differences. For example, the plants involved are from very different species, and the methods of working differ significantly. We shall explore later these differences and similarities. There is, however, one major difference between the two that captured my interest.

The Druidic tradition has, since its beginnings, been maintained and developed through an oral tradition. Lore was passed on to a chosen successor, from generation to generation. Until relatively recent times, little if any of the true tradition has been recorded in any written form whatsoever.

Even now, as we experience a renewal of interest in Druidic practices and paganism in general, very little of the true tradition appears within the innumerable books currently being published. Many are based on either the romantic notion of the Druid in the long white robe, golden sickle in hand and crowned with mistletoe, or the cultural bardic tradition, which is and always has been a far cry from the practical Druidism with which I grew up.

The Druidic tradition taught to me is the product of generations of personal training and learning by Druidic master and student. Usually both are members of the same extended family and live within the same community. Training is given through a unique personal dialogue and by example, presented by the master in a way particularly designed to suit the individual needs and abilities of the student. Nothing is standardized, nothing is written down; the tradition remains an oral one, changed and adapted to the generation and times in which it is being applied.

In contrast, the traditions, ethos, and practices of alchemy have been recorded in infinite detail over the past twenty-five hundred years. Each philosophical theory, each concept, and the processes and results of every experiment are meticulously recorded and the product of this combined body of knowledge provides us with our current understanding of the alchemist's science and art.

Most of the modern books dealing with Druidic history and the apparent ancient Druidic practices tell us (incorrectly) that it takes between seven and fourteen years for the student to become an accomplished, initiated Druidic master, priest, or priestess.

The true tradition tells us that seven "ages" or "periods of learning" are required to achieve full understanding and initiation into *all* the disciplines of the Druidic tradition.

Each period of learning is unique to the individual initiate or student. Some individuals may complete their training in as little as two to three years; others may take an entire lifetime. The time taken depends on the aptitude of the student, the ability of the Druidic master, and how much time each can dedicate to teaching and learning. There is no limit imposed; nor are there any awards for completing the training in double-quick time. It is a question of mutual agreement and compatibility of student and teacher. Thus, it is easy to see that with the only form of teaching being through direct contact between student and master and with no textbooks or reference material available, it can be a very time-consuming journey to become a Druidic master.

Many students find it extremely difficult to commit the entire body of knowledge to memory. None is allowed to take notes or draw permanent diagrams to help. Nothing may be permanently recorded during the entire period of training, and even after initiation, only certain pieces of information may be preserved in writing, such as significant dates, certain time-related charts, and records of processing dates.

Imagine, then, my excitement when I began to read centuries-old texts describing the very same kinds of practices I had been taught, but in this case written by an alchemical master on the other side of the world. Imagine, too, my astonishment at seeing detailed illustrations of equipment and processes that I had committed to memory many years before in the belief that this knowledge was the sole property of Druidic scholars. Had I actually been an alchemist all these years without realizing it?

The answer would turn out to be no. It was much later when my initial excitement, tempered with conflict, gave way to a greater understanding of the original Druidic tradition I had been taught. Researching alchemy would raise my understanding of Druidic practices to another level and give me insight into some of the "missing theories" taken for granted within the received wisdom of the Druids.

In order to share this experience with the reader, it is necessary to begin at the beginning by being aware of the origins and history of the art and science of alchemy.

13
Initial Research

A Brief History of Alchemy

This section is by no means a definitive history of the development of alchemy. There are innumerable publications covering this subject in much more detail than I have room to do here. It is designed instead to give the reader insight into some of the most influential alchemists, their work, and the contribution they have made to the existing body of knowledge.

To explore the history of alchemy in greater detail—it is a fascinating and illuminating subject—I suggest you begin with the more contemporary commentaries before reading what copies of the original texts you may be able to obtain.

For me, the initial difficulty was knowing where to begin. The greatest difficulty was knowing when to stop. For the purpose of this book, we shall begin our account in ancient Egypt.

The majority of academics would agree that alchemy began its history in Alexandria as a synthesis of Egyptian sacred mysticism and ancient Greek philosophy. The origin of the very word *alchemy* was the ancient Arabic *Al-kemia,* meaning "the black land," a common name for Egypt at the time.

The father of alchemy was said to be the Egyptian god of wisdom, Thoth, called Hermes in Greek. So strong is the influence of Hermes on the origins of alchemy that it is still referred to as the hermetic tradition, the way of Hermes, or the hermetic art.

Hermes Trismegistus (thrice great or thrice blessed) was reputedly an alchemist, sage, and philosopher. History tells us he was the bearer of secrets and knowledge. In his day his fame was so great and spread so far that he was simply known as "the Egyptian." He is credited with writing the *Hermetica,* a collection of mystical, philosophical writing upon which all Middle Eastern and Western alchemy is based. He also wrote the Emerald Tablet, the most profound document of the hermetic tradition. These writings later became the cornerstone of medieval alchemy in Europe.

Many of these early writings tell us that alchemy was chiefly devoted to manufacturing or discovering an elusive substance that would not only transmute base metals into gold or silver but also provide the means to prolong human life indefinitely. The search for this elusive substance has preoccupied alchemists ever since.

14
Alchemy: Its Relationship to the Druidic Tradition

In an effort to understand the structure and meaning of nature and thereby use this understanding to transmute metals and prolong life, alchemists have made major contributions to today's knowledge of science, medicine, chemistry, and philosophy.

Magic also played a dominant role in early alchemy, and every Egyptian alchemist would also have been a magician. The most famous of these was Imhotep, the renowned Egyptian high priest, physician, and magician who features in many accounts of ancient Egyptian history and remains a cult figure even today. The secrets of the ancient Egyptian practice of mummification may have been part of the developing Egyptian alchemical art as well.

Although alchemy may have seen its beginnings in Egypt, it undoubtedly took many of its ideas from what was then the "new" Greek philosophy. At the time, many of the Greek philosophers were developing what were to become the first established chemical theories, and by the fifth century B.C.E. Empedocles had advanced the theory that all things are composed of air, earth, fire, and water. Aristotle was later to add ether as the fifth component.

This theory would profoundly influence the work of alchemists for the next two and a half millennia.

Aristotle made further contributions to the fundamental theories of alchemy by suggesting that "nature and God are working toward an end; striving for what is perfection" and that "[e]verything is striving to gain perfection, that ultimate union of the All in the One."

Aristotle tells us that each of the four original elements has two characteristics:

Fire	=	hot and dry
Air	=	hot and moist
Water	=	moist and cold
Earth	=	cold and dry

He then explains that there are therefore really only two characteristics—namely, hot and moist. The remaining two are simply their opposites.

Hot is the product of fire and moist is the product of water. Therefore, the most important of the elements are fire and water. One opposes the other. One is combustible, the other is liquid. One is male, one female. Here we gain our first glimpse of the balance and harmony of opposites, a principle of profound significance, as we shall see later.

Alexandrian alchemy was also influenced by the melting pot of eclectic philosophical and religious movements that were burgeoning at the time. Neoplatonists, Gnostics, Egyptian priests, Jewish rabbis, Pythagoreanists, and the later Christian cults, all had their effect on the alchemy of the day.

Women also played an important role in the developing art and science of Egyptian alchemy. Two women in particular had such a significant impact that their legacy remains with us today. The alchemist Cleopatra (not the queen of the Nile) created works on cosmetics and poisons, developed standard weights and measures and became an experienced alchemist in the hermetic tradition.

The other woman was Maria the Jewess, also known as Maria Prophetissa, who worked to combine the Egyptian hermetic theories with her own tradition of Jewish alchemy. Also an inventor of apparatus and working equipment, Maria invented a bath containing water to gently heat the vessels immersed in it. Now known as the *bain-marie* (Marie's bath), the same apparatus may be seen in almost every laboratory and commercial kitchen in the world. Through her inventiveness and skill as an alchemist, Maria made a major contribution to both alchemy and chemistry, not to mention the worldwide food industry.

The last significant writer of Egyptian alchemy was Stephanus of Alexandria. In the seventh century C.E. he wrote the final Egyptian Tracts on alchemy, which, by that time, had been undermined by the conquest of the Egyptians by the Greeks, then the Romans, and the eventual arrival of Christianity.

And so it was in the latter half of the seventh century C.E., as Egypt was taken by the Muslims, that alchemy took up a new significance as it was introduced to Arab culture.

At the same time as Egyptian alchemy began its development in Alexandria, a process of alchemical development was happening in ancient China, alongside a curiously simultaneous appearance in India. Over the years there has been much speculation on this apparently unconnected development of alchemy at more or less the same moment in time in Egypt, China, and India.

Each of these traditions has a similar story of the introduction of an ancient knowledge of alchemy by a visiting race, giving rise to theories of alchemy being the science of Atlantis or having been introduced by some super-race that has since become extinct. Some even suggest the introduction of alchemy by travelers from another planet.

Whatever the truth may be—and it is beyond the scope of this book to explore the various theories, however intriguing they may be—the fact remains that around 2,500 years ago something stirred the interest of these diverse civilizations and inspired the simultaneous, yet independent, development of alchemy.

Chinese alchemy is said to have developed from Taoism, China's oldest philosophy. The alchemy of the Chinese school is based entirely on this ancient Taoist philosophy and every Chinese alchemist is therefore a Taoist. Alchemy, however, is not an essential part of Taoism; rather it is an accepted part of this ancient and sophisticated belief system.

As with the Taoists, Chinese alchemists were in search of the secrets of longevity, immortality, and the processes of the transmutation of metals. Alchemists still refer to this epic pursuit as the *Magnum Opus,* the Great Work.

The first known practicing Chinese alchemist was Tsou-Yen, who, around 350–270 B.C.E drew on the Taoist principle of duality, the yin and yang (the fire and water or male and female of the Egyptian tradition) and based the Chinese alchemical philosophy on the three fundamental principles of the cosmos as defined by Taoism. These fundamentals are:

- **The chi.** The universal energy that is apparent in all aspects of the cosmos as the life force.
- **The Tao.** The Tao, or the Way, is divided into two fundamentals, the yin and the yang. The harmony of the universe and of each individual's existence depends on the harmonious balance of the yin and the yang.
- **The concept that all matter and processes in the cosmos are made up of five principal elements.** These are not the elements of early Western philosophy (fire, water, wind, and air), as contained within the Druidic tradition, but rather unique elements of the Taoist, and therefore alchemist, philosophy. They are defined as *sense, essence, vitality* (Ching), *spirit* (Shen), and *energy* (Chi).

17
Initial Research

At the heart of Chinese alchemy is the belief that this complex interaction and interdependency among all the aspects of the cosmos comes together to make up the whole, or the Tao. The pursuit of the Great Work is achieved through two traditions, the *exoteric* and the *esoteric*. Chinese alchemists called these two traditions *Wai-tan* (the outer elixir, or the exoteric) and *Nei-tan* (the inner elixir, or the esoteric).

Wai-tan looks for this outer elixir in the world of nature in an effort to use nature's gifts of plants and minerals to prolong life. It is the practical tradition, involving experiment and workings within the physical substances of the cosmos. It has played an important and undeniable part in the history and development of science and was arguably the birthplace of modern chemistry. There is little doubt that this early experimentation and its subsequent development resulted in the discovery of many new substances and the invention of a wide range of scientific processes.

Nei-tan focuses on the inner elixir and sees the physical transformation of the Wai-tan as a metaphor for the transformation and refinement of the base human into an elevated spirit being. Taking much of its philosophy from Taoism, it has in turn made a major contribution to the understanding of the natural world and the human psyche.

Eastern alchemists had a name for the elusive agent that could bring about these transformations of both the inner elixir and the outer elixir and thereby aid longevity and produce immortality: They called it the pill of immortality. In the West it was to become known as the *lapis philosophorum,* the philosopher's stone. The Alexandrians of ancient Egypt first called it the stone of light. Here the Egyptian alchemist Zosimus describes it: "This stone which is not a stone, this precious thing which has no value, this polymorphous thing which has no shape, this unknown thing which is known by all . . ."

The fabrication or discovery of this pill of immortality or philosopher's stone became the prime goal of all alchemists, in the belief that this substance, the purest in the universe, is so perfect that it could instantly elevate base metal to gold. In the same way, this agent of ultimate purity and power could raise the base human to the spiritual being through the process of enlightenment and eventual immortality.

Alchemy has been defined in many ways: "the art and science of transformation," "the raising of vibrations," "the elevation of basic substances," to name just a few. However it is described, alchemy has two major goals—to transmute base metals into gold and to produce or discover an elixir to prolong life. Although it has also frequently (and correctly) been described as the forerunner to modern chemistry, it was, and still is, much more than that.

In addition to its practical facets, it is an art and science concerned with the body, spirit, and mind and therefore reaches far beyond the ubiquitous images of furnace, reaction vessel, and the relentless pursuit of infinite wealth.

Meditation, purification by fasting, and ritual cleansing all play an important part in the preparation preceding any alchemical work and the Chinese alchemists inherited their methods from the trance and ecstasy techniques of the early Taoist shamans. The Chinese alchemists also emphasized the importance of sex as a means to health and longevity. It is one of the most important aspects of the Nei-tan alchemy of the inner elixir as it mirrors the harmony of the cosmic yin and yang.

The Chinese tradition maintains that in order to prolong life, one must follow nature and, therefore, to have sex is to go with the flow of nature and increase the vitality of both partners. A similar tradition is maintained in the Indian alchemical tradition, and both these traditions have a strong resonance within the Druidic tradition.

As the Chinese alchemists were refining their science, a similar yet independent school of alchemy was developing in India. There, alchemy is a subsidiary of the cult of Tantrism, which in turn is one of the schools of Hinduism. The tantra emphasizes the female aspect of nature and employs many aspects of sexual symbolism within its workings.

Ancient Indian Hinduism is based on the spiritual powers of Shakti (female) and Shiva (male) which represent consciousness and energy. The Indian school of alchemy sought to recombine these forces to recover the original unity of the cosmos and thereby live forever. (The same philosophy may be observed in the Chinese school of alchemy, with its attempt to bring together the male and female principles of yin and yang into a unified harmony.) The Vedas, written between 1500 and 800 B.C.E., became the cornerstone of Hinduism. Their contents lead us to believe that Indian Hindus were searching for an elixir of immortality as far back as three thousand years ago. In India, this pill of immortality or philosopher's stone was called the Sphadick stone.

Indian alchemy developed alongside ayurveda, the science of longevity, one of the oldest existing systems of medicine and "lifestyle" in the world. Ayurvedic medicine uses mainly products of the plant kingdom and maintains that all substances are made up of five original elements: earth, water, fire, air, and ether (the same theory that Aristotle introduced to the Egyptian alchemists).

As the Indians traveled to China and introduced Buddhism, they brought back many of the Chinese alchemical beliefs. As a result, alchemy in India developed at a great speed. The father of Indian alchemy was a Buddhist by the name of Nagarjuna. He reputedly extended his own life to the age of one thousand by alchemical means. During this extended lifetime he wrote the first notable Indian book on alchemy, the *Rasasatnakara,* around 200 C.E.

For the most part, Indian alchemists used the same techniques and methods as their Chinese counterparts but stressed the intuitive aspect of its development along with the use of yogic visions. However, in the south of India a second school of Indian alchemy was developing alongside the Siddha medicine tradition. Both Siddha and ayurvedic systems share beliefs, but Siddha concentrates on the use of minerals, salts, and metals as opposed to the ayurvedic emphasis on the use of herbs and plants.

Siddha and ayurveda represent the practical aspects of alchemy, the outer elixir, the exoteric, or the Wai-tan of the Chinese tradition. Tantra is concerned with spiritual alchemy, the inner elixir, the esoteric, or the Nei-tan of the Chinese tradition.

As the Chinese and Indian traditions of alchemy continued to advance, the doctrines of the Alexandrian hermetic tradition were being carried into the Islamic world through Iraq. Hermes was already known to the Muslims as the prophet Idris and was acknowledged by all three main branches of Islam, Shiite, Sunni, and Sufi.

Khalid ibn Yazid established himself as the first major Muslim alchemist, but by far the most noted was Jabir ibn Hayyan (720–815 C.E.), known in the West as Geber. As a Sufi, Jabir was an Islamic mystic, and his main influences appear to have been Hermes, Pythagoras, Socrates, Plato, and Aristotle.

He cultivated Aristotle's theory that all minerals contain two characteristics, or exhalations—"moist" and "dry" vapors—and identified them in the form of mercury and sulfur. These are not the mercury and sulfur of modern-day chemistry, but rather specifically alchemical definitions of the same words. This theory of vapors continues to be at the core of alchemical work.

Jabir maintained, as did Aristotle, that matter is composed of four elements—earth, fire, water, and air—with the qualities of dryness, heat, moisture, and cold, each in differing proportions. By altering these proportions, matter may be transmuted from one form to another. Jabir believed that this transmutation may be achieved by using a grand elixir, the philosopher's stone. In his search for the grand elixir, Jabir devised his famous method of balances. He developed balances for minerals, vegetables, animals, and stars. These balances attempted to create an equilibrium between the external appearances (the exoteric) and the hidden inner reality (the esoteric).

Jabir also had a fascination for numbers and occult geometry, and his related theories became more and more complex and cryptic, making little sense to anyone but Jabir himself. This confusing and convoluted writing gave rise to the word *gibberish,* now applied to anything that seems impossible to understand.

Jabir played a major role in introducing Egyptian alchemy to the Arabs and in forming the foundation for European alchemy, which was to follow some time later. His interpretation of Aristotle's theory of the four elements and his additional theory of mercury and sulfur were revised once more by the Persian alchemist Abu Ali al-Husain ibn Sina, known in Europe as Avicenna.

Agreeing with Aristotle's four elements, Avicenna added a third substance—salt—to Jabir's mercury and sulfur as the constituent parts of all matter. He believed, like Jabir, that substances might be transmuted by varying the amounts of these constituent parts through the employment of an "elixir."

Another famous Islamic alchemist and physician who made a significant contribution to alchemy was the Persian Abu Bakr Muhammad ibn Zakariya, or Al-Razi, known in Europe as Rhazes. Rhazes was a renowned healer of his day and wrote a famous treatise on smallpox and measles, which is still referred to in medical history texts. His main interest was in the practical work of the outer elixir, and he was responsible for defining the first classification of substances into animal, vegetable, and mineral. Through a combination of his medical and alchemical work, Rhazes made a huge contribution to both medical science and chemistry.

Following the Muslim conquest of Spain in the eighth century C.E., Eastern alchemy was imported to Europe from Syria, Persia, and Iraq, and the new synthesis of

European alchemy was born. With them the Muslims brought the new vocabulary of Eastern alchemy, all of which remains with us today. Just a few examples are

alchemy *(Al-kemia)*	the name for Egypt; literally "the Black Land"
alcohol *(Al-kohl)*	original meaning, "fine powder"
elixir *(Al-iksir)*	medicine
alembic *(Al-anbiq)*	the head of the still, as known to all alchemists
athanor *(Al-tennur)*	the furnace, as known to all alchemists

European alchemy began its history in Spain at the turn of the first millennium and more particularly in Córdoba, where the first prominent European alchemist, Abu'l Qasim Maslamah ibn Ahmad, known as Al-Majriti, was born (later he was called simply "the One from Madrid"). His work focused primarily on the outer elixir and he wrote mainly on practical alchemy and laboratory techniques.

The alchemical tradition was maintained in Spain for centuries and included the works of such prominent practitioners as Muhammad ibn Umail, the Jewish philosopher Rabbi Moses ben Maimon (Maimonides), and the cabalist Moses of León.

By the thirteenth century C.E., European alchemy was well established and Albertus Magnus, known as Dr. Universalis, was producing numerous alchemical manuscripts. His most famous pupil, Saint Thomas Aquinas, was also a believer in the transmutation of metals.

In Britain the intellectual and magician Roger Bacon began his works on alchemy. Later called Dr. Mirabilis, he emphasized the need for experience over argument and described alchemy as an experimental science. His practical alchemy produced many benefits, particularly in the area of medicine.

Ramon Lull, Dr. Illuminatus, was born in Majorca around 1230 C.E. and went on to develop his famous Lullian Art. Much used by later alchemists, the Lullian Art is based on geometric symbols and letters, which he alleged reflected the structure of the universe. Lull also maintained that in addition to the four elements or essences, there is a fifth essence—the quintessence—found in all matter, which is responsible for their generation, activity, and eventual corruption. Much of the work of the Lullian adepts involved the attempted manipulation of this quintessence in order to increase its activity in the material world.

Another medieval alchemist involved in the exploration of the quintessence theory was Arnald of Villanova, who was credited as the first to distill alcohol from wine and then use it to dissolve plants and herbs as a means to extract their quintessence. This is a direct parallel to the Druidic tradition.

He also used magic in his treatments for illnesses, just like the Egyptians and Muslims before him, another parallel with the Druids. Arnald agreed with Jabir and Rhazes that ill health is caused by the upset balance of the humors, which may be rebalanced by the use of magic and specific elixirs. This theory has also been carried forward and forms one of the fundamental principles of modern homeopathy and the famous Bach Flower Remedies (see page 45).

Arnald's writings also give us a method of separating the elements of matter using a ferment and then recombining them to form the elixir. This too is fundamental to Druidic plant magic. His works have been revived time and time again, particularly in the sixteenth and seventeenth centuries, and it is in the practical work of Arnald of Villanova that we see the first major parallels between the hermetic art and the practical traditions of the Druids.

It is worth noting that although Arnald's work began in the mid-thirteenth century, the Druidic tradition was well established by the time of the first written accounts of their activities by the Romans in the first century B.C.E. and the even earlier account by the Greeks in the mid-fourth century B.C.E.

In Britain, Elias Ashmole (reputed to have written under the name Geoffrey Chaucer—the Ashmolean Museum, Oxford, England, bears his name) further developed Bacon's work, along with Sir George Ripley and the influential Thomas Charnock of Feversham.

In France, Nicolas Flamel and his wife, Perennelle, two of the most famous names in the history of alchemy, claimed to have made the great elixir, upon being initiated into the secret by an anonymous Jewish cabalistic master.

23
Initial Research

Almost a century after Flamel died, probably the most celebrated alchemist in history was born near Zurich, Switzerland, in 1493. Philippus Aureolus Theophrastus Bombast von Hohenheim took the name Paracelsus, meaning "beyond or greater than Celsus," the first-century Roman writer on medicine and healing. Paracelsus created his own school of alchemic practice, which he called Spagyric, from the Greek *spao* (to divide) and *ageiro* (to bind or combine), based on the ancient alchemical methodology of "dissolve and coagulate."

Along with his fellow spagyrists, he pursued the universal solvent, which he called the *alkahest*. He also expanded the mercury, sulfur, and salt theory of matter to become the core of subsequent alchemical practice. Paracelsus believed that by using magic it was possible to influence the hidden forces of the cosmos and emphasized the role of "energies" in the healing process. Both of these principles may also be seen as fundamental in the Druid credo.

He proclaimed the *Tria-Prima* (fundamental Trinity) of salt, sulfur, and mercury, representing the body, the soul, and the spirit, respectively, and maintained that if these three fundamentals were not correctly balanced in the body, illness would result. His assertion that "like cures like" has not only been the foundation of contemporary alchemy but has also formed the basis of a wide range of alternative or complementary medicines.

Paracelsus revitalized alchemy and gave it a new direction. His research and experimentation also revolutionized traditional medicine. His followers include all the prominent alchemists of the sixteenth and seventeenth centuries, as well as the legendary alchemist Basil Valentine (Basilius Valentinus).

Many of Paracelsus's followers met together in secret societies and the Rosicrucians, or The Brotherhood of the Rosy Cross, developed primarily as an alchemical group. Members of the Rosicrucians included the English philosopher Robert Fludd, Francis Bacon, Robert Boyle, and Isaac Newton, who spent much of his life studying alchemy.

European alchemy is said to have reached its peak in the late sixteenth century and early seventeenth century when the city of Prague became the focal point of alchemical practice. At the time, Prague could boast more alchemists than any other city in Europe. Among these were Michael Maier, a notable figure in the Rosicrucian movement; Oswald Croll, a prominent cabalist; the physicist Johannes Kepler; the English cabalist John Dee; and the famous mystic Jacob Boehme. Each made a significant contribution to the developing ferment of European alchemy.

The eighteenth and nineteenth centuries saw a major suppression of alchemy in general. Suffering from the ridicule of the emerging new sciences, alchemy became less popular and European alchemy in particular began to divide into two groups. One group was composed of alchemists who pursued a purely scientific approach to discovering new processes and compounds, and it may be argued that these "scientists" were the true ancestors of today's chemists. The other group followed a more metaphysical approach and maintained the more mystical elements of the original alchemy. This group is part of the unbroken chain of alchemists who remain to this day.

It may not be surprising, then, that Marie and Pierre Curie, the discoverers of radium, were reputedly involved in alchemical practices at the time.

The advent of the twentieth century saw a revival in alchemical theory and practice, possibly as a result of the work of the New Zealand scientist Ernest Rutherford. Prior to Rutherford's work it was generally held that elements could not be altered by transmutation. Through pioneering work in his laboratory in England, Rutherford transmuted nitrogen into oxygen and hydrogen. By doing so, he established the now accepted theory that transmutation is possible. In fact, it has now been identified as part of the natural process of decay. As a consequence of Rutherford's work, a number of new elements, not found in the natural world, have been created in the laboratory using nuclear energy.

Rutherford's work revitalized the interest in alchemy, as it suggested that the ancient alchemists might well have known more than they had previously been credited with. Indeed, Rutherford himself claimed that it was possible to produce gold by the transmutation of platinum.

This period saw the foundation of the Alchemy Society of France by F. Jollivet Castelot, the later establishment of the Paracelsus Research Society in the United States by the famous Frater Albertus in the early 1970s, and the Philosophers of Nature in France by Jean Dubuis.

It also created an atmosphere conducive to the work of such renowned alchemists as Fulcanelli and Archibald Cockren, the psychoanalyst Carl Jung, and Frenchman

Armand Barbault, who worked primarily with plants to create his "liquor of gold." Barbault applied alchemical techniques and methods to medical practice. His use of plants and particularly his use if dew may have been the starting point of Edward Bach's work; it certainly has resonance in the Druidic tradition.

We must now consider the philosophical and practical achievements that have brought alchemy to its present-day sophistication before we begin our comparison of the alchemical art with the Druidic tradition.

The Workings of Alchemical Preparations

The workings of alchemy are divided into two principal areas of activity: the Greater Circulation and the Lesser Circulation.

The Greater Circulation refers to the alchemical workings of the mineral kingdom. It involves the use of minerals and metals in the pursuit of the philosopher's stone. This is what most people instantly imagine when one mentions the work of the alchemist—the quest to transmute base metals into gold using the *lapis philosophorum,* or philosopher's stone. As we have seen above, this is a vastly oversimplified definition of the alchemist's work; the Greater Circulation involves itself with both the outer and inner elixirs.

Although I continue to find the subject of the Greater Circulation truly fascinating, there is no equivalent to be found in the Druidic tradition.

The Lesser Circulation refers to the workings of the plant kingdom, and it is the methods and processes of the Lesser Circulation in relation to the Druidic tradition that we shall be concerning ourselves with for the remainder of this book. In particular, we shall be exploring the area of alchemical workings within the Lesser Circulation concerned with the preparation and production of medicaments through the methodology that Paracelsus called spagyria. We shall see as we progress that the two activities from which the term derives—to divide and to bond—form the beginning and end of every alchemical working, as they do in this same area of work within the Druidic tradition.

Spagyric Theory

All spagyric medications are prepared in the same way, using three stages: separation, purification, and cohobation (recombining the separated parts). By preparing their medications in this way, spagyric practitioners believe they are actively intensifying the potency of the plants being used while releasing additional healing powers in a way that is not possible by any other method. They believe that the more usual methods of preparation such as infusions and tinctures extract only part of the potential curative properties of the plant from which they are prepared. Spagyric remedies, on the other hand, release the entire curative potential of the plant as a result of their unique method of manufacture.

Alchemy has been variously described as the "raising of vibrations" and "the elevation of basic substances," and it is in this context that spagyrics believe that their preparation methods release the full potential of the plants they use.

Within the realm of alchemy, spagyrics employ a similar range of plants for the same effects as most other curative and preventive systems that have their basis in natural medicine. This range of plants is, of course, much wider than that used in Druidic tradition, as the history of alchemy has covered a much wider area of plant habitats and encompasses the use of many plants beyond the reach of the Druid/Celtic cultures.

Spagyrics use the medicinal parts of the plants they harvest. These may include the bark, roots, seeds, flowers, leaves, fruits or berries, or combinations of these. The plants are gathered at various seasons of the year, depending on their individual life cycle and overall planetary influences. The selected parts of the harvested plants are then used as the *prima materia,* or raw material, for the subsequent processes of manufacture.

As we have seen above, this manufacturing process begins with separation, but first we must ask, What are we going to separate and for what purpose?

All substances belong to one or another of the three kingdoms or principalities: animal, vegetable, or mineral. Our focus is on the vegetable kingdom.

The first step in the spagyric process is to extract the essence from the plant employed. This essence contains the alchemical mercury of the plant with its sulfur adhering to it; the remaining plant matter contains the plant's salts. We have seen previously that all substances, including plants, contain mercury, sulfur, and salt. This alchemical mercury is not what is normally understood as mercury or quicksilver. The sulfur is not common sulfur or brimstone. Nor is this salt common sodium chloride. Each has a separate and specific alchemical meaning removed from the accepted "scientific" interpretation of the name.

In most of the alchemical processes involved in the Greater Circulation, it becomes necessary to separate the sulfur from the mercury in order that the spagyric adept may work with all three alchemical substances separately. This is not the case in the plant processes of the Lesser Circulation, wherein the spagyric practitioner may work equally effectively with the combined mercury and sulfur liquid (the extracted essence) together with the salts contained in the remaining plant matter.

At this point it is important to note a few of the essential principles of the Lesser Circulation, principles that are for the greater part consistent with Druidic tradition and practices.

The essence (or quintessence) of the vegetable kingdom is the same in all plant life. It is the common force or energy of all plants. It does not vary from species to species. (The Druidic tradition maintains that different parts of the plant contain different "manifestations" of this force or energy. See page 59.) The salt or ashes produced differ from one plant to another. Each plant yields a unique salt with its own unique attributes. These two principles hold equally true for all essences (mercuries) obtained from the animal and mineral kingdoms.

Following the extraction of the essence, the remaining plant matter, or *caput mortum* (dead head), as alchemists call it, is burned to ashes (calcinated) in order to extract the remaining salts. The calcinated ashes are then reunited with the previously extracted essence and, following a period of digestion and maturation, the alchemical medicine or elixir is formed.

We can see, then, that all alchemical elixirs are produced through the three main steps of the spagyric process: separation, purification, and cohobation, or reunification. It is apparent, therefore, that alchemical elixirs are not the result of natural phenomena but of artificial production.

This is the theory of the preparation of spagyric medicines. Let us now look at a practical example of the preparation of an elixir from any common herb.

Practical Processes

Unlike Druidic plant lore, alchemical practice allows for the use of fresh or dried plants. Whichever form is used, the first stage as we have seen above is the separation of the extract. This may be achieved in any of three ways.

- **Maceration.** The fresh or dried herb is steeped in liquid for an extended period.
- **Circulation.** The fresh or dried herb is percolated in a fashion similar to coffee percolation.
- **Extraction.** The fresh or dried herb is placed in a specialized extraction system such as a Soxhlet Extractor, a specialized piece of laboratory equipment used mainly in the process of extracting essential oils.

Any of these methods may be used to obtain the extract, but for the sake of simplicity we shall adopt the maceration method for our example.

The appropriate herb is first ground to a fine consistency, either with a mortar and pestle or by rubbing it firmly between the hands. The ground herb is then placed in a suitable glass vessel, one with a tight lid, and covered with the maceration liquid, or *menstruum,* which will extract the essence. The most common menstruum is any form of strong alcohol (40 percent or more by volume), usually brandy (called "spirits of wine" by alchemists). The vessel is now sealed and set aside in a warm place to allow the menstruum to do its work.

After two or three weeks the menstruum will have taken on the greenish hue of the herb, showing that it has achieved the extraction of the essence. The clear liquid is then poured off into another vessel for later use. This is the herb's essence, containing its properties of mercury and sulfur.

The remaining herbal matter, containing the salts of the herb, is placed in a flameproof dish and ignited. As it has been steeped in alcohol, it will burn readily and quickly reduce to black ashes. These black ashes are then repeatedly heated and ground until they become a light-colored powder. This is the process of *calcination.*

The calcinated powder is then recombined with the essence (the salts are recombined with the mercury and sulfur) by placing the calcinated powder into the vessel containing the essence and tightly sealing the vessel to prevent the escape of any vapors. The vessel is then set aside in a warm place for about two weeks to allow the liquid essence to "digest" the salts of the calcinated ashes. This process is called *digestion.* This completes the manufacturing procedure, and the herbal elixir and medication are ready for use.

By using this method of preparation, spagyric practitioners maintain that the elixir produced is more potent and efficacious than any other form of herbal medicine.

Now, how do the history, theory, and practical processes of alchemy relate to the ancient and contemporary Druidic tradition, and what may we learn from alchemy that will enrich our understanding of Druidic practices?

Harmonious Associations

When I began to focus my research on the details of the spagyric methods of the alchemical tradition, I was instantly overwhelmed by its similarities to the Druidic practices I had grown up with. I was, and still am, amazed at how both these traditions have survived and developed for so long, yet there is no mention of either the Druid's work in the history of alchemy or the alchemist's work in the history of the Druids. There is, in fact, no equivalent word for *alchemy* in the Welsh language, although in modern Irish it may be translated as *ailceimic.*

So let us begin our comparison of the two traditions by looking at some of the main differences between them. This will lead us to a fuller understanding of how each may—given the correct concordance—inform and influence the other.

Western alchemy has, since the Middle Ages, progressively shed its mystical and magical aspects in favor of a more physical, scientific approach—in other words, abandoning the inner elixir for the outer elixir. Although retaining some of its spiritual elements and continuing to acknowledge the transmutation of base metals into gold as a metaphor for spiritual elevation and enlightenment (the outer elixir as a metaphor for the inner elixir), it remains preoccupied with chemical experiment and the science of transforming and elevating matter.

Having said that, no alchemical experiment is ever completely devoid of some form of spiritual and moral dimension. True alchemists continue to purify themselves before they begin their experimentation, and there are still established fasting and cleansing rituals used by each adept in preparation for his or her work. There are, however, very few modern adepts who continue to make use of the spells and invocations of the ancient alchemists.

32

Alchemy: Its Relationship to the Druidic Tradition

Given the religious and political history of Europe leading up to and during the Middle Ages, the Inquisition, and the persecution of those not subscribing to the Christian faith, it is not surprising that alchemy in Europe abandoned a large portion of its original pre-Christian, mystical beliefs. Some areas even developed a strange style of Christian alchemy, merging the arcane pre-Christian practices with mainstream Roman Catholic doctrine. The results of this imaginative coalition may still be seen today.

In contrast, the Druidic tradition has retained the union between the physical and the mystical in the belief that the two are inseparable and that neither may be effectively employed without the other. While accepting the physical curative properties of the plants it employs, it also believes that the physical (chemical) benefits of potions and remedies can reach their full potential only if they are prepared and administered by mystic ritual.

This being the case, Druidic potions of all kinds are used in many applications other than purely medicinal remedies. They have a fundamental role to play in most Druidic rituals, and their use stretches far beyond their curative capabilities.

Later, we shall see just one example of how Druidic potions derived from the plant kingdom are used to energize, stimulate, and enhance sexual potential and performance during sex magic rituals. From this example you will gain an understanding of how Druidic potions may be employed in sympathy with the mystical and spiritual elements of the tradition.

The Elevation of Basic Substances

All alchemical texts speak of the elevation of natural substances. They describe the work of the Greater Circulation as the elevation of base metals into gold and the Lesser Circulation as the elevation of the natural products of the plant kingdom into energized substances and the vegetable stone. The ultimate goal of both circulations is the manufacture or discovery of the elusive philosopher's stone.

It may well be that this attempt to improve on nature is based on a doctrine of Aristotle, who maintained that all things, including nature, are striving toward perfection. If this were the case, it would appear that, given enough time, all things would reach a state of perfection through the process of natural progression. It has been suggested that the work of the alchemist in his or her workshop is really just an effort to speed up this natural process in order to arrive at the perfect state (the philosopher's stone) without having to wait for nature to take its course.

Whether alchemical work is intended to elevate nature's products or accelerate nature's development, it appears that in some cases the alchemist is contradicting and working against the natural balance of the cosmos. It could also be argued that the alchemist's "practical" work in the workshop, where he or she applies him-or herself to the development of the outer elixir, in fact contradicts the search for the balance and harmony of nature apparently sought by the work of the inner elixir. It is for the reader to explore this thesis and arrive at his or her own conclusion.

As a Druid I consider it impossible to improve on nature's products and unthinkable to contemplate speeding up the course of nature. The Druidic tradition that I

know holds nature to be in a constant state of perfection and to be moving in a cyclic continuum that may not be interrupted by anything or anyone.

The purpose of Druidic work within the plant kingdom (the equivalent of the spagyric's Lesser Circulation) is to release and concentrate the latent energies and attributes of the plants with which we work. There is never any suggestion that our work actually elevates or improves anything that nature provides. The work is concerned with the attempt to understand what is already inherent in nature and uses nature's gifts in sympathy with nature's laws.

The gifts of the natural cosmos are immensely rich, complex, sophisticated, and at all stages *complete*. By this I mean that even if we consider nature to be progressing in the form of evolution (and that too is a thesis for the reader to consider), each manifestation of this evolutionary process is complete in itself as it appears. To gain some understanding of this natural cosmos is the ultimate goal of every Druid, not to attempt to elevate something that is already sublime and perfect.

Let's look at an example that we are all familiar with, that of our own individual "evolution" from single cell to adult person. In normal circumstances this is, as we all know, a wholly natural process, one of nature's greatest and most amazing gifts. If we look at this process in a Druidic light, it must not be interrupted in any way. We may, however, look at the evolving person at any stage of his or her development, search for the individual's strengths and attributes, and gently nurture them for the benefit of the individual and the rest of society as a whole.

When a person's life comes to an end, it is only the corporal being that is lost. The individual's personal energy is reunited with the collective energy and her store of knowledge and experience is passed on to others. In this way, although each life cycle is finite, it forms a part of nature's evolving continuum.

In contrast, it could be said that it is the work of the alchemist to take the newborn baby and, through a series of brutal physical and profoundly mystical processes, transform that baby instantly into a physically and mentally enhanced mature adult (improving, elevating, and accelerating nature).

Of course, the Druidic tradition strives to understand the processes involved in the physical and mental development of the individual and to some extent enhance them in the light of the knowledge and experience it has at its disposal. Druidism also seeks to address and remedy any impediments to this development but never to elevate or accelerate nature itself. This may well be an overly simplified analogy, but it serves to demonstrate how the two traditions differ in relation to their perceived ability to "alter" nature.

I am convinced that it is this belief in the inability to improve upon nature, or to speed up its progress, that provides us with the reason that Druidism has no equivalent to the Greater Circulation and does not involve itself in the attempt to raise or elevate base metals into gold. Practitioners of the Druidic herbal lore, however, do share some of their fundamental methods and techniques with the alchemical tradition and in particular with the techniques of the spagyrist. For example, among other things, the preparation of Druidic potions, remedies, and complexes follows the same three-stage process that is used by the spagyrist: the separation, the purification, and the amalgamation (the equivalent of the alchemical cohobation).

The techniques of the alchemists, and in particular the work of the spagyrist adepts, though with similar foundations, diverge from those of the Druidic tradition in some very important ways. As I continued my research, I was struck by the brutality of the methods alchemists employed. I felt offended by the use of such harsh incineration and the application of excessively high temperatures to "force out" the substances they were searching for. It all seemed to be such an unnatural process when compared to the much more gentle and sympathetic procedures of Druidic plant lore. Even so, I could not ignore the similarities between the two and became convinced that somewhere there would be a common ground where some form of combined practice would benefit both traditions.

Thus, maybe at this point we should look a little more closely at the actual techniques employed and compare the methods of preparation and motivation of the spagyrist and the Druid.

We have seen how the spagyrist goes about preparing his or her herbal elixir. We understand the theory of the five elements (earth, water, air, fire, and ether), the three components of matter (the *Tria-prima,* or fundamental Trinity), mercury, sulfur, and salt, representing spirit, soul, and body, respectively.

In the Lesser Circulation the mercury and sulfur remain joined in what is referred to as the essence. This *essence* contains the life force of the plant and is the same in all plant life (the spirit and soul of all plants). The separated salt—that is, the body of the plant—differs from one plant to another, and it is these salts that contain the various attributes of each plant within the plant kingdom. These three components are first separated into the essence and the salt, then purified and finally recombined to form the elixir, or medicament.

The separation is achieved by maceration (soaking), circulation (heating and condensing), or extraction (a process similar to percolation). The purification occurs by further evaporation and incineration; the cohobation is achieved by combining the previously purified components to form the elixir.

The spagyrist makes no attempt to influence the work or the products by using spells, incantations, or any form of ritual during their preparation. This, then, suggests that although there are spirit and soul components contained within the material of the spagyrist's elixir, there is no spiritual energizing or potentializing process involved in the manufacture. The elixir *may* then work only on a material plane and have limited effect on the internal energy of the individual using it.

In contrast, Welsh Druidic lore maintains that there are four elements (earth, water, air, and fire) and that these are manifestations of the *collective energy,* the single cosmic energy that unites all of nature. Everything in Creation contains a part of this collective energy in the form either of *internal energy,* as in animals and humans, or as the *latent energy* contained in plants and natural inanimate objects. This internal or latent energy is returned to the singular collective energy once the life cycle of the person/animal/plant is completed.

When considering the plants used in Druidic lore, we see that they are composed of two constituent parts: the *latent energy,* as described above, which we can see is the same for all plants, and their *attributes,* which are unique to each plant.

The attributes of each plant may be further divided into the *physical attributes*—these are the purely "chemical" properties of the plant as used in scientific pharmacology—and the *magical attributes,* whose effect is beyond our current scientific understanding but nevertheless equally efficacious.

The two subdivisions of the attributes work in constant harmony, which is not surprising as they form part of the same plant. We can, however, choose to use one or other of these natural phenomena to a lesser or greater extent in our work without damaging their natural harmony.

To recap, every plant has three components that are at our disposal:

- **Latent energy.** Common to all plants and to ourselves, as we all draw our energy from the common collective energy.
- **Physical attributes.** Unique to each plant and may be employed as medications.
- **Magical attributes.** Available to us in our work to channel as remedies, potions, and influences.

How, then, do we *release* the potential of this latent energy, *extract* the physical attributes, and *channel* the magical attributes of these plants in order to use them for our work? This is achieved through a combination of the practical manufacture and ritual energizing of what are called the plant's *complex* and the plant's *incense.*

The complex may, in some ways, be compared to the spagyrist's elixir. It is the sum total of all of the chosen plant's beneficial components—its energies, its physical benefits, and its magical benefits. It is this complex, and its corresponding incense, that we employ in all our remedies, potions, spells, and intentions. Unlike the spagyrist's elixir, the complex also has spiritual and magical aspects and is used in a much wider range of applications.

In order to create our complex, we must first extract the *cardinal essences* of our selected plant. As we shall see, each plant has either two or three cardinal essences.

Following the harvesting of the chosen plant, its *cardinal components* are separated. These are the various individual components of the plant that contain its range of energies together with its physical and magical attributes. These components vary according to the type or part of the plant we use. For example, in the case of flowers, we separate the petals from the flower head. These provide us with the two cardinal essences of the flower. In the case of trees, we separate the leaves, bark, and wood of our harvested branch. These will provide us with the three cardinal essences of the tree.

The initial stage in extracting the cardinal essences is *leaching,* in which the first part of the essence is steeped out of the plant. This yields the *leached essence.* The second stage is called *fermentation,* during which the second, deeper attributes of the plant are extracted by fermentation within a natural must. This yields the *fermented essence,* along with the residual, almost exhausted, plant matter *(the incense).*

The leached essence and the fermented essence are then combined *(unification)* to form the two (or three) cardinal essences. The incenses are stored for subsequent use in conjunction with the essences.

The cardinal essences of the plant are stored separately for a period of maturation and recombined only during the ritual or working for which they are destined. It is only at this stage, when the cardinals are recombined to form the complex and the corresponding incenses are combined and heated, that the full potential of the plant is made available. We shall look at this process in great detail later (see page 164).

During the process of creating the Druidic complex there are a series of rituals, which are absent from the spagyrist's preparation techniques. These are placed at various stages of the process and acknowledge the *separation* and *recombination* of the component parts of the plant. The first ritual is at the time of harvesting, when we separate the harvested branch or flower, for example, from its donor plant. The second takes place as we separate the cardinal components of the harvested branch or flower. The third is the ritual unification of the leached and fermented essences to form the cardinal essences. The fourth and normally the final ritual is the amalgamation of the cardinal essences and the heating of the incense during the eventual ritual or working for which it is employed.

You will already see that this technique is a complicated one, requiring dedication, concentration, and a great deal of patience. It involves both the physical creation of the complex and its spiritual or magical empowerment. The entire creative process (called the *complex refinement*) enshrines a great respect for nature and employs only natural processes. It is harmonious with the seasons of nature and uses only that which is provided by nature. It is governed by the time it takes for these natural processes to run their course and makes no attempt to accelerate or improve on the natural forces of the cosmos.

Refinement, in the context of the complex refinement process, does not suggest improvement. It describes the process of cultivating the overall qualities, both physical and magical, of the plant and channeling them in a way that may be beneficial. The Oxford Dictionary defines the word *refined* as "Characterised by polish, elegance or subtlety," and the words *lluniaidd* (elegant) and *cyfrwys* (subtle) are used constantly in this context throughout the modern Welsh Druidic tradition as well as in many other schools of natural magic.

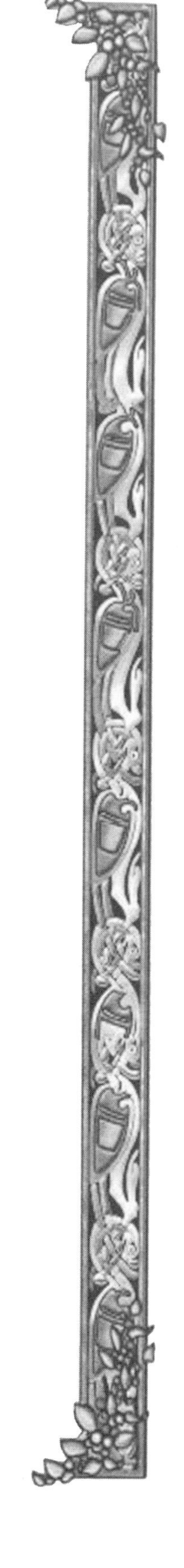

Are Druids Actually Alchemists?

So far we have seen that the traditions of alchemy and Welsh Druidism share many of their fundamental beliefs. Among these are:

- the simple but profound belief that the plant kingdom provides us with the means to influence and remedy many of the physical, mental, and spiritual ills within both individuals and society as a whole;
- the equally simple belief that there are two realms of activity required in order to address these ills: the spiritual (magical) and the physical, and the inner and outer elixirs, the esoteric Nei-tan and the exoteric Wai-tan of the Chinese tradition;
- the theory of the four basic elements, earth, water, fire, and air and the fifth alchemical element of ether, which may correspond to the Druidic collective energy;
- the latent energy of the Druidic tradition, shared by all plants, may well equate to the alchemical plant "essence" of combined mercury and sulfur—the common spirit and soul that alchemists believe are shared by all members of the plant kingdom;
- the physical and magical attributes of Druidic plant lore, unique to each plant species, may also equate to the body or salt of the plant as defined by the alchemist;

- all of the aspects of the plants listed here may be extracted by a remarkably similar three-stage process (in the case of the alchemist, separation, purification, and cohobation; in the case of the Druidic tradition, separation, purification, and amalgamation); and
- the techniques for separation, in some cases, are the same in both traditions; the purification techniques vary, as does the process of amalgamation (cohobation), but the underlying principle remains very much in tune.

What is missing—or rather what has been abandoned to a great extent within the alchemical tradition—is the emphasis on the spiritual (magical) aspects of the work. Conversely, there is no equivalent to the work of the Greater Circulation within Druidic lore. Nor is there a real equivalent to the philosopher's stone, the ultimate goal of the alchemist's Great Work. Or is there?

At this stage it is difficult to conclude whether Druids are actually alchemists (spagyrists, to be more accurate). We can assume, however, that there has been very little, if any, contact between the ancient Druids of the Celtic races and the alchemists of the Egyptian, Chinese, Arab, or any other ancient school. That alchemy arrived in Europe and the Celtic nations at a time when the Celtic pagan religions and the influence of their Druidic priests and priestesses was in decline suggests that none of the alchemical traditions would have had an effect on the arcane systems and beliefs of Druidic plant lore.

Before we can address this question in its full light, we must look in more detail at how the Druidic tradition creates and employs its plant complexes, the theory behind their use, and what benefits may be expected from their application. As the Druidic tradition does not have the benefit of the vast wealth of written text available to the alchemists, we must for the very first time commit Druidic lore to print. Historically, Druidic lore is maintained through an oral tradition, so all of what follows is singular in its content.

For the time being, then, we will leave our task of comparing these age-old traditions in favor of exploring just the Druidic component. We shall do this in a way that will allow the reader, should he or she wish, to facilitate or enact any or all of the rituals and workings being described. We shall return to our work of comparison once we have completed our exploration of the Druidic plant lore tradition.

The Principles of Arriving at the Complex and the Incense

The ancient Druids used the variety of plants and trees available to them in a unique way, employing not only the physical benefits that the plants may provide, in the same way as many other herbal traditions, but also the spiritual attributes held within the plant. This was, and still is, achieved by two principle and inseparable techniques: first the gentle extraction and refinement of the plant's physical benefits in the form of "complexes" and second, the spiritual energizing of these complexes in order to release and focus the natural spiritual attributes of the plant. These arcane techniques are, by definition, quite detailed but by no means beyond the capabilities of the average reader. We shall then begin our exploration of these techniques by looking at the refinement process, the first stage of preparing our complex.

An Introduction to the Refinement Process

The objective of our work will be to craft the cardinal essences, which, during the course of our ritual, will be combined to produce the specific complex that we require for our needs. Part of this process will also produce the incenses that will, in conjunction with our complex, enhance and energize our ritual. For the purpose of our exploration, we shall be looking at some of the specific complexes and incenses used in the working of sex magic rituals (see page 221).

43
The Principles of Arriving at the Complex and the Incense

To begin our understanding of the materials and processes involved, we need to define exactly what each of these various components is and the part each plays in our ritual, but perhaps first I should explain exactly what the *ritual* is.

I am often asked to explain the difference between the ritual, the working, and the ritual working, and the only really accurate answer to this question is that it depends entirely on the context in which the words are used and on the individual using them. Some practitioners and adepts speak of ritual workings, others of working rituals, yet more of workings in the preparation of rituals. For my part, I can only explain the way in which I was trained to use these words and therefore how they will be used throughout this book.

The ritual is the enactment of a predetermined sequence of events in a stylized fashion, with the intention and expectation of producing an accurately defined outcome. Therefore, if I and a number of my Gathering decide that we wish to undertake a particular ritual in order to project and bind a particular spell, we come together and enact a predetermined sequence of events designed to achieve that particular spell's projection and binding.

The next time we wish to achieve the same results, we will repeat the same sequence of events and in this way—by repeated enactment—the sequence of events establishes itself as the ritual.

The ritual may, and often does, seem quite theatrical in its enactment and this is deliberate on behalf of the priest or priestess facilitating it. The purpose of ritual in this context is to coordinate the activities and progress of the members of the Gathering, which happens quite naturally as the participants eventually become familiar with the sequence of the ritual. In the same way that the ritual facilitates the physical progress of the Gathering's activities, it also synchronizes the Gathering's spiritual and emotional progress. In the case of the sex magic rituals we'll be looking at later, it also synchronizes the progress of sexual arousal and works toward the desired collective orgasm.

The theatrical-like presentation or facilitation also plays a role in the collective understanding of the ritual, allowing the priest or priestess to communicate not only by verbal means, but also through the nonverbal communication or body language of the facilitation. This again is extremely important in sex magic rituals, where switches in focus between the sensual and the spiritual elements need to be clearly emphasized and communicated at the appropriate times to the Gathering as a whole.

The working is a more commonplace activity that is frequently very unceremonious indeed. It refers primarily to the activities undertaken in the workshop in preparation for the ritual or in the manufacture of compounds, potions, complexes, ritual tools, and so on, that may be stored for future use. There is, by definition, no direct element of magic or of the spiritual in these activities. Most workings are conducted by the Druidic priest or priestess, adept, or practitioner in the isolation of his or her workshop or the seclusion of a forest grove. On such occasions the priest or priestess may be accompanied by his or her assistant, apprentice, or student—workings provide ideal opportunities for the aspiring practitioner to learn the craft.

The fermentation of essences, the grinding of compounds, the filtering of liquids, all these "manufacturing" processes may be called workings. Only when there is the requirement of some form of magical or spiritual element in these workings do they become *ritual workings*—that is, a working that includes a ritual as a part of its process.

A typical example of this is the *cleansing* of ritual tools and equipment. There is, of course, the physical cleansing of the items involved, but to complete the cleansing the item must also be spiritually cleansed. This is done through a brief spiritual cleansing followed by a further spiritual energizing, yet another spiritual element.

So this cleansing activity when viewed as a whole consists of both the physical working and the cleansing ritual. It may therefore be called a *ritual working.*

The Gathering, in its form as a collective noun, is a group of practitioners assembled for the purpose of enacting a ritual. It is also the name given to the period at the beginning of an assembly when the participants come together, or gather, for the ritual.

Having covered the definitions of these more general terms, it is now worth returning to our original objective as outlined in the introduction on page 42 in order to define some of the less familiar terms it contains.

As we will discover later, each individual species within the plant kingdom yields two or three cardinal essences. Each of these unique essences contains some part of the energy and attributes inherent in the species. The processes involved in the extraction of these cardinal essences and how these essences are subsequently used are explained in greater detail in part 3.

45
The Principles of Arriving at the Complex and the Incense

At the appropriate point in the ritual, the cardinal essences produced from each plant are brought together to form the complex. It is this complex, in its newly reunited and highly energized condition, that becomes the first of the prime elements at the core of the ritual.

These cardinal essences are extracted in the form of liquids and, once combined in the form of the complex, are used mainly as libations, or potions, or applied to the skin. In order to use all of the potential energies and attributes contained in the specific plant, we must also release the potential contained within the solid material remaining following the extraction of the liquids.

These plant solids are dried, reunited, and heated on charcoal as incense during the ritual. The heating of the incense frees the potential of the solid plant material, and it is this releasing of the plant's energies and attributes that forms the second of the prime elements at the core of the ritual.

The concept of extracting and using the potential curative properties and beneficial attributes of species within the plant kingdom is by no means unique to the Druidic tradition. Similarities may be drawn to many areas of ancient and modern herbalism, the more modern practice of homeopathy, along with the ancient practices of the alchemists as detailed earlier. There are, however, as we have seen, fundamental differences that make the Druidic tradition stand apart from the other practices mentioned.

Having already looked at the more ancient forms of herbalism and alchemy, we now will look at some of their more modern counterparts. A number of modern alternative or complementary medical practices speak of harnessing the curative properties and beneficial attributes of plants. The most common and widespread of these is without question homeopathy.

Homeopathy

Homeopathy shares a number of its basic principles with some of the oldest medical practices in the world. Along with acupuncture and ayurvedic medicine, it is based on the belief that the body has the innate ability to heal itself. Homeopathy, however, is a relatively modern practice. Developed around 1796 by the German physician

Samuel Hahnemann (1755–1843), homeopathy was hailed as a new medical science. It is based on two fundamental principles.

The first principle of homeopathy is "Like cures like," the second is the Doctrine of Infinitesimals, that being the administration of the smallest possible dosage. The first principle is based on Hahnemann's belief that certain medicines induce the same symptoms in the healthy body as they appear to relieve in the sick person. This can be closely compared with the much more ancient theory of *correspondence* as practiced in both Chinese and Indian herbalism. The second principle was of Hahnemann's own invention, he called this the Doctrine of Infinitesimals. It can be understood as "the smaller the dose, the more likely it is to be effective." He believed that the process of dilution actually refined the original substance, making it more pure and therefore even more potent.

In his *Organon of the Healing Art,* Hahnemann explains that in the healthy person, the body is held in balance by the spiritual vital force, which he calls the *Dynamis*. This vital force rules over the spiritual body, which in turn maintains the equilibrium of the physical body. The purpose of homeopathic medicine is to help the body's vital force restore itself to balance and, by doing so, allow the physical body to use its natural ability to cure itself.

Homeopathy continues to be controversial and skepticism has grown even greater since recent scientific analysis suggested that homeopathic remedies appear to contain no active ingredients whatsoever. All the same, homeopathy remains a relatively popular form of alternative medicine, and its advocates provide regular reports of its medical successes.

It is possible to draw some parallels between Hahnemann's homeopathy and the way in which the Druidic tradition deals with plant remedies. To explore these similarities in greater detail is beyond the scope of this book, but the reader may gain insight into these similarities by further research on this subject.

Flower Remedies

By the early part of the twentieth century, the British physician Edward Bach had developed some of these principles to arrive at his famous Flower Remedies.

47

The Principles of Arriving at the Complex and the Incense

Edward Bach (1880–1936) developed his range of Flower Remedies from a belief that they are infused with healing energies absorbed from the flowers from which they are prepared. He maintained that all disease is the result of imbalance between the soul and the mind and that his Flower Remedies redress this internal conflict.

The Flower Remedies were originally created from dew collected from a variety of flowers that Bach considered to have healing properties, the dew having absorbed the healing energies of the flowers upon which it had formed. Bach simplified the overly laborious task of collecting this dew from the selected flowers by introducing the process of floating the same flowers on a bath of water in sunlight, thereby extracting their healing energies in a more productive fashion. This energized water was then further diluted with brandy to produce the cure as it is now sold. The remedy is then once more diluted with a high proportion of water or wine before it is taken.

This method of preparation is very similar to that in the Druidic tradition, and it is no surprise to discover that Bach spent much of his time in the north of Wales searching for new ingredients for his remedies and exploring Welsh folk traditions and the ancient herbal cures of the Welsh culture. One does not have to stretch the imagination too far to envisage that Bach would have come into contact with the Druidic tradition during his wanderings and absorbed the ancient Druidic techniques into his burgeoning theories.

He then appears to have married this Druidic technique with the more conventional homeopathic theory of the Doctrine of Infinitesimals by diluting these energized waters with large quantities of brandy. Bach also aligned some of his techniques and theories of the administration of his remedies with those of conventional homeopathy, arguing that his Flower Remedies redress an imbalance in the body's equilibrium, thus allowing the body to cure itself. In the case of Bach's remedy, it acts on the emotions rather than on the physical body.

So whether Bach created a new form of treatment or effected a union among the three existing traditions of Druidic remedies, homeopathy, and alchemy is for the reader to decide. Whatever the case may be, Bach's Flower Remedies continue to be very popular and may be purchased in most countries of the world. They are used extensively as an alternative therapy in the treatment of stress-related ailments, for which they appear to be particularly appropriate.

In comparison, while Druidic practice shares some of its methods for extracting the vital energies and attributes from the plants it employs with both homeopathy and Bach's techniques, it does not subscribe to the two basic principles of homeopathy and Bach's Flower Remedies—namely, "Like cures like" and the concept of the Doctrine of Infinitesimals.

One of the greatest aspects of the Doctrine of Infinitesimals is, of course, its infallibility. If Hahnemann's theory is correct and dilution equates to purification and an increase in potency, then it is the right thing to do. If it is not, then at least the remedies are so dilute as to be harmless.

In stark contrast to Hahnemann's theory, Druidic plant lore tends to advocate the concentration of its essences and complexes as a means of focusing the attributes and increasing the potency of the plant's natural benefits.

Hygiene

The process of arriving at the plant complex and incense begins with the correct harvesting of the part(s) of the plant we intend to use. This seems to have little relevance in other traditions, but to the Druid, knowing the provenance of all the materials he or she works with is essential. The process of harvesting is so important to the Druid that it is actually enacted as a formal ritual. As we shall see, the first step is the identification of suitable donor plants, establishing a rapport with them, and ensuring their suitability (and willingness) as donors.

In Druidic lore there is no argument for using bought or found source materials. It is not just the simple question of whether fresh or dried plant material is more effective; it is a much more involved principle than that. It is fundamental to the effectiveness of any of the plant's derivatives that the location, environment, general health, approximate age, and even the compass orientation of the part of the plant used is precisely known before it may be utilized to its full potential. It is also essential to know that the time, date, and method of harvesting are appropriate and that the harvested plant has been correctly preserved between its time of harvest and when it is used. This is why most Druidic priests and priestesses insist on harvesting all of their materials personally. Only in this way may the plant material be guaranteed suitable for its planned use.

49

The Principles of Arriving at the Complex and the Incense

As many of the complexes yielded by the plant will be used internally or on open wounds, cuts, and abrasions, it is essential that the highest standards of hygiene be maintained throughout.

Following its harvest, the plant material will be cleansed either in a fast-moving stream or in a bath of moon-cleansed water (see page 235). There are no scientific cleansing agents used in either of these processes. The ancient Druids had no "scientific" understanding of hygiene. They did, of course, have experience of the effects of poor hygiene, but had no real understanding of their cause.

Purists would argue against the need for proprietary sterilizing agents, particularly at this early stage of the process, as it interferes with the natural essences and attributes of the plant. But as always, the choice is yours. If your plant materials are harvested from a clean, unpolluted environment and the stream used for initial cleansing is pure, you may consider this sufficient, as the purists do. I suggest you read through the rest of the details of the plant's treatment before making your decision. These involve soaking in alcohol and fermentation, and you may decide that these processes prove sufficient for your needs. Alternatively, there is a range of natural, herbal sterilizing agents that you may choose to use.

However, the need for sterile vessels, bottles, and equipment for the refinement of the complexes and incenses is unequivocal—not only because of the health hazards involved in using unsterile equipment but also because the refinement process itself involves the controlled use of certain bacteria, which will undoubtedly be impaired by the introduction of uncontrolled bacterial agents.

The traditional sterilization methods taught to me are immersing the vessels in rapidly boiling water for a few minutes or baking them in a hot oven for half an hour before use. These methods are equally effective; use the facilities you have available to you at the time.

As far as workshop cleanliness is concerned, the Druidic tradition has nothing to say on the matter. Many of the workshops I have seen and used are a long way from what I would call hygienic. Often they are in corners of sheds, outhouses, or spare rooms. Very rarely are they designed specifically for their Druidic applications. The ancient Druidic practices survived despite these conditions, but you may choose to plan a suitably hygienic environment for your activities from the outset.

When asked about the standards of hygiene required for the safe practice of Druidic "workshop" activities in general, I always refer people to the standards required for the commercial preparation of food. These health and safety standards are normally defined by law and copies of the standards may usually be obtained from your local government authority. Adherence to these standards will ensure that the products of your workshop are risk-free.

Conservation Issues

Most of the plants we shall be using are common to all the northern European countries where the Celtic races are found. (This is why they have their place within the Druidic tradition.) Many of the plant materials used in the wide range of schools of alchemy vary significantly from those found in the Celtic nations, due mainly to their very differing climates and natural history. There are, however, many similarities to be found.

Depending on where you live, you may have to vary the materials to suit your own natural resources. I have deliberately selected two very common plants to illustrate the complex refinement processes, both of which may be harvested in most areas without undue stress on the environment. However, should you decide to use other plants for your initial experimentation, or widen the range of plants you use as your skills develop, make sure that they are an abundant, renewable resource within the areas from which you harvest them. Never harvest plants you know or suspect to be classified as endangered species. Remember that as Druids we are striving at all times to be in harmony with nature; therefore, we should harvest only what we are confident that nature can restore without difficulty. If in any doubt about the classification of a plant you intend to harvest, contact your local conservation organization.

Morals and the Law

As Druids we have a moral obligation not to interfere with the processes of nature; harvesting, in whatever form, may seem to contradict this principle. We must remember, however, that we are also part of nature ourselves and our very existence depends on our consuming her bounties. As we are at the top of the food chain, and as we are endowed with a sense of reason and intelligent thought, it behooves us to exercise a high degree of responsibility for the future conservation of our planet and everything that exists on it.

Responsible harvesting for food and other essential needs in a way that does not endanger or disturb the balance of nature is necessary for our continued survival. It is with this in mind that I urge everyone who uses natural resources in his or her work to exercise the utmost responsibility in harvesting, both in the quantities harvested and in the methods used. Since the beginning of its known history, conservation has been a prime principle in Druidic lore. The Druidic rationale for conservation is based on two simple philosophies.

The first is a great *respect* for nature. Druidic lore acknowledges that the gifts of nature are provided unconditionally. Druids (for the most part) never actually *cultivate* their resources but instead harvest them from their natural habitat during the season in which they naturally become available. (I say "for the most part" because I have known some Druids who feel comfortable in planting specific species of plants into wild environments in the belief that it is the growing process and the atmosphere that imbue the plant with its attributes. I believe that only naturally occurring specimens, which form part of the natural cycle of their environment, hold the true attributes of the species.) It is, however, this powerful respect for nature that underpins all the harvesting methods used in the Druidic tradition.

The second criterion is the belief that for everything that is taken, something has to be returned. This act of returning may, on many occasions, be a ritual of symbolic action. We see this in most Druidic rituals where "offerings" are made by spilling wine or scattering bread onto the ground, or in the symbolic return of ashes to the earth or the leaving of "gifts" at ritual sites following Gatherings. (See my book *Celtic Sex Magic* for more about "taking and giving" as fundamental to all Druidic rituals.)

In Druidic lore, nature is seen as self-sufficient and self-renewing, the greatest and most complex manifestation of the collective energy, much akin to the anima mundi, or World Soul, of the ancient alchemical tradition. To interfere with nature's works or to deplete her resources would be contrary to all that Druidic lore holds dear.

This philosophy was explained to me in very simple terms as I began to learn the

Druidic tradition as a young boy. "You cannot keep taking from a pot without putting something back in or eventually you will starve" is what I was told. And by way of proof, I was introduced to the fermentation processes we will be looking at later (see page 157), in particular, the perpetuation of what I now know to be the yeast culture, which is never used in its entirety and always is fed (or replenished) for the next occasion of its use. I can remember a number of times when searching for young leaves and branches hearing the words "Remember the yeast" being spoken over my shoulder. "If something is not left, there will be no renewal."

Taken together, these two principles form a sound conservation philosophy. *Respect* and *renewal* are excellent watchwords for your relationship with the rest of nature as a whole.

In addition to these moral principles of nature, there is also the law of man to be taken into account. Trespassing, harvesting plants from privately owned property, harvesting endangered species, taking plants from national parks and reserves, growing and/or using "illegal" plants, causing damage to hedges and fencing—all these are criminal activities that may result in prosecution, fines, and even imprisonment. Be aware of the status of the area from which you harvest. Take advice from people who know the area, talk to rangers, study local maps, do whatever it takes to become familiar with the sites you visit. There is no need to break the law. With a little patience and perseverance, you will always find a suitable donor plant for your needs.

Another aspect that many herbal practitioners often overlook is their legal responsibility for the safety of the products they produce and the methods they employ.

Wherever you live, there is no doubt that you will be held responsible should anyone or anything suffer from the products you prepare or the methods you employ. A mild case of poisoning may put someone off work for a few days, and that's your fault! A simple allergic reaction may cause skin irritation; that's your fault! Inhaling incense fumes may cause an asthmatic reaction; that's your fault! A participant may hurt herself during a Gathering; that's your fault!

Are you getting the picture? It is your responsibility to ensure that everything you make and everything that you organize is done in the safest and most considered fashion possible. Leave nothing to chance. You owe that much to yourself and to the other members of your Gathering. Here are some guidelines:

- **Never** be tempted to use yourself or anyone else as an experimental vehicle for your workings or products. This is irresponsible and illegal!
- **Never** use any ingredients if you are not entirely certain of their effect and safety.
- **Never** use any plants you know to be poisonous or that you suspect may produce ill effects.
- **Never** experiment with that which you do not know without due care and attention.
- **Never** consider using your work for anything other than good. In that way you will set the scene for responsible and considerate actions and avoid any of the tribulations of malpractice.
- **Always** work safely and within the limitations of your knowledge and experience. I was taught, "Never use anything on anyone else that you would not first use upon yourself," and "Never wish yourself anything other than good health and vitality." Put these two pieces of wisdom together and you have the building blocks of the Druidic Code of Practice.

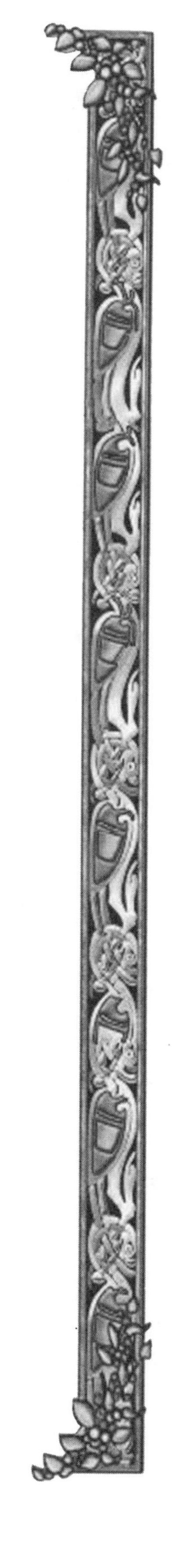

Part 2

Assessing the Natural Resources

Working within the Rhythm of Nature

Like many other natural magic traditions, Druidic lore makes full use of the many resources provided by nature. In its entirety, Druidic plant lore embraces mosses, grasses, flowers, herbs, trees, seaweeds, nettles, and mushrooms as well as a number of other, less ordinary plant species. From these plants we harvest leaves, flowers, barks, woods, roots, berries, and nuts together with combinations of these.

It is probable that wherever you live, some if not all of these resources will be available to you within your neighborhood or within a short walk or drive. Alternatively, you may need to plan short harvesting excursions in order to harvest the plant material you need. Whichever method fulfills your needs, it will be necessary for you to look carefully at the resources available before you begin your work.

Each plant complex is prepared with a specific use in mind. Considering that it may take up to three months for certain complexes to be crafted and then mature enough to use, it is a good idea to form a plan of how and when you intend to use each complex before you begin its harvesting and manufacture. Never harvest plant material that you do not intend to use and never begin manufacturing a complex that you do not have a use for. This may sound as if I am preaching my conservation sermon again, but if you think the whole process through, it contains a profound natural logic.

First, you need only to harvest whatever plant material you require for immediate use. All plant complexes are best made from fresh plant material and the best way to keep plant material fresh is to leave it on the plant until you are ready to use it. Second, whether you decide to manufacture the complex for a ritual, for a work-

ing, or for your own practical experimentation and development, the only measure of the success of your efforts is the effective use of the complex and whether it achieves the desired results. There is, therefore, no point in manufacturing a complex unless you intend to use it.

Another major factor to take into account in planning your work is the seasonal availability of the plants and parts of plants you require. For example, young leafy branches may only be harvested in the spring, while most berries only become available in autumn.

It is possible—indeed, it is a common practice—to harvest plant materials during the season when they are available (or when they are at their most potent), and then to manufacture the cardinal essences and incense from the freshly harvested material and store them until they are required. This does not affect the potency of the eventual complex because, as we have already seen, it does not achieve its full potency until the cardinal essences are amalgamated to form the complex during the ritual within which it is being used. In fact, the complex as such does not exist until the amalgamation itself takes place.

This may suggest that it is a good idea to manufacture as many cardinal essences as possible during the appropriate seasons and store them indefinitely until a use is found for them, and I must admit that this is a method used by a number of practitioners. However, this is not a methodology of which I either approve or to which I subscribe. I suggest (from personal experience) that if you adopt this practice of opportunist manufacture, you will soon be overrun with bottles and boxes of liquids and incense that have no part in the plans you have for your own activities or those of your Gatherings.

Your time is much better spent getting to know intimately the area from which you are harvesting, learning to identify the plants around you and how the environment in which they grow affects their "personalities," deepening your knowledge of the attributes and energies of the plants that are available to you and the benefits these attributes and energies may produce. In this way, and only in this way, will you deepen your understanding and develop your knowledge in pace with your practices. It will serve no purpose to frantically manufacture substances when you do not understand their composition or use.

So begin simply. Identify a single plant that is available to you. Do as much research on that particular plant as you possibly can before you even think about harvesting any part of it. Learn what you can about its botanical aspects, its natural history, what uses it may have already been put to. Has it been used by herbalists? If so, for what purpose? Are there any accounts of its effectiveness as an herbal remedy? Is it used in homeopathy? Does it have a place in mainstream "scientific" medicine? These are just a few of the questions you may ask yourself about the existing applications of the plant. Then there are questions about the environment in which the plant is growing, the community of plants that surround it, the age and health of the plant, its ability to renew the part or parts you intend to harvest, and so on. These are topics we shall be exploring in detail throughout the rest of this book. Be confident that you know all you need to know about the plant you have selected to harvest before proceeding.

The next step is to make yourself familiar with the technique and ritual of harvesting, as only plants that have been harvested in the correct manner will yield the essences and energies you desire. Finally, you need to prepare your workshop for the process of refining the plant material following its harvest.

Once you have harvested your first plant material and begun the extraction of its cardinal essences, you may address a second plant for study while you wait for the processes of extraction of the first plant to take their course. You have by no means finished your work on the first plant, but you may and should take advantage of the periods of inactivity as the extraction and maturation of the plant's essences take place.

Do not try to harvest and refine more than eight plant species in your first year. By working with only eight plants during the course of a year, you can develop a thorough knowledge about the uses of each plant. In broad terms, this equates to two species during each season. It may also benefit if during each of the four seasons you focus on different parts of the plant. For example, in spring work on the young branches of the oak and the flower of the primrose. In autumn, try the fruits of the blackberry and the leaves of the common mint.

You will, of course, have to plan your own initial range of plants and timetable of work. If you try to include a variety of plants and are selective about the parts of the plant you harvest, you will gain experience in the various methods of refinement used to extract their individual essences.

Understanding the Nature of Your Donor Plants

As we have seen above, knowing the energies and attributes of the plants you use is fundamental to Druidic lore. The energies and attributes of plants vary, not only from one plant species to another but also according to the parts of the plant of which you make use. Without knowing the individual energies and attributes of each plant and the effect these will have when used in the context you intend, it is impossible to channel them toward their intended purpose.

Each plant is imbued with the energies of its species. These may then be enhanced or subdued according to a number of factors affecting the plant during its life cycle. We have already listed some of these factors, such as its location, the plants surrounding it, its state of health, and its age, and we shall explore these again when we look in detail at selecting a plant for harvest.

Thus, we may designate certain energies to each plant according to its genus and species and identify any external influences on these energies by looking at the health of the plant, its neighbors, and its surroundings. But what of the various parts of the plant: How do these energies vary from one part of the plant to the other?

To begin to understand this we must look at the simple astrological system that Druid lore applies to the plant kingdom. Contrary to general opinion, the Druidic tradition—at least the Welsh Druidic tradition—has a very simple system of astrological beliefs. Although most books on the subject talk of Druidic "astrologers," no such

people exist in the tradition I was taught. Druidic divination does not embrace star charts or astrological tables; it works on a much more terrestrial level.

The suggestion that Stonehenge and other standing stone circles are actually forms of complex Druidic astrological clocks/calendars/calculators/compasses was discredited some time ago. Nearly all the stone circles in the United Kingdom predate the Druids by centuries. It may be true that Druid priests or priestesses used these convenient "circles" for their rituals, and indeed many still attempt to do so, but this was (and is) for two main reasons. First, the stones form the basic circular shape required for every Druidic ritual; some even have distinct entry portals as required for the Druidic Protective Circle. Second, most are constructed on ley lines (a narrow, invisible line of energy that runs across the landscape below the surface of the earth) of immense power, which work on a conscious and subconscious level, and these powers are often channeled for use during Druidic rituals.

The fundamental universal power of the Druidic tradition is the collective energy, which exerts its influence through two celestial bodies only: the sun and the moon. These represent the eternal balance and harmony of the cosmos. The sun represents the male influence; the moon, the female. The balance of these influences is sought in all things. These are equivalent to the yin and yang of the Chinese Taoists, the Shiva and Shakti of the Hindus, and Aristotle's fire and water.

Each of the four basic elements (or essences) is governed by its corresponding celestial body—air and fire by the sun, earth and water by the moon. The fifth element (essence), the quintessence (fifth essence), is the combination of them all, the collective energy of Druidic lore. In the Druidic tradition, every plant comes under the influence of either the sun or the moon and is therefore ascribed with the aspects and nature of its governing celestial body. These aspects and nature have a profound influence on the plant's energies and attributes and dictate how we should interact with the plant from harvesting to the eventual use of its complex and incense.

In wand making, for example, trees under the sun's influence must be harvested only during daylight and the wands they yield are used by priests; on the other hand, trees that are influenced by the moon are harvested under moonlight and are used only by a priestess. In the Celtic sex magic rituals we shall be looking at later (see page 224), each potion, complex, and incense we use will vary depending on the gender of the person on whom it is used and whether it is a priest or a priestess facilitating the ritual. This selection will be governed by whether the plant comes under the influence of the sun or the moon.

The various parts of the individual plant are also designated as being within the realm of one or the other of these two celestial bodies. In general, the parts of the plant associated with the moon are either those that are dependent on the elements associated with the moon (earth and water) or the reproductive organs of the plant concerned. These female parts of the plant are seen to be the *producer.* The male parts of the plant are dependent on the elements associated with the sun (fire and air) and are the *provider* of the plant.

Therefore the roots, wood, and stem of the plant are under the influence of the moon, as they are within the soil (the element earth) and carry the water supply to the plant (the element water), respectively. These, then, are the female parts of the plant.

The leaves, petals, and bark of the plant are under the influence of the sun, as they are most closely associated with the elements air and fire (for *fire,* read *light/sun* in this context). These parts of the plant either gather light (the element fire) or allow the plant to breathe (the element air). These are the male parts of the plant.

Most of the plants we shall be dealing with are hermaphrodites, carrying both the male and female reproductive organs. The location of these organs will vary according to each species, and we will look at each one separately later in this book. Most hermaphroditic plants produce male and female organs at different times of the year to ensure cross-pollination. For our purposes all the plant's reproductive system is classed as female and comes under the influence of the Moon.

These designations may be questioned by modern-day science, as the work of the various parts of the plant are not so simply defined by the botanist. Yet this system of classification has been used within the Druidic tradition for millennia and has been proved to work well within the context that we require.

So, to recap: We have seen that each plant species has its own unique energies. These may be strengthened or weakened by the plant's overall growth environment and its health. These may be further enhanced or suppressed by the effects of its neighboring plants. This energy is the plant's own individual share of the collective energy that we find in all things.

Each plant comes under the overall influence of either the sun or the moon. We call this its *central influence.* The various parts of the plant are further influenced by one or another of these celestial bodies, depending on the element or elements it is most closely associated with. We call this its *associated influence.*

When we manufacture our complex, our first thought is to select the plant with the correct central influence for the purpose of our work. Having done this, we then select the plant species with the most potent energies that are necessary to carry out the work intended to best effect. Next we attempt to find a particular plant whose energies and attributes will have been enhanced by its neighboring community of plants.

Once we have targeted the particular plant we intend to harvest, we must select the parts of the plant that best serve our needs. In doing this it is possible to emphasize the male or female aspects in order to serve our purpose, but each complex *must* be manufactured from a combination of male (sun) *and* female (moon) essences to maintain the balance of nature's power. We must therefore harvest at least some parts that come under the sun's associated influence and some that come under the moon's.

Later in the workshop these parts are separated and become known as the cardinals, from which we extract the cardinal essences. It is these cardinal essences that are amalgamated during the ritual to form the potent complex we desire.

For the purpose of refining our cardinal essences (and subsequently our complex and incense), all of our plant matter will be processed by one of two methods. The first is known as the *complex of the flower;* the second is called the *complex of the tree.*

Everything prepared through the complex of the flower method will have two cardinal essences, and the solid plant material will also undergo a process of *fermentation.* Everything prepared through the complex of the tree method will have three cardinal essences, and there will be no fermentation process.

This may sound as if we are able to use only flowers and trees in our work, but this is not the case. A plant may be refined "as a flower," for which we use the complex of the flower method. This method, therefore, will not be used only on what we commonly know as flowers, but will also be used on the flowers of flowering trees, herbs, shrubs, and thistles. Alternatively, a plant may be refined "as a tree," in which case we employ the complex of the tree method. We would use this method, then, not just on trees but also on plant stems, woody sprigs of herbs (woody stem and leaf groups), sprigs of bushes and shrubs.

How, then, do we decide which process to use on which plant or plant part? The answer is that you will need to commit to memory the method for each plant and each part of the plant. This prospect may be off-putting to some students, but do not be deterred. Remember, although there is a great volume of plants and plant parts, there are actually only two refinement methods, so it may not be as tedious as it first seems.

In general terms, flowers are divided into petals and flower heads, which form the two cardinals of the flower. Trees are separated into leaves, wood, and bark, which provide the three cardinals of the tree. There are then some obvious guidelines to follow.

If we harvest a new young branch from an oak, we detach the *leaves,* strip the *bark* from the branch, and shred the remaining *wood* of the branch. This gives us the three cardinals we need for the cardinals of the tree method of refinement. If we harvest a dog rose flower, we separate the *petals* from the *flower head* to give us the two cardinals we require for the cardinals of the flower method.

This simple process of division allows you to account for the vast majority of the plants you will be using. But in some cases, a category may not be so obvious. For instance, the dog rose bush from which we harvested our dog rose flower to refine through the cardinals of the flower method may at the same time yield a leafy sprig for harvest. This sprig will be refined through the complex of the tree method by separating its leaves, bark, and woody stem. The two resulting complexes will be used in different ways to produce different results, and it is these subtleties of treatment that must be committed to memory.

To ease this process, I have included two tables of comparison for most of the plants available for use in Wales, Ireland, Scotland, and England. Many of the plants listed also grow as wild or cultivated plants in the United States. Alternatively, they may well be available as seeds from seed suppliers should you wish to cultivate them for yourself. These tables list, among other things, the traditionally designated method of refinement assigned to each plant and plant part.

We can see from the above that the dog rose yielded two very different harvests in the form of its flowers and its leafy sprigs, but this is not quite the end of the story. At a certain point in its life cycle, the dog rose will also produce its seed in the form of what we call the rose hip, a cluster of seeds held in a berrylike casing. Traditionally, this rose hip is made into a syrup and used to treat coughs and sore throats, but how is it refined in Druidic lore: Is it a flower or a tree?

This raises the question of the designation of all types of seeds—those contained in fleshy fruit, berries, hips, and nuts and acorns. Fortunately, the answer to this is a simple one. All are treated as "flowers" and therefore have just two cardinals. The cardinals are divided as follows.

- **Fleshy fruit.** The kernel, pips, or seeds are the female cardinal, equivalent to the flower head. The fleshy outer part of the fruit is the male cardinal, equivalent to the petal.
- **Berries.** Single-seed berries are treated in the same way as fleshy fruit. For berries with "clusters" of seeds, the fleshy cluster containing the seeds is treated as the female cardinal, while the sepal (the small leafy "cup" in which the berry rests) is treated as the male.
- **Hips.** The seeds forming the core of the hip are the female cardinal; the fleshy shell surrounding them is the male cardinal.
- **Nuts.** The kernel of the nut is the female, and the shell and sepals are the male.
- **Acorns.** The kernel is the female cardinal, and the cup and sepals are the male.

These divisions may in some cases seem to contradict the cardinals of the flower definition, where the petals are male and the flower head (which includes the sepals) is female. The reason is that the prime constituent of the female flower head of the flower is the reproductive organs; the sepals in this case just represent the "body" of the plant. Similarly, the main function of the male petal is as a receptor for the influence of the sun (male).

In the case of nuts and berries, the fertilized "seed," in whatever form, is the product of the plant's reproductive organs (female producer) while its nourishment and security are provided by the fruit's fleshy covering or its "umbilical" connection through the cup or sepals of the plant (male provider).

Now there is just one remaining major anomaly—herbs. If we wish to harvest the flower of the herb, we treat the flower the same way we do all other flowers. If, however, we need to harvest the leaves and stems of the herb (which is often the case), we need to know how to refine its cardinal essences.

Woody herbs are the simplest to deal with. Herbs, such as rosemary that have a woody branch system, are harvested and refined by the cardinals of the tree method. The leaves are removed, the bark stripped, and the inner wood ground or shredded. This is the perfect method for extracting the cardinals of the tree. The difficulty comes with herbs that have fleshy stems.

Let's take the common mint as our example. We can remove the leaves as we did with the rosemary, but it is impossible to strip the outer "bark" of the stems from the inner stem. The answer is that we keep the stems whole. Rather than use the cardinals of the tree method, we use the cardinals of the flower method.

We separate the leaves from the stems, treat the leaves as the male cardinal (due to their interaction with the sun and air), and treat the stems as the female cardinal (due to their interaction with the earth and water). In this way we keep the same male and female associations with their elements and also arrive at a practical way of refining the plant parts.

Thus, we can see that herbs in particular are refined using either the cardinals of the flower or cardinals of the tree method depending on the "woodiness" of their stems. Bearing in mind that plant stems are "woodier" at some times of the year than others and that in general most plants' stems will become woodier as the plants grow older and larger, we may end up with cardinal essences from the same plant refined by different methods at different times. This is fine as long as we remember their differing energies and attributes when we put them to use.

Understanding the nature of your donor plants is imperative to understanding how plant material is used in Druidic lore. Here we have learned a number of the fundamental principles that have an effect on how we select our donor plants and how we then use them. It is crucial that you take time to absorb this information before moving on. Normally, this amount of new information would take months to be taught through the traditional oral method, so do not be disheartened if you need to reread the previous section a number of times before it begins to make sense. Gaining a true understanding of these concepts and coming to grips with the vocabulary is a major step forward. Without this knowledge, you may well find what follows difficult or even incomprehensible.

Knowing and Identifying Plants

Knowing the qualities of the energies and attributes of the plants you use is essential. Even more fundamental to any work you may wish to do with plants is having the knowledge and ability to distinguish between one species and another and to identify the plant you need growing in its natural habitat.

Plant species identification is beyond our scope here, but there are many books on this subject. There is a wealth of field guides that will provide you with photographs, illustrations, and descriptions of local plants, the habitat in which they are most likely to be found, and the time of year they appear. Just arm yourself with one or two of these books and venture out into the area where you suspect you'll find the plants you need. With a little practice and experience, you will soon be able to identify those plants and recognize the other species surrounding them that may affect their energies and attributes.

Very often local bookstores and libraries have specialized books on the plant species that grow in your particular area. This can make the job of identifying plants much easier, by eliminating most of the species that are not found locally.

One of the first things you encounter as you read through any book of plants is the often confusing system of nomenclature. Most plants were named centuries before the official Latin names that were introduced by Linnaeus in 1735 were adopted. Many of these original names refer to the general appearance of the plant, some form of symbolism associated with it, or the use to which the plant was most often applied.

The difficulty was—and still is—that many of these old names had some form of significance that varied from place to place. It would not be uncommon, therefore, to see exactly the same plant referred to by a number of different names depending on where you were at the time. In order to eliminate this confusion, Linnaeus devised a system of categorizing plants using the common academic language of the time: Latin.

Each plant had a binomial categorization—a family or surname (genus) and a first name (species). The plant's family name (genus) is usually of ancient Greek, Persian, or Latin origin. The genus is always a noun, and, due to its antiquity, it is often impossible to "translate" into modern English.

The species name of the plant may have been created from a number of sources. Sometime it indicates the plant's country of origin, other times the plant's natural habitat, its color, or its fragrance, or even on occasion the discoverer's name. One very interesting genus is *officinalis,* which indicates the plant's use as an ancient herbal medicine.

In Welsh Druidic lore, plants are identified by their ancient local names, as Welsh tradition predates the Latin classifications by centuries. Like many names in the Welsh language (ancient and modern), those of plants are usually descriptive, saying something about a plant's appearance, natural location, or use. For example, the Welsh poppy *(Meconopsis cambrica),* is known in the Welsh tradition as *llysiau cwsg* (the herb of sleep).

To ease the reader's understanding and to ensure concordance with botanical publications throughout the world, whenever plants are mentioned in this text and the accompanying tables they are referred to by their common name (Welsh poppy), their Latin name *(Meconopsis cambrica),* and their Welsh or Irish traditional name, together with the literal translation where possible (*llysiau cwsg,* the herb of sleep). In this way the reader may refer to the plant's Latin name to confirm the identity of the plant even if the local common names differ from the ones given.

Now, armed with your botanical guide and your knowledge of the names of plants, you should be in a position to venture forth and begin your work in seeking the plants you require. Remember, though, that in most cases we shall not be harvesting the entire plant, nor will we be haphazardly harvesting plants at just any time in their life cycle. Thus, our next step is to gain an understanding of the physical structure and life cycle of the plants we will be using. We shall, from this point on, focus on the two types of plants most commonly used in the Welsh Druidic tradition of plant lore—that is, the flower and the tree.

While other traditions rely on herbal remedies, Druidic plant lore employs mostly flowers (mainly from flowering herbs) and trees. Druidic lore uses most of the herbs used by other traditions, but it distinguishes itself by using only the flower of the herb as opposed to other herbal traditions, which use the entire herb but rarely the flower. And even when we do use other parts of herbs, berries, and nuts, for example, they are treated as flowers or trees during the complex refinement. This further emphasizes the Druidic significance of these two groups of plant.

Let us now explore the flower and the tree.

The Flower

Flowers, or, more accurately, flowering plants, play a large role in ancient Druidic lore. Many flowers have been ignored for centuries as the development of medicine focused on herbs, shrubs, and roots rather than on flowers. As we have seen, Edward Bach brought the curative properties of flowers back into public focus, and his range of flower remedies remain popular to this day. The Druids, however, had a different approach to using flowers, and to begin to understand this we must first look at the flower life cycle and its place in the natural world.

The Life Cycle of the Flowering Plant

More than a quarter of a million flowering plants have been identified and classified. Each flowering plant matures through one of three life cycles. It will be defined as either annual, biennial, or perennial. In all cases the life cycle consists of the same stages of development: germination, growth, flowering, and seed production.

Annuals complete this life cycle within one year. They flower only once, produce their seeds, then die. *Biennials* do not flower until their second year of growth, then they produce their seeds and die. *Perennials* flower and produce seed for many years, sometimes dying back after seed production only to send out fresh growth the following year.

Various plants trigger the beginning of their life cycle at different times of the year. Some flower in summer and produce their fruit in autumn, others develop earlier, still others develop later in the year. A plant's life cycle is further affected by climate, number of daylight hours, the soil in which it grows, and its general environment. It is

important first to gain knowledge of the *theoretical* times of a plant's life cycle and then to get to know the actual plants you are working with in their natural habitat, as this may affect dramatically the triggering and rate of progress of their individual life cycles. Only in this way will you learn to harvest your flowers at the best possible moment.

The ancient Druids had a thorough understanding of the life cycles of the plants surrounding them, based not on any scientific theory, but rather on the practical necessities of survival. Knowing when plants yielded their various fruits, berries, and nuts and at what time of year vegetables were able to be harvested and stored could make the difference between life and death for the hunter-gatherers of the Celtic races.

Flower Structure

The most significant aspect of the flower is that it carries the reproductive parts of the plant, and although flowering plants differ dramatically in their appearance, they are all constructed of three basic component parts: the root, the stem, and the leaf. The part of the stem that carries the plant's flower is called the *inflorescence*. The flowers themselves form on the inflorescence in a variety of ways, depending on the particular genus and species involved. There are, as always, a collection of Latin names for the different types of formations. You may find these names in any good botanical book, but for our purposes they are not important. As the shape of the flower formation will be one of the identifying features you will use, there is no real need for you to know the scientific names of the various forms.

The parts of the flower may be seen as modified leaves and usually form in a series of circles around the stem base. It would be useful to read this next section with a flower close by for reference. If we begin at the base of the flower, where it joins the stem, we can look at each of the individual circles as we progress to the center.

The first (outer) ring is most commonly separated into green *sepals* (the *calyx*). It is these sepals that protect the flower bud before it blooms. In an open flower they usually appear as a green "cup" underneath the flower where it joins the stem. Above the sepals we see the inner circle of usually brightly colored *petals* (the *corolla*). It is these petals that usually hold the *nectar-producing glands* (the *nectaries*) that attract insects and aid pollination. These two outer rings (the sepals and the petals) form the *floral receptacle* (the *perianth*) containing the reproductive parts of the flower.

Moving inward toward the center of the flower, the next thing we see is a circle (or sometimes circles) of *stamens,* the male part of the flower (the *androecium*). Each individual stamen consists of a fine *filament* tipped with an *anther.* It is these anthers that produce the *pollen* necessary for the reproductive process of the plant.

The final and innermost circle is the female part of the flower, the *pistil* (the *gynoecium*). The pistil consists of at least one *carpel,* and frequently more. Each carpel contains one or more *placentas* with an *immature seed* (an *ovule*) attached to it. The pistil as a whole is divided into the *ovary,* the *style,* and the *stigma.*

The plant reproduces by means of a *fruit,* which develops from the ovary after pollination. Pollination typically occurs when the pollen of one plant is transferred to the pistils of another by adhering to the surface of an insect or by being carried by air currents. The fruit protects the seeds until they are ripe and often plays a role in the seeds' dispersal.

In many flowers the associated parts vary in their relative position. Descriptions and explanations of the distribution of the parts of most flowers may be found in any good botanical publication. Once again, it may be necessary for you to commit the various compositions of the flowers you use to memory. Alternatively, you may choose to build an information base of your own, containing the more common plants of your area, so that you may refer to it regularly.

You will note in the section above that I have deviated from my general rule of not using scientific (usually Latin or Greek) names for the parts of the flower. This is deliberate, so that as you seek further information in other, more detailed botanical publications, you will be able to identify the relevant parts of the flower by the "official" names that will undoubtedly appear within the text. It also may be useful to refer to the illustration below identifying the various elements of a typical flower.

Having read and understood the above, you now possess a greater "scientific" knowledge of the flower and the reproductive cycle of plants than the most learned of ancient Druid priests.

Component parts of the flower
Stigma
Filament
Petal
Sepal
Style
Receptacle
Ovule
Ovary
Stem
Switzer

Ancient Druids viewed plants as much more than just physical objects and saw their attributes as extending far beyond the physical properties of today's "scientific" approach. As we have already seen, the tradition we have inherited acknowledges that plants have latent energies along with their physical and magical attributes. It is this fundamentally holistic appreciation of the plant and its flowers that provides us with the basis of our contemporary Druidic plant lore.

The ancient Druids understood that a plant has certain physical characteristics that may be readily observed, and in understanding these characteristics it is sometimes possible to predict the behavior of the plant through the seasons. In the same way, they also realized that they could reproduce the beneficial results of using the physical, medicinal properties of certain plants over and over again when they were used in the same circumstances. But unlike modern-day medical practitioners, they believed these beneficial results were achieved to their full potential only if the latent energies and magical attributes of the plant were employed with equal vigor.

Understanding the Druidic conception of the flower's structure, its reproductive cycle, and its energies and attributes is essential to understanding how flowers are used in Druidic plant lore. Druidic plant lore holds that the flower itself consists of two basic components once it has been separated from the plant stem—the petals and the remaining flower head.

The petals are the male part of the flower. All petals come under the associated influence of the sun no matter what the particular central influence of the genus or species may be (see page 62 to recall the difference between central and associated influences). As the receptors of the sun's energies and the sun's influences, the petals assume the male provider role.

The ancient Druids appreciated some flowers' functions both in following the sun's progress across the sky and in opening and closing as the sun rises and sets. This was seen to be the result of the petals' relationship with the sun, responding to the energies they absorb from the sun's light and heat and the magical attributes given to the plant by the sun and collected through the flower's petals. The energies of the sun provide the fuel for the plant's movements, and the magical attributes give the plant the spirit and "intelligence" to control its animation.

In their role as receptors, coupled with the Druidic theory that plants and flowers breathe through their leaves and petals, the petals of the flower are associated with the two elements of fire (the sun's heat and light) and air (the breathing function of the petal). These two elements are considered male and are themselves associated with the central influences of the sun. The Druids also recognized that the petals give the flower its captivating appearance, its intoxicating fragrance, and its (sometimes) sweet taste. With the combination of all their virtues, it is from the petals that we refine the first of the plant's cardinal essences.

Once we remove the petals, the remaining components of the flower, in the Druidic tradition, comprise the flower head. We now know that this flower head contains both the male and female reproductive organs of the plant, but to the ancient Druids this was the female component of the flower.

Even though they had no knowledge of the plant's reproductive system, they understood that it was the core, or central part of the flower, that yielded the eventual seed. This can be seen from the Druidic name for the flower head, *croth,* meaning "womb." As there was also no real understanding of the various component parts of the flower head, the whole flower, minus its petals, was seen to be the reproductive organ. It gained its nourishment from the earth and from the rain that fell upon it, which it then "drank." It was also significant that in some plants, notably the dandelion, the flower head swells before releasing its seeds (the dandelion "clock"). This was associated with the female pregnancy and further reinforced the femininity of the flower head. But as the Druids were mostly concerned with the plant's energies and attributes, it is the flower head's association with the elements of earth and water that define it as female and bring it within the associated influences of the moon. It is, then, from the remaining flower head that we refine the second of the plant's cardinal essences.

The Two Cardinals of the Flower

We have seen that the flower yields two cardinal essences—one derived from the flower's petals and the other from the remaining flower head—one male and the other female. Both cardinal essences are released through the complex of the flower method, which we shall look at in detail later (see page 141).

This process involves each of these cardinal essences in two forms of refinement.

The physical refinement, through a series of operations, produces a liquid containing the physical (chemical) attributes of the plant. The spiritual refinement, accomplished through a series of magic rituals and ritual workings, imbues this liquid with the energies and magical attributes of the plant. In this way, each of the cardinal essences contains the greatest possible measure of the energies and attributes of the plant.

Following the refinement of both cardinal essences, the remaining, almost exhausted plant matter is itself physically refined and magically energized to form the incense containing the final potential of the plant. These three components of the flower—the male (petal) and female (flower head) cardinal essences and the refined and energized incense—are then stored in separate containers until it is time for their use.

I was taught to store these elements together in a closed box. The box is placed away from direct sunlight, in a cool, dry place. You will see later that when working with plants in our workshop, we always keep a detailed account of the dates and times that the various steps in our refinement processes take place, and we also precisely label each flask and bottle we use. In this way we can refer to our records to determine how and when each item was crafted, and every vessel and container we use will be accurately labeled.

The three separate components are eventually taken from storage to play their part in the ritual for which they were created. It is during this ritual that the two cardinal essences of the flower are reunited in the act of amalgamation. It is only when the two cardinal essences are brought together to form the complex that the full potential of the flower and all your hard work become manifest.

Before the complex is used, a small amount is poured onto the ground in the symbolic act of returning part of what has been given. In most cases, the remainder of the complex is mixed with moon-cleansed water to form a libation. In this way we acknowledge the authority of the elements of earth and water. This is the part of the ritual that invokes the influence of the moon upon our ritual Gathering.

The incense is then placed on a charcoal brazier. As it has been thoroughly dried as one step in its refinement process, part of the incense matter ignites in flame, but the whole quickly subdues and releases the remaining potential of the flower into the air. This acknowledges the authority of the remaining two elements, fire and air. This part of the ritual invokes the influence of the sun on the work of our Gathering.

In some cases the flower's incense is used in the crafting of a ritual "cake," which is placed onto the charcoal brazier in the same way as the incense. This practice is an old one, which I always use if possible. It harkens back to the making of cakes and breads to use as offerings during special seasonal celebrations. These cakes were usually made from cereals, grain, and local produce, and after a little had been scattered on the ground as an offering, the remainder would have been eaten by the participants as a celebratory feast.

In the Druidic tradition, however, the cakes were made primarily of plant material and flour and called *Teisen Iâr,* or "Hen's Cake" in English, probably because those cakes that weren't heated on the brazier in the ritual would have been fed to the hens afterward (very little was wasted in the mainly subsistence existence of the Celtic nations). The *teisen iâr* are formed into a small disk shape, about three inches (7.5 cm) in diameter, and marked with a circle containing a cross with arms of equal length (as shown below).

The circle and cross marking of the teisen iâr

Part of a standing Ogham stone showing the circle and cross of the Celtic Pagan earth symbol.

This circle with a cross is the ancient pagan symbol for the earth and may be seen on a number of standing stones throughout the Celtic regions and on some of the Ogham stones in Ireland, including one close to my home in County Kerry.

It has been argued that these *teisen iâr,* with their circle and cross symbols, were

Hot cross buns.

mainly eaten by the ancient Celts at their springtime ceremonies and that this tradition was subsumed by the later Christians in the form of today's hot cross buns, eaten throughout Europe at Easter, as a symbol of the story of Christ's crucifixion and resurrection. In fact, many of the cross and circle combinations seen in Christian churches and graveyards today, including the Celtic cross, are most likely relics of the pagan/Christian symbolism used by the early Christian church as a means of easing the introduction of their new doctrine.

Returning to the use of our cardinal essences and incense, we can see that following the point in the ritual where the incense is placed on the charcoal brazier, we have invoked the influences of both the sun and the moon and acknowledged the authority of all four elements. Having done this, and having simultaneously converged the influence of the two celestial bodies with the four elements, we are brought into contact with the fifth element or essence (the quintessence), the collective energy of the Druidic tradition. It is from this point in the ritual onward that we may connect to and channel the supreme potential of the collective energy itself.

This, then, is how the influences of the sun, moon, and elements affect the potency of the ritual. We can see from this that the two cardinal essences of the flower represent the associated influences of the sun and the moon. What effect, though, do these influences have on the complex that we produce, and how do they affect the eventual use?

Flowers of the Sun and the Moon

Each genus and species of plant is designated as coming under the central influence of either the sun or the moon. This central influence determines the way in which the plant may be used, who uses it (to best effect), how and when the plant must be harvested, upon whom the plant is most likely to have the best effect, and what other plants may work with or against the plant's own energies and attributes.

As we are looking at flowers in this section, we should first note that flowers themselves are better suited to some applications than are other parts of the plant. They reflect the softer, gentler uses of plants, often used in works where children are the focus. They also appear in rituals concerned with spiritual love and affection, emotional matters, fertility, birth, and death. They generally are used in a happy way and as a means of commemoration.

Many of these symbolic uses relate to their visual appeal and the delicacy of their structures as much as to their latent energies and attributes. What, then, may we expect from plants that fall under the central influence of the sun?

Plants of the Sun

It must be noted here that other traditions may have alternative and sometimes contradictory symbols for the celestial bodies. For example, the symbol for the sun in the hermetic (alchemical) tradition is a circle with a single dot at its center, and the zodiacal sun symbol is the lion. On occasion, it may be important to be able to distinguish the symbols of the Druidic tradition from those of other traditions.

The Druidic symbol for the sun is the Circle.

We now know that the sun is the center of our "solar" system. This is a concept of which the ancient Druids had no comprehension. They did, however, recognize that the sun is central to all life, that its light and heat have a profound effect on all living things. They knew that if plants were deprived of the sun's light, they would cease to flourish and that in winter, when the sun's heat diminished, many of the plants around them died away, only to return with the heat of the sun the following spring. They no doubt enjoyed the heat of the summer sun on their bodies and missed its comfort during the cold winters of northern Europe. They would have used the daylight hours to hunt and to gather crops and would have felt threatened as the sun set and darkness descended, not knowing whether the sun would return. The sun was therefore seen as the universal provider.

The sun was the main controlling factor in the ancients' lives. The long, warm days of summer allowed them an existence totally different from the short, cold days of winter. The sun also played a major role in the way in which they organized and planned their lives, their day-to-day work and rest, the availability of plants and animals for food, and their harvesting and gathering activities.

It also influenced the cycle of reproduction of all living things. Spring saw the birth of many young animals, along with the arrival of new plants and new growth on old ones. Conversely, many things die in winter when the sun is at its lowest ebb. The sun was therefore linked with energy, vitality, and sexual vigor.

So within the Druidic tradition, the sun casts its influence over the functions of control, organization, and planning. It therefore has an influence on the mind, the thought processes, and willpower. We invoke the sun's influence if we wish to exert power and control over something or somebody or if we wish to imbue the recipient of a spell with similar powers.

The sun's influences are linked with generosity and giving. Its influences are all embracing, engendering wholeness and completeness—hence its circular symbol. Its energy is central to all things, and all things radiate from it. Its main areas of influence in relation to the body are the heart, the mind, the nervous system, and the male genitals. Its main contact points in the body are the head, the heart via the chest and pulse points, the solar plexus (literally, "the complex of the sun," the system of radiating nerves at the pit of the stomach), and the genitals.

We have seen that the sun is masculine, so plants falling within its central influence are best used by priests and their intentions targeted toward male recipients. If a priest needs to target his intentions toward a female recipient, then the parts of the plant with female-, or moon-associated, influences should be used or emphasized. The plants of the sun are best harvested, refined, energized, and employed in daylight, as they are purified and energized by exposure to sunlight.

You may see from the above that the influences ascribed to the sun are founded in the observation of the practical effects of the sun on the world around us. Druidic lore is, in all cases, pragmatic at one level and spiritual on another. However, when it comes to ascribing magical influences, the pragmatic informs the spiritual and the spiritual then enhances the practical.

Plants of the Moon

The moon is the earth's only satellite, and its appearance in the night sky changes dramatically over the course of the lunar month. The Druids recognized the moon's influence on the waters of the world, causing the tides to ebb and flow. The apparent variation in the moon's shape we now know to be caused by its ever changing relative angle to the sun and the amount of the moon's surface exposed to the sun's light from below the horizon. The ancient Druids, however, thought the moon actually changed its shape, swelling and shrinking in a cycle of fertility that was emulated by the earthly female.

The Druidic sign for the moon is the crescent.

The moon, then, imbues distinctly female characteristics. It influences fertility, conception, and the reproductive process in general. The sun influences the conscious mind; the moon influences the subconscious and inner feelings. It influences growth and the rhythm of reproduction. We shall see later that in the application of Celtic sex magic, the moon exerts the influence of passion (often wild passion) and raw, physical instincts, while in other applications it may have a loving, motherly influence on an individual or a family. This again ties the ever changing appearance of the moon to the changeable aspects of its influences.

The main areas of the moon's influence on the body are the subconscious mind and the reproductive system. Its main contact points in the body are the head, the breasts, the womb, the ovaries, and the female genitals. We invoke the moon's influence if we wish to affect fertility, sexual energy, sensuality, and adventure, and alternatively—and I am aware of the contradiction here—motherliness, family feelings, reflection, purity, and the subconscious.

Plants falling within the central influence of the moon are best used by a priestess and their intentions targeted toward female recipients. If a priestess needs to target her intentions toward a male recipient, then the parts of the plant with male-, or sun-associated, influences should be used or emphasized.

The plants of the moon are best harvested, refined, energized, and employed in moonlight, as they are purified and energized by exposure to the light of the moon.

One of the most important influences of the moon is that of its purity. This is channeled in the crafting of moon-cleansed water, used extensively in most Druidic rituals and potions.

Flower Attributes

Having seen how the celestial bodies may influence the energies and attributes of flowers, we must now look at the actual physical and magical attributes of the various genera and species of flowering plants. The table below shows the range of flowers and flowering herbs (treated as flowers) that are used commonly in Druidic plant lore and that are indigenous to the Celtic regions of northern Europe.

The Influences and Attributes of Celtic Flowers

Name				Attributes	
Common	Scientific	Welsh (translation)	Celestial Influence	Physical	Magical
Anemone (Wood)	*Anemone nemorosa*	*Blodyn y gwynt* (flower of the wind)	Moon	Poultice treats strained muscles	Healing, protection, sincerity
Angelica (Wild)	*Angelica sylvestris*	*Llysiau'r gwrid* (the blushing herb)	Moon	Digestive disorders	Purification, healing
Bird's-foot Trefoil	*Lotus corniculatus*	*Traed yr Oen* (lamb's foot)	Sun	Poultice reduces bruising	Sexual potency, fertility

Name			Attributes		
Common	Scientific	Welsh (translation)	Celestial Influence	Physical	Magical
Bluebell	*Hyacinthus non-scripta*	*Clych y eos* (bell of the nightingale)	Moon	Used externally to ease sprains	Faithfulness, modesty, truth
Brooklime	*Veronica beccabunga*	*Llysiau Taliesin* (Taliesin's herb)	Moon	Reduces swelling, treats throat and mouth infections	Protection; improves visionary capacity
Buttercup (Meadow)	*Ranunculus acris*	*Blodau y menyn* (yellow flower)	Sun	**Poisonous;** said to cure the plague	Increases self-esteem and confidence
Celandine (Greater)	*Chelidonium majus*	*Llym u llygaid* (sharp of eye)	Sun	**Poisonous;** treats corns and warts	Brings joy, cures depression
Chickweed (Starwort)	*Stellaria media*	*Gwlydd* (potato stem)	Moon	Treats coughs and heals wounds	Love and relationships
Cinquefoil (Marsh)	*Potentilla palustris*	*Pumbys* (five leaves/ petals)	Moon	Treats mouth ulcers and sore throats	Protection and purification; love and wisdom
Clover (White)	*Trifolium repens*	*Meillionen wen* (white clover)	Sun	On skin increases sensitivity	Empowers projection; increases psychic power
Coltsfoot	*Tussiago far fara*	*Carn yr ebol* (colt's hoof)	Moon	Treats coughs	Brings love and peace
Cotton Thistle (Scottish thistle)	*Onopordon acanthium*	*Ysgall* (thistle)	Sun	Treats nervous complaints	Protection, vitality; increases libido

Name				Attributes	
Common	Scientific	Welsh (translation)	Celestial Influence	Physical	Magical
Cowslip	*Primula veris*	*Llysiau'r parlys* (herb of paralysis)	Sun	Externally, acts as mild local anesthetic	Protection, healing, youthful energy
Cuckoo flower or Lady's smock	*Cardamine pratensis*	*Blodyn llaeth* (milk flower)	Moon	Taken as a digestive	Fertility, passion, and sexual energy
Daffodil (Wild)	*Narcissua pseudonarcis-sus*	*Gwaew'r brenin* (the blood of the king)	Sun	The bulb is narcotic; used externally to reduce swelling	Increases self-esteem; binds fidelity and love
Daisy	*Bellis perennis*	*Lygad y dydd* (the day's eye)	Sun	Treats strains and bruising	Protection, binding, devotion
Dandelion	*Taraxacum officinale*	*Dant y llew* (teeth of the lion)	Sun	Treats jaundice and coughs; purifies the blood	Rejuvenation; increases psychic abilities; cleansing
Feverfew (Common)	*Tanacetum parthenium*	*Wermod wen* (white wormwood)	Moon	Treats headaches; regulates menstruation	Immortality, love
Figwort (Common)	*Scrophularia nodosa*	*Meddyges ddu* (the black medicine)	Moon	Treats sore throats and toothache	Protection, happiness; the Irish "queen of herbs"
Forget-me-not (Field)	*Myosotis arvensis*	*Llys cariad* (the darling herb)	Moon	Externally, acts as cleanser	Love; increases memories
Foxglove	*Digitalis purpurea*	*Menyg yr ellyll* (glove of a fiend)	Moon	**Poisonous** DO NOT USE	Very strong magical properties

NAME				ATTRIBUTES	
Common	Scientific	Welsh (translation)	Celestial Influence	Physical	Magical
Fumitory (Common)	*Fumaria officinalis*	*Mwg y ddaear* (smoke of the earth)	Moon	Antiseptic	Purification and cleansing
Garlic (Ramsons Wild)	*Allium ursinum*	*Garlleg* (Garlic)	Sun	Treats loss of appetite; digestive problems	Protection; guards against evil
Gypsywort	*Lycopus europaeus*	*Llysiau'r sipsiwn* (Gypsy's herb)	Sun	Yields strong black dye; treats heart, nervous conditions	Healing; relaxation; aids divination and scrying
Honeysuckle	*Lonicera periclymenum*	*Gwyddfid* (honeysuckle)	Moon	Treats headaches and coughs	Increases psychic ability
Iris (Yellow)	*Iris pseudacorus*	*Enfys* (rainbow)	Moon	Used externally for skin irritations	Purification; invokes wisdom and courage
Lavender (Common)	*Lavandula angustifolia*	*Lafant* (lavender)	Moon	Treats migraine, exhaustion, and nervous disorders	Invokes love, peace, joy, and healing
Marjoram (Wild)	*Origanum vulgare*	*Mintys y creigiau* (mint of the rock)	Sun	Treats coughs and intestinal problems	Happiness; re-lieves depression
Marigold (Pot)	*Calendula officinalis*	*Aur y gors* (gold of the marshes)	Sun	Antiseptic, antifungal; treats cuts and wounds; use as mouthwash	Increases prophetic dreams; increases love and passion
Meadow-sweet (Bridewort)	*Filipendula ulmaria*	*Brenhines y waun* (queen of the meadow)	Moon	Treats flu, headaches, and stomach ulcers	Love; lifts depression

Name				Attributes	
Common	Scientific	Welsh (translation)	Celestial Influence	Physical	Magical
Melilot (Common Ribbed)	*Melilotus officinalis*	*Mel y ceirw* (honey cherry)	Sun	Treats headaches; antiseptic	Protection
Milkwort (Common)	*Polygala vulgaris*	*Llaethlys* (milk herb)	Moon	Purifies the blood	Health, longevity, immortality
Mint (Round-leaf)	*Mentha sauveolens*	*Mintys* (mint)	Moon	Treats stomach complaints and nausea; antiseptic	Protection, healing; the Druids' most sacred herb
Mistletoe	*Viscum album*	*Uchelwydd* (most lofty of herbs)	Sun	Treats high blood pressure, arthritis, eases menstrual flow	Not really a flower/herb, but the "all powerful" Druidic plant
Mugwort	*Artemisia vulgaris*	*Llwydlys* (Gray herb)	Moon	Regulates menstruation; treats loss of appetite	Brings prophetic dreams; aids divination
Mullein (Great)	*Verbascum thapsus*	*Clust y fuwch* (goat's ear)	Sun	Treats coughs, chills, and earache; poultice treats wounds	Increases psychic awareness and vision; used to make "hag's tapers" or enchanter's candles
Nightshade (Deadly)	*Atropa belladonna*	*Llewg yr iâr* (makes hens faint)	Moon	**Poisonous** DO NOT USE	Very strong magical powers

Name				Attributes	
Common	Scientific	Welsh (translation)	Celestial Influence	Physical	Magical
Pansy (Heartsease)	*Viola tricolor*	*Trilliw* (pansy)	Moon	Treats skin complaints, respiratory problems	Love and affection; aids divination
Parsley (Cow)	*Anthriscus sylvestris*	*Troes y dryw* (wren's foot)	Sun	Increases stamina	Peace and affection
Pennyroyal	*Mentha pulegium*	*Brymllys* (pennyroyal)	Moon	**Poisonous;** used externally to combat fleas	Used in scrying and divination to sharpen the wits
Pimpernel (Scarlet)	*Angallis arvensis*	*Lysiau'r cryman* (the sickle herb)	Sun	**Poisonous;** used as a weatherglass and clock	Dispels melancholy (also called "the laughter bringer")
Poppy (Welsh)	*Meconopsis cambrica*	*Llysiau cwsg* (the herb of sleep)	Moon	**Poisonous;** used externally for skin disorders	Fertility, sleep, relaxation, meditation
Rose (Dog)	*Rosa canina*	*Rhosyn y berth* (the valuable rose)	Moon	Used as a general pick-me-up and tonic	Healing, love; said to cure the bite of a mad dog (dog rose)
Sage (Wood)	*Teucrium scorodonia*	*Sage gwyllt* (wild sage)	Moon	Treats catarrh, nasal infections	Wisdom, immortality
Selfheal	*Prunella vulgaris*	*Craith un nos* (scars like night)	Moon	Treats throat and tonsils, heals cuts and wounds	Healing, aids self-confidence
Scullcap	*Scutellaria galericulata*	*Gras Duw* (God's grace)	Sun	A strong nerve tonic	Strengthens sexual potency

Name				Attributes	
Common	Scientific	Welsh (translation)	Celestial Influence	Physical	Magical
Sorrel (Shamrock Wood)	*Oxalis acetosella*	*Suran y cwn* (dog's acid)	Moon	Treats liver and kidney disorders; heals cuts and wounds	Healing; a bringer of good fortune
Sneezewort	*Achillea ptarmica*	*Tafos yr wydd* (goose's tongue)	Moon	Treats toothache, clears head, counters fatigue	Increases sexual energy and attractiveness
St.-John's-wort (Perforated)	*Hypericum perforatum*	*Y gantwll fawr* (leaves with large holes)	Sun	Treats depression, wounds, sprains, and bruises	Wards off evil; the predominant healing herb
Tansy (Common)	*Tanacetum vulgare*	*Tansi* (tansy)	Sun	Used as a mouthwash and eye lotion	Divination; increases psychic powers; longevity
Thyme (Common)	*Thymus vulgaris*	*Gruwlys* (royal heather)	Moon	Treats digestive disorders, coughs, and bronchitis; used as mouthwash	Purification and cleansing; helps in seeing other worlds
Valerian (All-heal)	*Valeriana officinalis*	*Gwell na'r aur* (better than gold)	Moon	Mild sedative, treats insomnia and nervous disorders	Purification, peace and calm, tranquillity and meditation
Vervain	*Verbena officinalis*	*Llys hudol* (enchanter's herb)	Moon	Hair tonic; aphrodisiac	Enhances spells, increases vitality
Violet (Sweet)	*Viola odorata*	*Crinllys* (violet)	Moon	Antiseptic; used in perfumes and toiletries; treats earache	Protection, calming, healing

Name			Attributes		
Common	Scientific	Welsh (translation)	Celestial Influence	Physical	Magical
Woodruff	*Galium odoratum*	*Llysiau'r eryr* (the eagle's herb)	Moon	Treats circulatory disorders	Cleansing; aids divination
Wormwood	*Artemisia absinthium*	*Chwerwlys* (bitter herb)	Moon	Treats loss of appetite, digestive disorders, fevers	Increases psychic power
Yarrow (Woundwort)	*Achillea millefolium*	*Llysiau'r* gwaedlif (the herb of blood flow)	Moon	Digestive tonic; treats colds and flu; heals cuts and wounds	Relaxation, love; increases attractiveness

There are a number of things to note from this table. The plants marked "poisonous" should not be harvested or used in any way. They are included purely because they are used by experienced herbalists and form part of the overall picture of plant medications. Never use any plant that you suspect to be poisonous.

The physical attributes of each plant are those that are expressed through the Druidic complex—here, the complex of the flower. They do not necessarily express the same therapeutic and healing attributes of remedies and medications prepared through other means. Even though herbalists and homeopaths may prepare remedies from the same genus and species, they generally use different *parts* of the plant, such as roots and leaves, to prepare their medications. This has a profound effect on the nature of the remedy.

One of the unique features of Druidic complexes is that because of the method of preparation (see page 141), all internal medications are taken in the same doses. These doses and the most suitable dilution agent (carrier) are considered later in this book. The "carriers" for external use of the complexes, such as salves, balms, and poultices, are also considered later as are the details of how these complexes are used in Druidic rituals and in particular in Celtic sex magic rituals.

Each plant has a binomial categorization, beginning with its family name (genus), followed by its individual name (species). Each genus is made up of a number of species. The plant's family name (genus) is usually of ancient Greek, Persian, or Latin origin. The genus is always a noun, and, due to its antiquity, it is often impossible to translate a name into modern English. The species name of the plant may have been created from a number of sources. Sometimes it indicates the plant's country of origin, other times the plant's natural habitat, its color, its fragrance, or even the discoverer's name. On some occasions the species name indicated the common use of the plant as in the species name *officinalis,* which indicates the plant's use as an ancient herbal medicine.

Once again I will stress the importance of absolute identification of the plants you are using. Some plants are very confusing and many are similar to other, sometimes deadly plants. Cow parsley, for example, has the common country names of adder's meat, devil's meat, and bad man's oatmeal because it is easily mistaken for hemlock and fool's parsley, both of which are deadly poisonous.

Of course, when considering which plants to use for a particular physical or magical benefit, it is possible to combine the complexes of a number of plants to obtain the attributes you desire.

Harvesting Ritual

This is the first of a number of rituals that we shall be exploring, so let's look at the basic ideas and methods that inform all Druidic rituals. The idea of a ritual is to undertake a predetermined sequence of events in order to obtain a predetermined outcome. Therefore, all Druidic rituals have a common sequence of events, or framework. Individual rituals will vary within this framework in whatever way is necessary to conduct the ritual to best effect. The framework of the ritual may be defined as follows.

The Gathering. The informal gathering of the participants in the ritual, a time when people meet and greet each other and the participants come together physically and mentally in preparation for what is to follow. This informal assembly then progresses into the Gathering proper, which is the first part of the ritual, focusing the participants on the purpose of their assembly. This is where a conscious, metaphorical line is drawn between the events and preoccupations of the mundane world and the focus of the ritual as well as when participants transcend from the mundane to the magical.

Casting and Sealing the Protective Circle. The Protective Circle provides spiritual and magical protection for the participants. It is drawn by the priest or priestess, and once all the participants are gathered within its circumference the Circle is sealed, providing a concentration of energy within and keeping any unwelcome or hostile influences out. Different priests and priestesses draw the Protective Circle at different times during the early stages of the ritual. This is a matter of personal preference, as long as the Circle is drawn and ready to be sealed once the participants are inside it; then it may be drawn or "cast" whenever best suits the priest or priestess. In the rituals we shall look at later in this book, I describe the casting of the Protective Circle at a point in the ritual where I would normally undertake it. You will see from the description that this may be altered, within reason, to suit the individual priest or priestess without any significant change in the ritual's progression.

The giving and receiving of the first libation. This is the opening part of the main body of the ritual. The participants are welcomed and share a ritual libation to acknowledge the coming together of the Gathering and its unity of purpose.

The protean core of the ritual. This is the focal point of the ritual, the reason for its facilitation. It is the most flexible part of the ritual and may take many forms. In Celtic sex magic rituals, for instance, this is where the seven successions of the ritual begin, and the successions may then continue for a number of hours. Alternatively, in the harvesting ritual this is the simple act of harvesting, which takes just a few moments to complete.

The final libation. A last libation, taken at the end of the main body of the ritual, is an act of the unity of intention of the Gathering and consecration of the prime purpose of the ritual.

Unsealing the Circle. This is the reopening of the Protective Circle on completion of the ritual.

The scattering. The participants leave the place of ritual following a brief period of socializing and discussion.

The gift. In recognition of the basic Druidic concept of returning what has been taken, and as a final act of giving and receiving, a token gift is left at the site of the ritual before the priest or priestess leaves.

This, then, is the framework of most Druidic rituals. There is, of course, the need for some preliminary preparation by both the priest or priestess and the individual participants. These, for the greater part, consist of cleansing and purification processes, together with mental and spiritual preparation. All of these processes of preparation are discussed in detail in my book *Celtic Sex Magic,* and I refer the reader to this source rather than repeat these elaborate processes here.

We must now return to the harvesting ritual. The means by which you harvest your selected plant (or plant part) is of prime significance and has a major effect on the eventual complex and incense that you derive from it.

We have seen how the plant's environment and state of health, for example, affect its energies and how we may target a specific donor plant in order to extract its physical and magical attributes. The actual selection of the donor plant may be a lengthy process. In this case, we shall look at the particular peculiarities of flower harvesting and the ritual this involves through the use of a practical example.

Here follows an account, with some additional explanations, of the harvesting of a crop of bird's-foot trefoil *(Lotus corniculatus),* used later in this book as the basic material for the demonstration of the refinement method of the complex of the flower. For the moment we shall not discuss its energies or particular attributes but rather focus on the harvesting aspect.

Finding the bird's-foot trefoil is not difficult, at least in the south of Ireland, where I live. It is a very common plant—in fact one of the most prolific wildflowers of the region. It has been known to country folk for as long as we can tell and it has attracted a number of country names, such as "lady's shoes and stockings," "thumb and finger," and "crow's toes," to name just a few. In the Welsh Druidic tradition it is known as *Traed yr Oen,* "lamb's foot," or, more significantly, *cala Duw*, "God's penis," and it is used primarily in sex magic rituals. As this is an application we shall be exploring in detail later, the bird's-foot trefoil makes an excellent example.

The bright yellow flower does not take the typical radiant petal form. Some of the petals are in fact fused together to form the shapes that have given it its vernacular names. Notice that the two central petals of the flower are linked to form a beak shape. It is from the appearance of this formation—and from a principle held by Druidic tradition that through my research on alchemy I have also come to know as

The bird's-foot trefoil, the primary flower used in Celtic sex magic.

Paracelsus's Doctrine of Signatures—that the bird's-foot trefoil takes its place as the primary flower used in the art of Celtic sex magic.

Paracelsus explains his Doctrine of Signatures in this context: "Nature marks every plant that issues from her for what it is good" and "There is no thing in nature created or born that does not also reveal its form externally; because the inner always works toward manifestation." In his Doctrine of Signatures, Paracelsus is restating an ancient Druidic belief that every plant will itself indicate the best way in which it may be used to serve or benefit others. In other words, if we look closely at a plant, it will indicate to us how we may best use it.

For example, St.-John's-wort *(Hypericum perforatum)* has been used in the Druidic tradition for millennia as a treatment for cuts and wounds. If you hold the leaf of the plant to the light, it displays translucent holes along its length. The Welsh Druidic name for the plant is *y gantwll fawr,* or "the plant with large wounds." The plant is therefore "showing" us its best use, its signature.

In the case of the bird's-foot trefoil, it is the phallic shape of the central male flower pair that gives us its signature. The occasional red streaks or blushes that appear on the petals also suggest the flushing of sexual excitement. Having taken heed of this indicator, years of subsequent application have demonstrated the effective use of the flower's complex and incense in sex magic rituals.

The bird's-foot trefoil may be found in abundance on pastureland, in open forests, and along roadsides and pathways. As it is a plant of the sun, I searched for it during the daytime and in a place where it would enjoy a good deal of sunshine. I eventually chose a community of trefoil growing alongside a large group of dandelions (another flower of the sun). The close proximity of the dandelions means that their compatible attributes would reinforce and enhance those of the trefoil. Having identified the flowers that I intended to harvest, I returned home to make plans and prepare for the harvesting ritual that was to take place the following day.

Early the next morning I gathered the tools I required from my cache and then undertook the usual cleansing and purification processes of my tools and body. Again these processes are explained in detail in *Celtic Sex Magic.* These processes include the physical cleansing of the body, often enhanced by the use of appropriate herbs to energize or calm the body, mind, and spirit, dependent upon one's mood at the time. This is accompanied by the purifying of the Internal Energy and the mental preparation/raising of awareness that is a necessary part of every ritual working. In addition to this bodily cleansing and purification it is also necessary to apply the same disciplines to the tools and accompanying equipment required for our ritual working. This again is done by the initial physical cleansing and purification of the tools in order to dispel any unwanted influences accrued since their last use.

For the harvesting ritual we need the following materials:

- **A stave** to cast the Protective Circle before harvesting.
- **A dagger or triple-knotted rope** to seal the cast Circle.
- **A ritual robe** to wear during the ritual; the harvesting may be done nude if you prefer.
- **A small vessel with an airtight seal** into which you will place the harvested flowers.
- **A compass** is essential so that you be aware of your orientation as you begin the harvesting ritual. If you are not familiar with your intended location, take a compass to find the cardinal points.
- **An earth gift.** A small token to leave at the harvesting site in return for the plants harvested. I often use the remains of libations or incenses used in previous rituals that I store in sealed bottles labeled "Earth Gifts."
- **A small cloth or working stone cover** on which to lay out the ritual tools and perhaps for you to sit on during the harvesting.

Armed with these few essential tools, I set forth to the harvesting site. By now it was about 9:30 a.m., and the bright sunlight pierced the forest canopy as I approached the group of trefoils growing deep within. (It is a good idea to harvest your flowers from secluded locations. This not only gives you privacy for your ritual—remember, you may choose to be nude to facilitate it—but also enables you to focus your concentration without fear of interruption. I find it very difficult to refocus on a ritual once I have been interrupted.) The ritual began by orienting myself so that I was standing due south of the flowers I intended to harvest. (If you are not familiar with the location, use the compass to determine the cardinal points.) I lay the cloth on the ground and placed all my ritual tools on it. I removed my clothing and put on my robe. (You may remain naked if you wish.) Standing facing the flower group (north) and holding my stave in both hands, I assumed the power position of the inverted pyramid stance. (Those of you who have read my book Celtic Sex Magic will be aware of this method of raising sensory awareness, and I refer those who have not to that publication rather than digress from the matter here at hand.) Very briefly, this is a process that allows the participant to focus on each of his or her prime senses in turn, raise their awareness of each, and then obtain a balance of all in order that the mind, body, and spirit are all in harmony before the ritual working begins.

When I felt prepared, I lifted the stave high above my head with both hands and said the opening words of every Druidic ritual:

"And so it begins."

I then cast the Protective Circle around the periphery of the flower group in the way described on page 237.

Sitting facing the flower group, I focused on the sensory experiences I had heightened a little earlier—smelling the fragrance of nature surrounding me, feeling the touch of the cool, smooth grass beneath me, listening to the sounds of the forest, tasting the airborne humidity and flavors carried on the breeze. I closed my eyes and began to look inward and to see myself as a part of nature, finding my place within the natural energies and frequencies of the forest that surrounded me.

Once I felt at ease, I began focusing on the plants that I was about to harvest, opening my senses to any negative or critical energy that may be generated by the donor plants. If at this point I had felt any negativity whatsoever, I would have abandoned the harvesting and looked elsewhere for more willing donors.

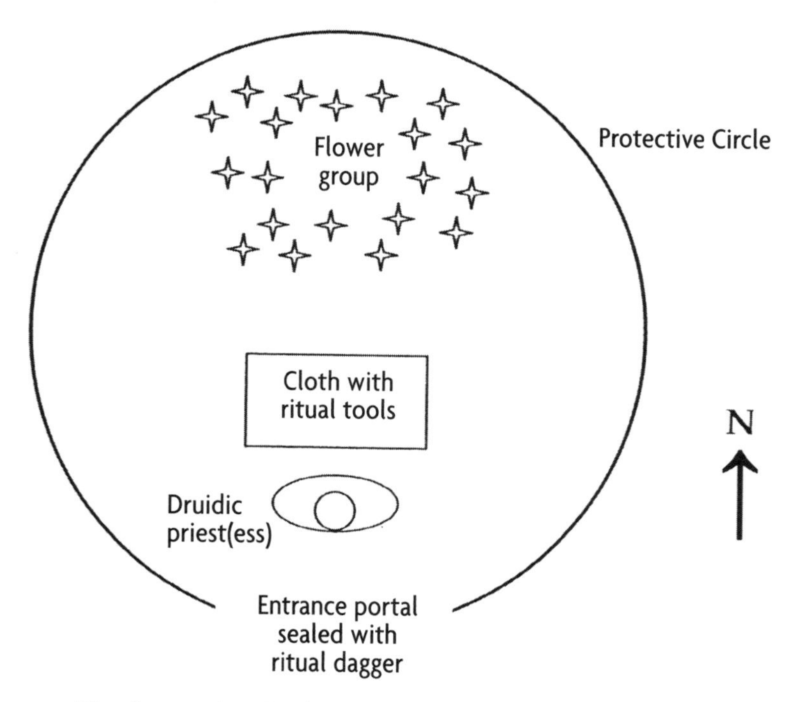

The Protective Circle encompassing the flower group.

As I felt nothing negative, I returned to a state of worldly consciousness and started gently to collect the flowers. I removed the flowers from the plants in the way I had been taught, by nipping them off immediately beneath the flower's head using the pinching action of my thumbnail against the side of my finger. (You will find this a natural action, although it is quite difficult to describe.) As I harvested each flower, I immediately placed it into the small, wide-mouth bottle I had brought with me for that purpose. As I continued to harvest the flowers I repeated the words:

"Thank you for your gift; I will use it well."

Once I had harvested sufficient flowers (a generous two handfuls yields about a cup of petals and half a cup of flower heads, enough for my needs), I sealed the bottle using its airtight top.

Placing the bottle of flowers safely to one side, I picked up the jar containing my earth gift, and as I scattered a little onto the ground of the harvesting site, I said:

"I take what you have given, and return to you what was once yours. May this always be the way."

At this point the harvesting is complete, so the ritual is closed in the usual fashion. I again lifted my stave high above my head with both hands as I said:

"And so it ends, at the beginning."

I then unsealed the Circle and erased it in the normal way, which is a reversal of the casting and sealing of the Protective Circle as described earlier. A more detailed description of these processes may be found in part 4, Unsealing and Erasing the Circle: The Ritual. Having changed into my everyday clothing and gathered all my ritual tools and containers, I returned home to my workshop.

This, then, is the ritual of harvesting flowers, and if you adhere to it closely, the flowers you harvest will retain the very best of their latent energies and attributes.

From Harvest to Workshop

It is important that you refine your flowers on the day of harvesting, as soon as possible. Always plan your harvesting to take place early in the morning (or at early moonrise for plants of the moon), and allocate time as soon as possible the same day (or night) to undertake the first two steps of the refinement process.

Keep the container of flowers out of direct sunlight and in a cool, dark place until you are ready to begin their refinement. If the flowers are exposed to heat, they will begin to wilt, and this both affects the potency of their essences and makes the separation part of the refinements more difficult. I always prepare my workshop beforehand so that when I return with my harvested plants I can begin the refinement immediately.

We have now discussed, in some detail, the physical and magical properties of the flower and how these may be utilized. We have also looked at the harvesting ritual and come to the point where we have returned to the workshop with our harvested flowers ready for refinement. We shall talk about the refinement of the complex of the flower in a later section, where we will focus on the work of the Druid in his or her workshop. For now, let's turn our attention to the other major group of plants used in the plant lore of the Druidic tradition, trees.

The Tree

Trees have long been associated with the Druids; in fact, most people's vision of the classic Druid would have him or her standing in a grove of trees of beneath a mighty oak. In addition to this almost iconic imagery, trees also play a major role in the plant lore developed by the Druids. But unlike many of the traditions found in the Far East and other areas of Europe, Druidic lore uses both the physical and spiritual (magical) properties of the tree. Once again, as with the flower, it is necessary to first look at the tree's life cycle and place in nature before we can begin to understand its use.

The Life Cycle of the Tree

Whether or not we appreciate it, trees play a major role in each of our lives. I am sure you would not have to look far from where you are reading this book to see at least one of the products of the trees we sacrifice for our convenience and pleasure. Wood has been one of humanity's most useful materials throughout our brief history on this planet, but few people appreciate the significance of the living tree in our lives and its place in the continued existence of all living things.

A single tree may have a life span of hundreds, even thousands of years, during which time it may take up to 440 gallons (2,000 liters) of water from the ground annually. This water, along with dissolved mineral nutrients, is transported from the roots, through the tree, to the leaves, where, using sunlight and carbon dioxide, the tree transforms them through a process called *photosynthesis* into the energy-rich sugars it needs for its growth. Eventually, most of the water taken up by the tree is released through the

leaves as water vapor. As this vapor enters the atmosphere, it is carried by the winds and will fall elsewhere as rain, which nourishes yet another plant or animal.

As you can see, each individual tree is responsible for the circulation of vast amounts of water during its lifetime, but if we take a moment to consider the effect that a whole forest has on our environment, we begin to see the importance of the tree in our ecology.

The reproductive process of most trees follows the same sequence as most other plants. Trees produce either flowers, cones, or catkins in order to reproduce. Most of these bear both the male and female parts and are called *hermaphrodites*. Alternatively, there may be separate male and female flowers either on the same tree or on different trees. In some cases, notably the ash, yew, and most of the hollies, the individual trees are either male or female. Conifers bear the male and female parts on the scales of separate male and female cones.

The structure and function of the flowers of the tree are the same as those for the flowers of the other plants we have seen in the previous section. Cones and catkins hold the same reproductive parts as the flower, though these may be found in various different locations.

All trees are perennial, seed-bearing plants and are either cone-bearing—most of the softwoods—or flowering plants, which account for most of the hardwoods. In general terms, trees fall into two broad categories: evergreen and deciduous. *Evergreen* trees are those that retain their foliage throughout the year, continually shedding their older leaves and replacing them with new ones. Most evergreens in the regions occupied by the Celtic races are needle-leaf evergreens. *Deciduous* trees are broad leafed and lose their leaves each year at the onset of winter.

Tree Structure

Trees, usually the tallest of all plants, differ from shrubs in that they produce a single, upright woody stem commonly known as the *trunk*.

The tree develops and grows by adding successive layers of woody tissues to the stem of the young plant. The stem of the young tree is made up of three main layers. The outermost layer, or *epidermis,* protects the inner layers of the stem. The middle layer, or *cortex,* is the storehouse. The innermost layer, or *stele,* is more complex. It consists of a number of layers, the tough *pericyclic* layer, the *phloem* layer, the *xylem* layer, and the innermost core, called the *pith.*

As a young sapling, the tree develops a layer of cells between the phloem and xylem, called the *cambium.* It is the cambium cells that constantly produce the new phloem and xylem cells that make possible the tree's growth.

As the tree matures and its circumference increases, the outer layer begins to crack and fall away. At this stage a new cork cambium, or *phellogen,* develops to protect the exposed phloem. As the tree continues to grow and its trunk expands and cracks, a new cork cambium develops to protect it. As the tree reaches maturity, the xylem layer makes up around 95 percent of its diameter. The xylem is commonly called the *wood.* The layers outside the cambium (growing) layer are collectively called the *bark.*

Because the xylem cells produced in the spring are larger than those produced in the fall, and because the tree halts its growth during the winter, the new wood develops in distinct concentric circles, called *growth rings.* The older growth rings are nonfunctional and usually dark in color. These are collectively called the *heartwood.* The younger growth rings, lighter in color, are used to transport the tree's sap. They are, therefore, called the *sapwood.*

The tree's bark forms a protective covering over its trunk, branches, and roots. It consists of an outer and inner layer and is used commercially in tanning, the manufacture of shoes and cork, and, most significantly for us, in medicines. The main European trees whose barks are used for medicines are the witch hazel and the yew.

Like the flowering plants we looked at earlier, trees have come to be known by many different names in different regions. Some are based on the appearance of the tree, for example, some on its common usage, some on its habitat. (The common names for native English trees have been standardized according to those published by the Botanical Society of the British Isles [Dony, Jury & Perring, 1986]. This is not a great deal of help to those people living outside the British Isles, of course.) The tree's botanical, Latin name is made up of two components, the genus and the species, just as it is in the case of the flowering plant classifications we saw previously.

By referring to the botanical name of each tree in any reference book, you ensure that you are in fact identifying the very same tree as is mentioned in the text that

Component parts of the tree
pith
Annual Rings
heartwood
bark
phloem
sapwood
Switzer

follows. By considering its common or "folklore" name, you may gain some insight into its "signature" as explained previously. Again, it is important to stress the need for absolute certainty in correctly identifying the trees you intend to target as donors. A mistake in identification could have disastrous consequences.

The Three Cardinals of the Tree

In looking at the three cardinals of the tree, we must first remember that we are not, at this stage, dealing with its flower, cone, or catkin. If that were the case, the tree's harvested flowers would be refined as the complex of the flower. Here we are considering the unique energies and attributes possessed by the tree *beyond* those of its flowers.

Unlike the flowering plants we're looked at so far, Druidic plant lore maintains that the tree is made up of three basic components, or cardinals. These are the *leaves,* the *wood,* and the *bark.*

The leaves are the male part of the tree and come under the associated influence of the sun, no matter what the particular central influence of the genus and species may be. As receptors of the sun's energy, they assume the role of the male provider. The leaves of the tree are linked most closely to the elements fire and air: fire in the form of the sun's light and heat, and air because they are the respiratory organ of the tree. These two elements are themselves considered to be male and under the influence of the sun. We therefore refine the first of the tree's cardinal essences from its leaves.

The wood of the tree is considered its female component and thereby comes under the associated influence of the moon. It was understood by the ancient Druids to be the generative part of the tree and therefore female. The tree's wood is linked with water and earth, the two female elements that come under the influence of the moon: water, because it is in the wood that most of the tree's water is stored and this was apparent to the ancients, who would have regularly harvested wood in its damp, "green" state when it contains large amounts of water; and earth, because the tree's wood penetrates below the surface of the soil and was seen to be the benefactor of its relationship with the earth. It is, therefore, from the tree's wood that we refine its second cardinal essence.

The third component of the tree, its bark, holds a unique position within all the Druidic cardinal essences. It is considered hermaphroditic, sharing both male and female traits. Thus, it also comes under the joint associated influences of the sun and the moon. The bark is linked with the elements fire (male/sun) and earth (female/moon): fire because of its male function of physical protection and earth because of its female functions of nourishment, nurturing, and motherly protection of the growing core within the tree. The bark, then, provides us with the third cardinal essence.

The three cardinal components of the tree were identified by the ancient Druids from their practical observation of the physical benefits they produce for the tree itself and for the humans and animals that use their various parts. They are also defined by their spiritual and magical benefits, which are linked with their association with the elements and celestial bodies that governed the everyday lives of the Celtic races.

The ancient Druid priest or priestess would have had no "scientific" understanding of the role that each of these cardinal components played in a plant's life cycle but could, and did, observe what physical effect each had on the plant's overall existence. Through experiment, priests and priestesses discovered how these energies and attributes could be channeled to benefit their own simple lives.

Each of the three cardinal essences of the tree is released through the same process, the complex of the tree method, which we shall look at in greater detail later (see page 174). This process involves each of these cardinal essences in two forms of refinement. The *physical refinement,* through a series of physical operations, produces a liquid containing the physical (chemical) attributes of the tree; the *spiritual refinement,* through a series of magic rituals, imbues these liquids with the energies and magical attributes of the tree.

In this way, as with the cardinal essences of the flower that we looked at earlier, each of the essences of the tree contains the greatest concentration of the energies and attributes that is possible.

Having refined the three cardinal essences, the remaining, almost exhausted plant matter is further refined to produce the incense of the tree. The four components derived from the tree—the three cardinal essences and the tree's incense—are then stored separately until the time comes for their use. The four separate components are eventually taken from storage in order to play their part in the ritual for which they were crafted.

It is during the ritual that the three cardinal essences of the tree are reunited in the act of amalgamation. It is only when the three cardinal essences are brought together to form the tree's complex that the full potential of the tree becomes available.

As with the complex of the flower, before the tree's complex is used, a small amount is poured onto the ground in the symbolic act of returning part of what has been given. In most cases, the remainder of the complex is mixed with moon-cleansed water to form a libation. In this way we acknowledge the authority of the elements of earth and water. This is the part of the ritual that invokes the influence of the moon on our Gathering.

The incense is then placed on the charcoal brazier. As it has been thoroughly dried as part of its refinement process, part of the incense matter ignites in flame, but the whole quickly subdues and releases the remaining potential of the flower into the air. This acknowledges the authority of the remaining two elements, fire and air. This part of the ritual invokes the influence of the sun on the work of our Gathering. As with the flower, the tree's incense is sometimes used in the crafting of the ritual *teisen iâr,* or hen's cake, that is placed on the brazier instead of the incense. This is a matter of personal choice of the priest or priestess concerned.

Trees of the Sun and the Moon

We have seen that each genus and species of plant comes under the central influence of either the sun or the moon. We have also looked at how this central influence determines the way in which the plant may be used, who uses it (to best effect), how and when the plant must be harvested, upon whom the plant is most likely to have the best effect, and what other plants may work with or against the plant's own energies and attributes.

In this section we are looking at the use of trees in Druidic plant lore, so we should initially note that trees provide complexes that are more suited to some applications than others. Their complexes reflect the more powerful and sturdy use of plants, often in magical work where mature people, as opposed to children, are the main focus. They are used most often in rituals concerned with wisdom, maturity, knowledge, decision making, community values and issues, and self-esteem. They are used in a powerful, forceful way and as a means of controlling events and circumstances.

We must remember also that certain genera and species of trees have individual male and female plants, and in these cases their gender overrides the central attributes of the genus and itself bestows the central attribute of the individual plant concerned.

These symbolic uses relate to the longevity of most trees and the experience and wisdom gained through such a long life span, to their massive size, to their raggedness, and to their domination of the habitat in which they live. Their essences are not without subtlety, however; and they are frequently used in love potions and the more physical aspects of relationships.

Trees of the Sun

The trees that obtain their central influence from the sun are imbued with the same characteristics as the flowers we looked at earlier in the section Flowers of the Sun—namely, their influence over the functions of control, organization, and planning and their characteristics of generosity and giving in their role as universal provider. I refer the reader to the section Plants of the Sun (page 78) for a more detailed discussion on these characteristics and their origins.

Trees of the Moon

The female influences imbued to trees by the moon are the same as those given to the flowers of the moon. Fertility, conception, and the entire reproductive process are all aspects of the moon's influence. Again, for a more detailed discourse, see page 80.

Tree Attributes

The table below shows the range of trees that is commonly used in Druidic plant lore and trees that are indigenous to the Celtic regions of northern Europe. This list, as with the list in the Flower Attributes section above, illustrates both the physical attributes that may be derived from a tree's cardinal essences and the magical attributes derived from the tree's energies.

The Influences and Attributes of Celtic Trees

Name				Attributes	
Common	Scientific	Welsh (translation)	Celestial Influence	Physical	Magical
Alder (Gray)	*Alnus glutinosa*	*Gwernen*	Moon	Used externally to treat swelling	Healing, protection
Apple (Crab)	*Malus dasyphylla*	*Afal*	Sun	Digestive disorders	Love, healing
Ash (Common)	*Fraxinus excelsior*	*Unnen*	Sun	Rheumatism and kidney disorders	Healing, protection
Beech	*Fagus sylvatica*	*Ffawydden*	Sun	Used externally for aching joints	Healing; increasing sexual potency
Birch (Silver)	*Betula pendula*	*Bedwen*	Moon	Antibacterial; treats kidney and liver complaints	Protection; invokes all feminine influences
Blackberry	*Rubus fruticosus*	*Mwyaren*	Moon	Treats mouth and throat infections; use as a mouthwash	Healing; invokes female influences
Elder	*Sambucus nigra*	*Ysgawen*	Sun	Treats hay fever, colds, and fevers; mild laxative	Enhances wish-fulfillment workings
Elm (English)	*Ulmus procera*	*Llwyfen*	Sun	Treats joint pain	Knowledge and learning
Hawthorn (Common)	*Crataegus monogyna*	*Draenen wen* (white thorn)	Sun	Treats nervous heart disorders	Fertility; protection from evil influences
Hazel	*Corylus avellana*	*Collen*	Sun	Treats muscular disorders and bruising	Wisdom, inspiration, Muses

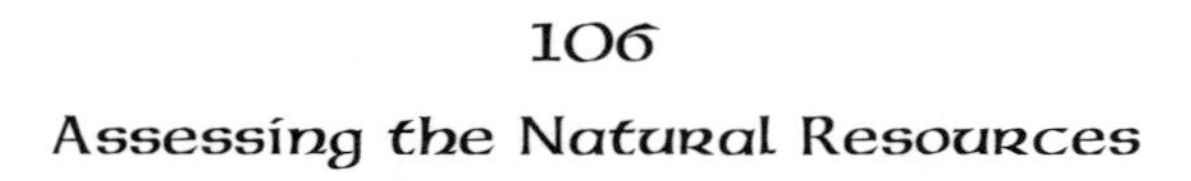

Name			Attributes		
Common	Scientific	Welsh (translation)	Celestial Influence	Physical	Magical
Heather (Common)	*Calluna vulgaris*	*Grug*	Moon	Antiseptic; mildly sedative; diuretic	Passion, loyalty, good fortune
Holly	*Ilex aquifolium*	*Celynene*	Sun	Used externally to treat bruising	The male to balance the female holly
Ivy	*Hedera helix*	*Eiddew*	Moon	**Poisonous**	The female to balance the male ivy
Oak	*Quercus robur*	*Derwen*	Sun	Antiseptic; reduces bleeding; treats cuts, burns, and sore throats	Abundance, fertility, longevity, protection; sexual potency
Rowan (Mountain Ash)	*Sorbus aucuparia*	*Cardinen*	Moon	Treats thrush; used as antiseptic gargle	Protection, healing; increases psychic powers
Silver Fir (Common)	*Abies alba*	*Ffynidwydden arian*	Moon	Treats rheumatic pains and swelling	Cleansing, purification, healing
White Poplar	*Populus alba*	*Poplysen gwyn*	Sun	Treats circulatory disorders	Contact with other worlds
Willow (White)	*Salix alba*	*Helygen*	Moon	Reduces inflammation	Protection, healing
Yew	*Taxus baccata*	*Ywen*	Sun	Increases sensitivity of touch; **poisonous:** DO NOT USE	Stability, divination, scrying

There are a number of things to note from the table above. The plants marked "poisonous" should not be harvested or used in any way. They are contained in the table purely because they are used by *experienced* herbalists and form part of the overall picture of plant medications. Never use any plant you suspect to be poisonous.

The physical attributes of each plant are those that are expressed through the Druidic complex. In these cases, the complex of the tree. They do not necessarily express the same therapeutic and healing attributes of remedies and medications prepared through other means. Even though herbalists and homeopaths, for example, may prepare remedies from the same genus and species, they generally use different parts of the plant, such as roots and leaves, to prepare their medications. This has a profound effect on the nature of the remedy.

One of the unique features of Druidic complexes is that because of the method of preparation (see page 174), all internal medications are taken in the same doses. These doses and the most suitable dilution agent *(carrier)* are considered later in this book. The carriers for external use of the complexes, such as salves, balms, and poultices, are also discussed later in this book. The details of how these complexes are used in Druidic rituals and in particular Celtic sex magic rituals are also explained later.

Once again, let me stress the importance of absolute identification of the plants you are using. Some plants are very confusing and many are similar to other, more deadly plants. When considering which plants to use for a particular physical or magical benefit, it is sometimes possible to combine the complexes of a number of plants to obtain the attributes you desire.

Harvesting Ritual

As we have seen, the three cardinal essences derived from the tree are refined from the leaves, bark, and wood of the donor plant. It is necessary to harvest these three cardinal components in the correct proportion, so that they will each yield the desired amount of cardinal essence for our use.

This is not as daunting a task as it first sounds. All we need to do is select a suitable young branch, about eighteen inches (45 cm) long with abundant foliage. Once this is

Example of a solitary tree.

harvested, it will provide us with the correct proportion of each part as determined by nature herself. What is important for us, then, is to make sure we use every part of our harvested branch for our refinement process. Every leaf, all of the bark, and all of the wood: leave nothing as waste; include every iota of the harvested branch to refine the complexes.

Targeting a donor tree and selecting an appropriate branch for refinement can be a much more difficult and time-consuming task than with the flowers we looked at previously. Trees are influenced to a much greater extent by their environment. If we accept, in general terms, that the mass of the plant below the ground is more or less equal to its mass above ground, and that the plant's area of influence extends to its farthest extremities, then we can see that the tree exerts its influence over a much larger area than do the smaller flowering plants.

This area of influence is further complicated by the way in which trees congregate in mixed forests with the taller trees forming a forest canopy covering and sheltering the growth of smaller genera and species beneath their lofty branches. To find a donor tree that is imbued with only its own energies and attributes, it will be necessary for us to locate a solitary tree, growing in isolation, such as the one pictured above.

If this same tree were growing in the middle of a dense forest, its individual energies and attributes would be profoundly influenced by the plants surrounding it. This

Areas of Influence
A Tree and a small plant
Upper areas of influence above ground
Lower areas of influence below ground
Switzer

need not be a bad thing; indeed, it is a feature we sometimes deliberately seek out. But it does complicate the issue of harvesting. It means that, in most cases, we need to get to know our donor trees much more intimately than we do other plants. We also need to study its environment much more critically.

Much of this detective work may be done with the aid of printed field guides and botanical reference books, though eventually you will discover the benefit of committing the contents of these books to memory. Remember that the ancient Druids (and the not-so-ancient ones like myself) were not allowed to write down this information or record it in any way, so we members of the old school had no option but to memorize all these facts as they were told to us.

What you need to bear in mind, whether you are using reference books or depending on your own recall, is that a plant exerts its effects on any other plant that comes within its area of influence. A neighboring plant's influence becomes stronger the closer it is growing to the donor plant. If the two plants are growing outside each other's area of influence, then they do not effect each other at all.

It is for the reader to develop his or her own skills in this facet of the art. Experience is the best way to learn this particular skill, so challenge yourself whenever possible to work out the influences exerted on any individual plant by its neighbors. We all have this innate talent; however, it is necessary to nurture it to the point where it becomes effective.

As we have seen, the plant's environment, state of health, and so on, affect its energies, and this influences us as we target a specific donor plant in order to extract its physical and magical attributes. One thing we did not need to take into account in harvesting flowers is the location of the branch on the tree's trunk in relation to the cardinal points of the compass. For maximum potency, it is necessary to harvest our branch from the north side of the donor tree. The branch is therefore growing in a south-to-north orientation, which allows it to absorb the maximum energy from the earth's magnetic fields (or as Druidic lore sees it, the earth's collective energy).

Now, having targeted a suitable branch on a suitable donor tree, we can prepare ourselves for the ritual of the harvest. Once again, as is common in the Druidic tradition, I shall use a practical example to illustrate the ritual of the harvest for the complex of the tree.

An oak from the oldest oak forest in Europe.

Here follows an account, with additional explanations, of the harvesting of a branch from the oak tree *(Quercus robur)* shown in the photograph above. This branch provides the basic material for the demonstration of the refinement method of the complex of the tree (see page 174).

This particular oak is growing in a secluded grove deep in the heart of the oldest oak forest in Europe. It is a place of supreme significance to me, and this huge, ancient oak has donated much to the physical and spiritual development of my work. This tree is surrounded by many other oaks, each of which reinforces and strengthens its energies. In the spring and early summer, large numbers of bluebells, foxgloves, and primroses grow under the dappled sunlight of its canopy. Its mighty trunk plays host to ivy and holly bushes growing at its feet. All that is missing from this king of trees is mistletoe. But the tree's potency is no lesser for that.

Druid lore reveres the oak above all trees, and it was a custom to carve a four-segment circle (the symbol of the earth we saw earlier) into the trunk of the tree to protect it from harm and to prolong its life.

I know this tree intimately, so it was not difficult for me to pick out one of its new branches as an ideal candidate for harvesting. Oak branches are best harvested in April and May, when tender new branches appear all over the tree, and it was one of these young branches, covered in leaves of the most delicate fresh green, that I selected to harvest. The oak is a tree of the sun, so I planned my harvesting to take place early in the morning of the following day.

For the harvesting ritual we need the following materials:

- **Your stave** to cast the Protective Circle before harvesting.
- **Your dagger or triple-knotted rope** to seal the cast Circle.
- **A sharp knife or pruning shears** to cut the branch from the donor tree.
- **Your ritual robe** the harvesting may be done nude if you prefer.
- **A suitable wood sealant or natural beeswax** to seal the stub of the branch left on the tree after harvesting and the end of the harvested branch.
- **A length of string or natural twine** to tie the harvested branch into a loop.
- **A compass.** It is essential that you be aware of your orientation as you begin the harvesting ritual. If you are not familiar with your intended location, take a compass to find the cardinal points.
- **An earth gift.** A small token to leave at the harvesting site in return for the plants harvested. I often use the remains of libations or incenses used in previous rituals that I have stored in sealed bottles labeled "Earth Gifts."
- **A small cloth or working stone cover** on which to lay out the ritual tools and perhaps for you to sit on during the harvesting.

Having gathered all my essentials, I set out on one of my many harvesting journeys. Walking deep into an oak forest is a spine-tingling experience on any occasion. But on this morning the floor of the forest was covered in a dense mist that thinned out as it rose to the treetops. It was cold but bright, and the shafts of sunlight pierced the mist and became diffused as they reached the dense lower level of the mist, illuminating the forest floor and making the huge oaks look as if they were floating on an iridescent sea. Apart from giving a distinctly "otherworldly" feeling to the forest, the mist was very disorienting, and I was surprised to discover just how much I depended on the contours of the forest floor to navigate through the many, very similar oaks.

As I walked farther into the forest the sun climbed higher and the mist began to evaporate. I soon found my way to the familiar glade and my favorite major oak. I knew the orientation of everything in the glade, as I had visited the place many times and had set my bearings during one of my visits years before. (If you are not sure of the orientation of the tree from which you are harvesting, use the compass to locate the cardinal points.) I had established earlier that the branch I intended to harvest was growing due north out of the northern side of the oak, so I positioned myself and my cache of tools to the south of the tree, facing the tree and the north.

I changed into my ritual robe (you may choose to facilitate the harvesting in the nude if you prefer) and, facing the tree with both my hands on the head of my stave, I adopted the power position of the inverted pyramid stance. Having raised my sensory awareness to a level where I felt prepared for the task ahead, I held the stave in both hands, lifted it high above my head, and began the ritual with the opening words of every Druidic ritual:

"And so it begins."

I then cast a Protective Circle, as shown below, around the base of the tree, allowing enough room for its perimeter to enclose my cache of tools, laid out on the cloth in front of me.

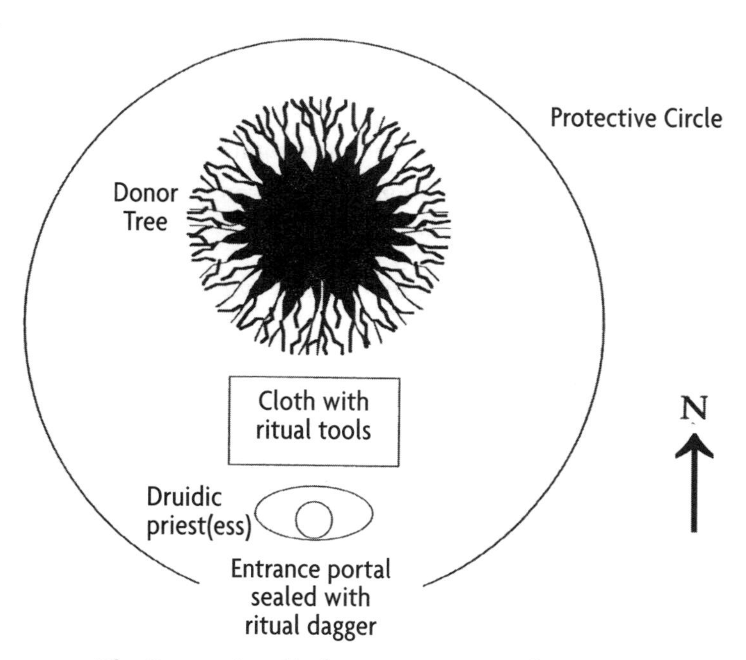

The Protective Circle encompassing the oak.

I put aside my stave and removed my robe before sitting at the base of the oak with my spine resting against the tree's trunk. As I sat, I began to focus on the sensory experiences I had heightened a little earlier, exploring my five senses and their interaction with the sounds, smells, airborne tastes, and feel of the forest that surrounded me.

Having established myself as part of the nature of the forest, I turned my attention to the donor oak. My spine became the conduit for the tree's latent energies as I "plugged in to" its core. I searched my inner feelings to see if there was any negative emotion placed there by the tree and continued to do so until I was convinced that the tree had no objection to my harvesting. Returning to a state of worldly consciousness, I stood up and walked to my cache to collect the pruning shears.

Back at the tree, I cut off the branch about one inch (2.5 cm) from the tree's trunk. I then quickly sealed the open ends of the stub on the tree and the end of the harvested branch to contain its natural energies. As I did so, I said:

"Thank you for your gift; I will use it well."

Next, I looped the harvested branch so that its tip touched the cut end at its base and tied it in position with the twine. This serves to contain the natural energies of the branch as it circulates around the closed loop. If the branch ends are left open, the energy quickly disperses. There is a risk that in looping the branch it may break or crack. If this happens, it is interpreted as a significant indicator that the branch has not been gifted to you in the proper way. Any such cracked or broken branches are returned to the base of the donor tree as you say:

"I take what is given freely and return to you what is yours. May it always be the way."

I then hung the looped branch from the stub left on the tree and walked back to my cache to collect the bottle containing my earth gift. Scattering a little of the earth gift onto the ground as I walked around the tree, I said:

"I take what you have given and return to you what was once yours. May this always be the way."

At this point the harvesting is complete, so the ritual is closed in the usual way. Picking up the stave in both hands, I raised it high above my head and said:

"And so it ends, at the beginning."

The end of this ritual is also the beginning of the cycle that will eventually produce the tree's complex and incense.

I then unsealed the Circle and erased it in the usual way (the details of which may be found in part 4, Unsealing and Erasing the Circle: The Ritual), and having dressed again in my everyday clothes, I gathered up my ritual tools, collected the harvested branch from the tree stub, and made my way back to my workshop.

This, then, is the ritual of harvesting trees. If you adhere to it closely, the branches you harvest will retain the very best of their latent energies and attributes.

From Harvest to Workshop

Having harvested the branch(es) that you require, it is essential that you begin the refinement process as soon as possible on the day or night of the harvest. The harvested branch should be kept in its looped configuration until you are ready to begin working with it. Hang it in a cool, dry place out of direct sunlight, and the tree's energies and attributes will remain their most potent.

We now have our harvested branch stored safely in our workshop, ready to begin its refinement. The next section looks in detail at that refinement process in anticipation of using the refined complexes and incenses in the rituals described in the final section.

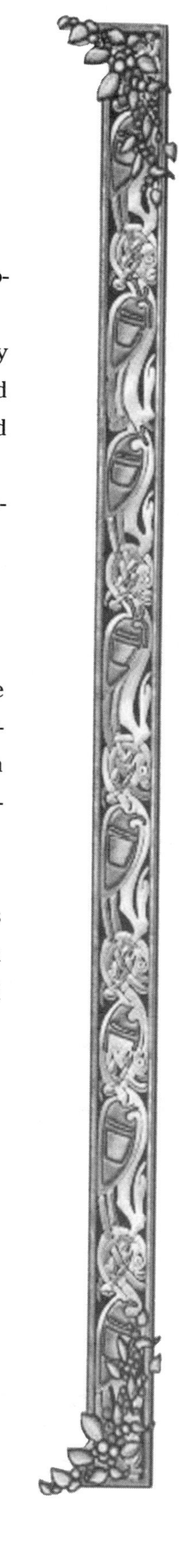

Part 3

The Druidic Workshop

Workplace and Sanctuary

For every practicing Druid, his or her workshop is the focal point of his or her activities, and therefore it becomes a place of immense significance. It is a place for private contemplation and meditation, a storeroom of all things precious, a place of ritual workings, and, most important, it is a practical work space where the practitioner may develop and practice his or her art and science.

As the Druidic practitioner's skills and capabilities grow, so the workshop grows, until eventually all the equipment, tools, and materials needed are within easy reach.

Many people begin their activities in a much more modest way, using perhaps a corner of a room, a spare bedroom, or an outdoor shed as a work space for some of the simpler techniques employed in the early stages of their learning. But before too long, the need for a dedicated and well-equipped work space becomes apparent. It makes sense that once you are convinced that you need to follow the direction of Druidic practice, the sooner you begin to contemplate where you can establish your own dedicated workshop, the better.

Later we'll look at the tools and equipment we'll need to begin the refinement of our complex and incense. As we do this, you will see that there are currently three basic "styles" of practice that we may employ.

Some people use traditional tools and equipment, which attach a degree of authenticity to the work being done. Others choose a scientific approach, using modern tools and laboratory equipment similar to that seen in any other laboratory. Yet

others prefer to use very practical, utilitarian tools and equipment borrowed from the kitchen, toolshed, or wherever they may be found in everyday life. If used and maintained properly, all are equally effective, and, if we look at it in a pragmatic sense, they all represent the same idea. The tools used by the ancient Druids—that is, the ones used in today's traditional school of practice—were the "modern" laboratory equipment of their day, the latest technology available to the priest or priestess at the time. Thus, there is no conflict of principles in utilizing today's technology just as the ancient Druids were doing in their day.

Similarly, many of the tools used by the ancient Druids were common household implements borrowed and adapted for their use in the workshop, only to be returned to general use once the ritual working was completed.

The best plan may be the one I arrived at during my forty years of practice—a combination of all three styles. If I am undertaking a process that depends on hygienic and sterile conditions, I use modern, sterile laboratory equipment. If the process is one of weighty ritual, I use traditional equipment to add authenticity. If I need something for a single, one-time purpose and it is sitting in the kitchen drawer, I borrow it and return it later.

This utilitarian approach is common in the history of the Druidic tradition. Druidic priests and priestesses were usually members of a large, extended family, often sharing living space with three or four generations of their own kin. In these circumstances, privately owned possessions were a rare thing; most of what was used belonged to the family.

Apart from one's clothes, the most common piece of privately owned property was a spoon and maybe a knife. In Wales, this gave rise to the tradition of the *love spoon,* one of the many unique aspects of Welsh cultural history.

The rural, agrarian society of Wales meant that young, single men had abundant leisure time in the long dark winter once the crops were stored and the autumn fruits and berries had been gathered. They used this time to carve decorative spoons that were presented to the young lady of their choice at their betrothal. As the tradition developed, the spoons became more and more elaborate, involving complex techniques of carving and establishing standard details representing love, chastity, and good luck. Small spheres contained in cages in the shaft of the spoon represented the

Welsh love spoons.

number of children hoped for from the union; linked chains represented the bonding of the couple. Later spoons even included Christian symbolism, changing the equal-sided cross and circle of the pagan earth symbol into the elongated cross and small circle of the early Celtic Christian cross.

Once given to the young lady, this spoon not only sealed their relationship until their marriage but also was often the only private possession of the young girl until she left the family home to live with her husband. Because of the symbolic importance of the spoon, it ceased to be a functional utensil and became the elaborately decorated love spoon known in today's Welsh culture. There are examples of love spoons in most Welsh museums, some dating back many centuries; on the other hand, there are still commercial manufacturers of love spoons working in Wales today, though the practice of carving one's own has virtually died out.

Love spoons were, and still can be, a part of the Druidic tradition. Originally, the woods used were selected for the same attributes they bring to wands, staves, and the complexes and incenses—such as healing and protection for the spoons made from the wood of the ash, or wisdom and inspiration for spoons made from the wood of the hazel. A more complete list of the attributes of wood from the trees of the Celtic Tradition may be found in part 2, The Tree: Tree Attributes. A fundamental part of the crafting of the love spoon was its "empowerment" by the Druid once it was carved, and many of the original details carved into the spoons were drawn from pagan imagery and the images of natural magic. Nowadays, all of these aspects of the love spoon have disappeared, leaving only an attractive souvenir and keepsake for the visitor to Wales.

In this atmosphere of communal living, it is easy to see that there was not much opportunity for the Druidic priest or priestess to live and work in the isolation that tradition sometimes demanded. The usual response to this problem was to erect a small building to be used exclusively as the workshop. This eventually became the place of consultation for students and patients, the place for the manufacture of ritual tools and for the crafting and storage of the priest's or priestess's materials and potions, and the private sanctuary of the priest or priestess for meditation and contemplation—in short, all the functions necessary for the modern-day Druidic workshop.

What, then, are the fundamental requirements for our workshop? First and foremost it must be a place of personal harmony. It is essential that the individual feel totally at ease and secure within his or her workshop environment. It needs to be a place of seclusion, somewhere where disruptions and interruptions are unlikely. Interrupting ritual workings or refinement processes can have disastrous results. Ideally, it will be at least large enough to contain your work table (the working stone), two or three chairs, storage racks, and side tables, and still leave enough room to move around comfortably. It must be well lit and equipped with the basic essential services (water, drainage, and electricity and/or gas).

Security will at some point become important to you. It's not that the contents of your workshop will contain overly expensive equipment, but it will house many things that will become extremely precious to you. The time and labor you will be investing in some of the compounds and materials stored in your workshop will make them very valuable to you, even in some cases irreplaceable. Make sure you are able to lock both your workshop and some of the cabinets within it, where you may store your most precious items.

Your workshop will need to be well ventilated, and you must be able to maintain a reasonable working temperature within it. Depending on where you live, and the season, this may mean either heating or cooling the interior. Remember that most of the time you are in your workshop you will be sedentary, so some form of environmental control is essential.

If you can find a space that fits all these criteria, the next step is to begin fitting it with the basic furniture and fixtures that you need. If you cannot, you may need to make some compromises.

One of the first things that can be eliminated is the water supply. Much of the work requiring water may be done in any kitchen or bathroom, assuming you know, understand, and adhere to the necessary hygiene procedures. If necessary, modest amounts of water may be carried to the workshop and stored until used. And if you have no water supply, you will not need drainage either. Without water and drainage, you are placing some restrictions on the potential of your workshop, but it may well be that you can add these services at a later date as your experience and knowledge demand.

An electricity supply is more important—indeed, almost indispensable. As a young boy I worked in a workshop lit by oil lamps and candles. I didn't find this too difficult as I knew no alternatives, but nowadays, electric lighting is ubiquitous, and you will find that the use of an electrical heating apparatus during your refinement processes helps provide a stable fermentation environment. Having said this, it is by no means impossible to work effectively without electricity. Most of the ritual workings depend on candle flame as a source of light and energy, and if the fermentation and refinement processes are carried out in the traditional seasonal cycle, they should be successful. At the same time, adequate ambient lighting can be provided by candlelight, gaslight, or battery light—as is always the case in outside rituals, particularly in remote locations.

The most important aspect of the workshop is its tranquillity and isolation. These are elements that cannot be compromised, and on that basis I have never found it possible to use a shared or temporary space as my workshop. For every practicing Druid, sooner or later it will become essential to find a dedicated workshop space.

The fixtures and fittings of the workshop are a matter of preference and may be as simple or as elaborate as you desire. The fitting of your workshop will always be a very personal expression, reflecting your inner nature and exercising your creativity. The basic contents must include:

- **A sturdy work table, known as the working stone.** This name remains with us from the ancient Druidic tradition, when all workings were done outdoors on a horizontal stone slab (similar to the altar of other traditions). Nowadays the working stone may be a portable table, a permanent rigid table, or in some cases the traditional stone slab upon which all the activities of refinement and crafting take place.
- **Two or three chairs.** For you and occasionally your students or consultees.
- **Storage shelves.** For all your general materials, tools, and equipment.
- **One or two lightproof, lockable cabinets.** For your more precious materials, complexes, and incenses (which must be stored out of direct sunlight).

With these simple fixtures and fittings in place you will be ready to gather the tools and equipment necessary to undertake the refinement processes and store the resulting complexes and incenses. But before we discuss the tools and equipment, let us take a brief look at the nature of the processes we shall be employing.

The Process of Obtaining Suitable Alcoholic Spirits

The word *alcohol* derives from the Arabic *al-kuhul.* This in turn refers to kohl, a fine powder of antimony used as an eye makeup throughout the Arab world and which remains in existence. Originally, the word *alcohol* was used to denote any fine powder, but during the Middle Ages, European alchemists applied the term to essences obtained by fermentation and distillation, and this led to the current usage.

Nowadays, the term applies to members of a group of chemical compounds and most often to the specific compound ethyl alcohol. Ethyl alcohol, or ethanol, more commonly known as grain alcohol, is a colorless liquid with a pleasing taste and, to most people, a characteristically agreeable odor. The ethanol found in wines and spirits has been manufactured since ancient times by the fermentation of naturally present sugars.

The techniques traditionally used to obtain alcohol, one of the principle ingredients in many of the refinement processes we shall be exploring, are by no means unique to the Celtic Pagan culture. Indeed it only fell upon the Druidic priest(ess) to become involved in these fermentation and distillation processes, as they both had the equipment and know-how necessary for the task. There are no special ritual workings involved in the manufacture of the alcohol spirit used and its production was, and still, is seen as a necessary "chore" rather than a priestly function. However, many people find great pleasure in fermenting wines, beers, and ciders, although the distillation of higher alcohol spirits is in fact illegal in most countries. In order to fully understand the processes (and dangers) involved, we must first gain an understanding of how both fermentation and distillation work.

125
The Process of Obtaining Suitable Alcoholic Spirits

Starch from potatoes, rice, corn, barley, rye, or other cereals is the most common raw material. The yeast enzyme *zymase* changes the simple sugars into ethanol and carbon dioxide through the chemical process known as fermentation. (This fermentation process is explained in more detail below.) The fermented liquid, containing from 7 to 12 percent ethanol, may be further concentrated up to 95 percent ethanol by a series of distillations.

Ethanol is miscible (mixable) with water and with most organic solvents and is used extensively in making perfumes, lacquer, celluloid, and explosives. It is the form of alcohol used in the Druidic tradition in both its fermented and its more concentrated, distilled forms.

It is extremely important, however, that this ethanol or grain alcohol is not confused with its close relative methanol. Methanol, methyl alcohol, or wood alcohol is the simplest of all the alcohols. It is made by the distillation of wood. Because of its low freezing point, methanol is used throughout the world as an antifreeze and as an industrial solvent. It is of the utmost importance to note that when taken internally, by either ingestion or inhalation, methanol is a powerful poison.

Many of the processes we'll be focusing on include wood, bark, and roots as their raw materials. Take great care in all of these cases to ensure that none of these woody materials is involved in any form of fermentation, as the risk of producing the toxic methanol, in however small quantities, should be rigorously avoided. Every single complex within the Druidic tradition has an alcohol base in some concentration or another, so it is worthwhile to gain a comprehensive understanding of the fermentation process in order to avoid accidental production of noxious compounds. Please take great care with fermentation. Mistakes may result in severe illness, and even death.

There is a strong argument to suggest that alcoholic beverages were enjoyed in prehistoric times, most probably through the consumption of fruit naturally fermented by airborne wild yeast. The earliest actual wine making dates from 10,000 to 12,000 years ago in the Mediterranean region. In the British Isles, it is likely that the first deliberately manufactured alcoholic drink was mead, with honey as its source of fermentable sugar. The use of fruits such as apples and pears as raw materials for fermentation became common by the Middle Ages. The ancient Celts would have consumed most of their alcoholic drinks through the technique of *cutting*—that is, diluting their wines with water in order to make the tainted water more palatable.

Many of these conventions are still followed within our Druidic tradition. You will see later that all our fermentations are started with a "ferment" called *apple must,* produced by mixing apples, honey, and yeast in the exact same fashion as did the ancient Celts. Another tradition that continues is that of the brewing wand, a stick kept by the community's Druid, who, during the appropriate seasons, went from one home to another to stir each family's brew in turn. Folklore tells us that the use of the Druid's magic brewing wand started the fermentation process through some form of supernatural act. Druidic lore tells us that this brewing wand is kept separate from other wands and is the only wand that is never cleansed or washed. It is most likely, then, that it harbored the live yeast and transferred it to each successive brew as it was taken around the village—yet another folk tradition based in practical science.

Fermentation

The term *fermentation* describes the chemical changes in organic substances produced by the action of enzymes. More often today, and certainly in our case, the term refers to the action of specific enzymes, called ferments, produced by minute organisms found in yeasts. In the context of the Druidic tradition, the most important type of fermentation is alcoholic fermentation, in which the action of the enzyme zymase, secreted by yeast, converts the simple sugars found in fruits and berries into ethyl alcohol and carbon dioxide.

The exact process used in the Druidic tradition is described in great detail on page 157, where the focus is on the fermentation techniques necessary to produce the alcohol bases needed for our workings.

Distillation

Distillation, in purely technical terms, may be defined as the process of heating a liquid until its more volatile constituents pass into a vaporous state and then cooling the vapor to return it to its liquid state by condensation.

127
The Process of Obtaining Suitable Alcoholic Spirits

If, for example, we wish to distill alcohol from a mixture of water and alcohol, we heat the mixture to 173°F (78.5°C), the boiling point of alcohol (as opposed to 212°F [100°C], the boiling point of water). The alcohol turns to vapor, then travels to the condenser, where it is cooled in order to return it to its liquid state. Thus, the liquid water remains in the original vessel and the alcohol, having been evaporated and condensed, is collected in the receiver vessel.

Even though we often refer to the entire distillation apparatus as a *still,* technically this applies only to the vessel in which liquids are boiled during distillation, prior to traveling through the fractionating column, the condenser, and to the receiver in which the distillate is collected.

Alcoholic spirits such as whiskey and brandy are usually manufactured by fermentation, followed by distillation, in order to increase the alcohol content of the drink. In normal cases, fermentation may create a liquid containing around 12 percent alcohol by volume—that is, 12 percent of the liquid is alcohol, and the remainder is principally water. By distilling this 12 percent liquid (usually more than once), manufacturers obtain the usual 40 percent alcohol (by volume) spirits that we see for sale.

The distillation process plays a major role in alchemical workings. Liquids are repeatedly distilled—ten, twenty, sometimes even hundreds of times—in order to purify and concentrate their potency. In the Druidic way, however, distillation is much less prominent. There is no great tradition of distillation of spirits within any of the ancient Celtic cultures. Fermentation of wines and the brewing of ales and ciders were much more apparent, and most households made their own brews from the fruits and berries gleaned from the surrounding countryside.

If the actual process of fermentation was considered a magical wonder, then the idea of distillation was an even more magical process. Distillation was practiced only by Druids, and even then by very few. The equipment needed to begin the distillation process was expensive and difficult to manufacture, and as there was no real understanding of the science involved, the results were haphazard and unpredictable. In fact, the same could also be said of fermentation, with many of the results yielding little if any alcohol content whatsoever.

All the same, alcohol spirits are used in nearly all Druidic herbal potions. Historically, the alcohol spirit (usually under the 40 percent by volume spirits we use today) would be distilled by the Druidic priest or priestess using various grains, vegetables, or fruits as his or her raw material. It was a dangerous process, sometimes ending in explosions and occasionally producing toxic results.

Much of the Druidic herbal tradition uses wood, bark, and roots as its raw material. If these wood-based materials are included in the distillation process, it is possible that the resulting alcohol will be methanol or wood alcohol, the poisonous relative of ethanol or grain alcohol.

Eventually, after what would have been many dangerous and disastrous experiments, most of the Celtic races managed to develop a rough, unpredictable spirit of some form or another. A more refined version of this spirit exists today in Ireland in the form of *poteen.* The manufacture of poteen for consumption within Ireland was illegal until very recently (1999). Today it can be made only by licensed manufacturers and is subject to government duty and taxation.

Needless to say, many Irish households, particularly the more rural ones, somehow manage to have a supply of homemade poteen from some long-forgotten source, which is usually stored away for "medicinal purposes." It may be a source of wonder to the reader that so many cases of severe colds requiring the use of this special medication appear in Ireland around Christmas, New Year's, and particularly around Saint Patrick's Day. In order to keep within the law and to ensure a consistent quality, we shall be using only the proprietary brands of poteen in our workings.

The distillation of alcoholic spirits, and in particular alcoholic beverages, is a very specialized and complex subject, far beyond the scope of this book. I strongly recommend that the reader use proprietary alcoholic spirits and stay well away from the distillation process unless he or she has a thorough understanding of the methods and the dangers involved.

Although poteen is now readily available anywhere in Ireland, I would not be surprised if it were difficult to obtain in some other areas of the world, in which case it is perfectly acceptable to use any relatively tasteless and clear spirit alcohol in its stead. Most countries will have their own readily available equivalent to poteen in the form of vodka or schnapps, for example, any of which will work as a perfect substitute for the classic Irish spirit.

The alcoholic spirit is merely the carrier of the essences we shall be producing (see page 211). So as long as they do not contain any conflicting ingredients, most spirits will fit the bill. Potentially conflicting ingredients may be identified either from our personal knowledge of what goes into the making of the spirit we are using or by reading the manufacturer's description of the contents on the bottle. A spirit should be avoided if the manufacturer's label identifies that the spirit contains wood or bark (such as many of the aniseed spirits), seeds (such as the cumin spirits), or berries (such a sloe spirits, or coffee spirits). Also avoid the use of spirits containing herbs (such as Martini and other vermouth), flowers (such as Chinese rose brandy), and the fruits of trees such as plum, pear, and the like. An exception is the apple as a fruit or a flower, as these are considered as neutral and one of the earliest forms of alcohol used in the Celtic nations. Most of the spirits listed in the above categories will contain unknown amounts of flavorings with rogue attributes from unknown sources that may conflict with the subtle attributes of the ingredients you will be carefully balancing in the crafting of your essences.

In looking for conflicting ingredients, we are first trying to avoid the use of any of the herbs or compounds listed in the Table of Attributes. Second, we want to avoid anything that includes an overpowering amount of any particular compound or taste such as highly flavored orange or coffee liqueurs. Finally, we are looking for a spirit that has been manufactured in the most natural way possible, avoiding large proprietary brands of malt and rye, for example.

All of these factors usually point toward a clear, relatively tasteless spirit, manufactured by smaller "local" distillers, and this usually means a traditional rural spirit of ethnic character.

Refinement Tools

Even to achieve the simplest results in the workshop, every practicing Druid must gather around him or her a collection of tools and equipment. Some may be everyday items borrowed from the kitchen or toolshed; others will, of necessity, be especially procured for the purpose. We have already mentioned some of the ritual tools, such as the dagger and rope, so what we need to look at next are the special tools and equipment needed to craft our complexes and incenses.

We have seen previously that there are three complementary schools of thought relating to the tools we need—the traditional, the functional, and the scientific—and I have already expressed my preference for a combination of these approaches in my own work.

In combining all three I believe we may maintain the traditional validity of the ritual workings while still ensuring that the most modern and effective methods of hygiene and conservation are not compromised. With this in mind, I have compiled the following list of tools and equipment from my own workshop, with a brief explanation of their use in the refinement of the complexes and incenses described later. In most cases, I have listed the option of a traditional or household alternative to the piece of scientific apparatus described.

1. For the separation and preparation of the harvested plants:

Practical Items

- **Cutting board.** During the initial stages of separating and preparing the various parts of the plants we have harvested, we'll need to cut or chop the

Traditional tools.

Functional tools.

Scientific tools.

plant material in order to fit it into the vessels we're using. In order to do this, we will need a durable cutting board. I use a marble cutting slab or sometimes a nylon cutting board. The important thing is not to use a wooden cutting board, as splinters from the board (which is often of unknown origin) may contaminate your material. Nylon cutting boards are practical and hygienic and do not blunt your knife blades, but they are unattractive and utilitarian. Marble is a little more aesthetically pleasing and equally as hygienic, but it does ruin the cutting edge of your knives if you don't maintain them regularly. Other synthetic materials may be used, but be sure they do not contain any materials that may conflict with the plant material you are cutting. The board will need to be at least big enough for you to cut up an eighteen-inch (45 cm) branch. Traditionally, this work would have been carried out on a stone surface, either a smaller stone slab in the workshop or on the actual working stone of the Protective Circle.

- **Knives.** You will find during the various processes and workings you undertake that you will need a selection of good-quality knives of various sizes. In most cases, however, all of the workings may be carried out by one or another of the three different knives that follow.

  A heavy, ridged knife with a blade of approximately eight inches (20 cm). This is used for cutting through branches and chopping branch wood and bark. I may also use a heavy cleaver for the same purpose.

  A light paring knife with a blade of approximately four inches (10 cm). You'll need this to strip bark, to slice, and for general-purpose cutting.

  A surgical scalpel with a straight, disposable blade. Used for the more delicate stripping operations and to separate flower parts.

- **Grater.** When reducing branch wood to a size suitable for maceration, it is often necessary to cut the wood into small, almost powderlike particles. This can be done through repeated chopping with a knife on the cutting board, but I have found that this is usually a tedious and time-consuming process (though traditional in its nature). I now use a grater on the "green" branch wood to achieve the correct consistency. Mine is a standard chef's manual grater, the type used in every kitchen for grating vegetables and cheese, and it does a fine job. There is no real traditional equivalent to the grater. I was taught to chop the branch using a knife as described above.

- **Mortar and pestle.** To reduce any of the materials that are mentioned above to a fine aggregate, it is best to use a mortar and pestle. The material they are made from is not really important; stone, earthenware, and glass are equally effective. Avoid wood, as this may contaminate your materials. The traditional alternative to the mortar and pestle is the *maen melin,* or millstone-two medium-size flat stones with the material placed in between. As the stones are moved back and forth, the material is slowly ground finer and finer.

- **Tweezers.** Not a traditional instrument, but useful for removing small petals, and so on.

Ritual Items

- **The candle triangle.** The familiar triangle of candles used in most rituals and ritual workings. The center candle, in the tallest candleholder, burns the flame that represents the collective energy. The flames from the other two candles represent the sun and moon, respectively. If a Druidic priest is facilitating, the sun candle is placed to the right of the central candle and the moon candle to the left. If a priestess is facilitating, the moon candle stands to the right of the central candle and the sun candle to the left. The sun and moon candles, along with their candleholders, are usually decorated to distinguish one from the other. The moon candle and holder are usually adorned with silver; the sun candle and holder are decorated in gold. The flames often represent the fire element in purification workings, as they do here.

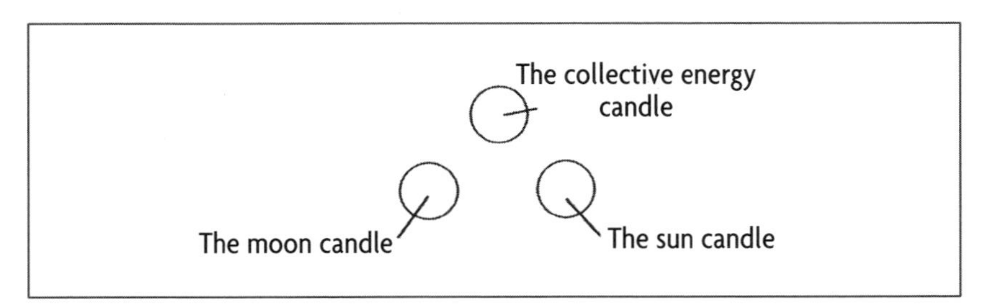

The candle triangle on the working stone of a male Druidic priest.

- **A vessel of moon-cleansed water.** Moon-cleansed water is used in most Druidic rituals, ritual workings, and potions. The process of its crafting is described on page 235. In this particular instance, the vessel of water is used to purify the harvested plant materials before their refinement begins, so the moon-cleansed water needs to be in a vessel around twelve inches (30 cm) in diameter and about two inches (5 cm) deep. Moon-cleansed water is used

instead of ordinary water in most Druidic practices. It often represents the water element in combination with earth, fire, and air. All four elements play their part in all purification workings, just as they do in this one.

- **An incense burner or crucible.** As the candle flames and moon-cleansed water represent the fire and water elements, respectively, so the smoke from the burning incense represents the air element. Traditionally in Ireland the incense is heated on a bed of peat, in Wales, charcoal is most often used. I prefer peat: First, the aroma of burning peat is wonderful in itself, and second, to be truly traditional the charcoal must be made from the same wood as the incense in order not to contaminate it. This can be difficult if working with unusual woods and impossible when working with flowers. In these cases, yew charcoal is considered neutral, but you will most likely have to make it yourself, as it is not a wood often used in making store-bought charcoal. Peat, however, is always considered a neutral agent.
- **A suitable incense.** As the purpose of the incense on this occasion is one of purification, it would not be appropriate to use one of the incenses crafted from the refinement of the complex. A simple purification incense such as lavender, pine, or rosemary is best.

2. For the maceration, maturation, and storage of the plant materials (cardinals) and their essences:

Practical Items

- **Measuring beakers.** I use 400 ml glass beakers, but any clearly marked measuring vessel will work just as well. A kitchen measuring jug is probably the most readily available functional substitute. Traditionally, any vessel of a suitable size would have been used, as the objective is just to measure equal quantities rather than specific amounts. Thus, as long as the same standard measuring vessel is used to measure all the liquids in equal amounts, the actual vessel is immaterial. It is worth considering, however, that you do not want the measuring vessel to be either too large or too small as to render it awkward to use. Something of a capacity of 400 to 500 ml will be most suitable. If you use a vessel with a pouring spout or lip, you will find it more convenient.

- **Glass bottles and stoppers.** These bottles will be used in nearly all stages of the refinement process, so they need to be of good quality. I use a variety of sizes of glass reagent bottles with ground-glass stoppers, mainly 100 ml, some in clear glass and others in amber. Any airtight vessel of a suitable size will work, but it must be made of an impervious material such as glass or ceramic. Avoid metal storage vessels of any kind.
- **Powder jars with screw-on caps.** The distinguishing feature of all powder jars is their wide neck. This means we can place plant material in them without difficulty. Bearing in mind that the plant material will expand during maceration as it absorbs the liquid it is being soaked in, we also need the wide neck to remove the plant material at the end of the process. I use 250 ml clear glass, wide-mouthed powder jars with a bakelite screw cap with faced liners. The liner is inside the cap and produces the seal. Any wide-mouthed storage jars will be adequate, such as kitchen storage jars, reused jam jars, and pickle jars, as long as they have an airtight seal. Traditionally, earthenware jars with cork and linen stoppers were used; in fact, I still regularly use the ones from my youth.
- **Spatula.** A long-shanked, small-cup spatula has many uses in the workshop. It may be used as a stirring device, to remove plant material from bottles and jars, and as an instrument to press plant material against the walls of a funnel to extract the last drops of essence. I use both a micro-spoon spatula and a Chattaway spatula, both of which fit the bill perfectly. A small, long-handled spoon would suffice, as would a glass stirring rod. From a purely functional point of view, a long cocktail spoon or drink stirrer borrowed from the kitchen or bar would also work well. There is a special bronze spoon that was traditionally used for this purpose, one of a collection of various spoons owned by most Druidic priests and priestesses, although I would think it very difficult to obtain a set like this nowadays.

The important thing is never to use a wooden spatula or stirrer, as again you will be contaminating your essences.

3. For the leaching and filtration of the cardinal essences:

- **Flat-bottom flask.** The stability of flat-bottom, conical flasks makes them ideally suited to be the receiver below the funnel when filtering liquids. I use 500 ml conical flasks with ground-glass stoppers. I prefer the standard-mouth aperture to the wide-mouthed version, as it can then double as a fermentation flask. You can, of course, use the measuring beaker mentioned above as a receiver, but then you will have to obtain some form of fermentation flask as well. Any glass or ceramic vessel of suitable size will work as a receiving vessel, and traditionally any handy vessel would have been employed.
- **Glass funnel.** Many of the operations of the refinement process involve the filtering of liquids. Today, this is usually accomplished with paper disks placed inside conical funnels. The exact method of doing this is explained in detail on page 153, but you will see that it employs a glass funnel. I use a 100 mm diameter glass funnel that I find best for the volume of liquids used. Funnels made of polythene, H.D.P.E. plastic, or ceramic are also suitable. A small kitchen plastic funnel will work, but I prefer the rigidity of glass. Traditionally, brass, bronze, or copper funnels were used, and there is also a filtering funnel used especially for this purpose.
- **Filter paper.** The circular filter paper is folded into a conical shape and placed inside the funnel in order to filter the liquid passed through it. It is important, therefore, to ensure that the correct grade of filter paper is used. As grades and definitions vary from manufacturer to manufacturer, the best thing to do is look for a filter paper with the following specification: "A general-purpose ashless filter paper with medium speed and particle retention."

  In order to fit the 100 mm diameter glass funnel mentioned above, you will need to obtain 150 mm or 185 mm diameter filter paper circles. From a functional point of view, I have seen some practitioners use coffee filtering cones, but I was not overly impressed by the results. Traditionally, the filtering processes moved progressively through a series of filtering mediums, usually a combination of linen and sheep's wool, until a clear essence was produced. This was a very wasteful process, as on each successive pass the filtering agents absorbed more and more of the precious essence. It was also unpredictable; if the filtering pad was too dense, the liquids would not percolate through, and if left too loose, the resultant liquid would not be sufficiently clear.

- **Retort stand with clamp.** I always clamp the filtering funnel into a retort stand and place the receiving vessel, usually a flat-bottom conical flask, below it. This makes the funnel rigid and totally independent of the receiving flask. It is possible, of course, to place the funnel directly into the mouth of the receiving vessel, but I have found from repeated experience that this produces an unstable and precarious situation. I use a retort stand with a rubber jaw clamp to hold the funnel securely above the receiver flask. This means I have a secure funnel to receive the filter paper and liquids, and I am able to remove or replace the receiver flask below it without hindering the process. This is not an essential piece of equipment, although it is very useful. With a little imagination and creativity, an alternative means of securing the funnel over the receiving flask could be devised with bits and pieces from the kitchen or toolshed.

4. For the fermentation of flower essences:

- **Flat-bottom flask.** See above.
- **Fermentation air lock.** Made of plastic or glass, the air lock prevents air from entering the fermentation vessel while allowing the gases created by the process to escape. The base of the stem of the air lock is designed to fit into a cork or rubber stopper, which in turn fits into the neck of the fermentation vessel. Because most fermentation equipment is designed for home brewing and fermenting homemade wines, the majority of the air locks and stoppers are made to fit demijohns and not the conical flasks that I recommend. It will then be necessary for you to trim down the cork

or rubber stoppers to fit firmly the neck of the fermentation flask. This is done quite easily using a sharp knife and a degree of care. Traditionally, a bung of linen was placed in the neck of the fermentation vessel, and that worked reasonably well. The gas produced inside the vessel leached out through the linen, and as the vessel is always under positive pressure, no air entered inside. The linen also prevented airborne bacteria from entering the ferment and disrupting the process.

- **Heater/temperature regulator** (optional). Fermentation heaters and temperature regulators, are too, designed mainly for the homebrew market, unless you are prepared to pay a large amount for a laboratory heat bath. They come in many different designs, but I prefer the collar or belt type. These fit around the fermentation flask and, when connected to the electrical supply, maintain the flask and its contents at a constant temperature suitable for optimum fermentation. A practical alternative is to place the fermentation vessel in an airing cupboard, or hot press, as it is known in Ireland, or any other place where it may be maintained at a relatively stable warm temperature. The traditional method is possibly a little unpleasant by modern-day standards. The fermentation vessel was placed in a bucket containing a mixture of straw and cow dung. As the straw and cow dung mixture decomposed, it generated a consistent heat source of exactly the right temperature to aid the fermentation. This is not a method that would go down well in most homes today.

That completes the list of equipment needed to begin our work. There will be one or two small additions as we go along, but the list above covers nearly all eventualities.

Almost all the "scientific" apparatus mentioned above may be bought at reasonable cost from any supplier of laboratory equipment. You will find these in your local telephone directory. It is often a good idea to try to source the equipment from suppliers that cater to schools and universities, as they usually stock a wide range of cheap, durable equipment designed to withstand the rigors of enthusiastic students. Alternatively, there is a range of mail-order suppliers available on the Internet. In my experience, it has never been difficult to obtain these items; every town has a school and every school buys its laboratory supplies from somewhere. If you have difficulty, call your local high school or a nearby college and ask where they source their apparatus—you can be sure they are buying good-quality equipment at a competitive price.

I have indicated above that some of the equipment is used in home brewing and in fermenting homemade wines. Where this is the case, the equipment may be purchased in any homebrew store, by mail order, or on the Internet.

None of the items listed above should cost more than a few dollars, but bear in mind that you may need more than one of each item, and in some cases you may need dozens. Build your stock of equipment as you develop your art.

The following shopping list provides all the necessary equipment to begin your work and allows you to craft two initial complexes concurrently.

Item	**Quantity**
Cutting board	1
Heavy ridged knife (8-inch blade)	1
Light paring knife (4-inch blade)	1
Surgical scalpel (straight disposable blade)	1
Kitchen grater	1
Mortar and pestle	1
Tweezers (fine tip)	1
Measuring beaker (400 ml)	2
Glass bottles with stoppers (100 ml)	12
Powder jars with screw caps (250 ml)	12
Spatula (Micro-spoon or Chattaway)	1
Flat-bottom flask (500 ml)	6
Glass funnel (100 mm diameter)	1
Paper filter	packet of 100
Retort stand with rubber clamp	2
Fermentation air lock	4
Heater/temperature regulator	2

You may substitute any or all of the above with their practical or traditional alternatives. It will be possible, particularly in the early stages of your work, to save quite a bit of money by raiding the kitchen and toolshed. However, if you discover that you

wish to continue in your work past the basic introduction, I strongly suggest you begin building up your equipment supply as soon as you can. There is no real substitute for the right tools for the job at hand.

I have not included any of the ritual tools in the shopping list, as you may already have much of this equipment. If not, again I recommend you begin gathering these items so that they are readily available when you need them.

Once again let me stress the need to maintain the highest standards of hygiene at all times, and here this means sterilizing all your equipment before and after it is used. This may be done quite easily using proprietary sterilizing agents bought from any drugstore. In every case, follow the manufacturer's instructions.

Now, having looked at the fixtures and fittings of the workshop and the equipment it contains, we are ready to begin our exploration of the refinement process itself.

The Refinement Process: The Complex of the Flower

You already know there are two specific types of refinement process, that of the complex of the flower, with its two cardinals, and that of the complex of the tree, which has three cardinals. Let us begin with the complex of the flower. The flower I have chosen for this example is the bird's-foot trefoil *(Lotus corniculatus)*.

The bird's-foot trefoil is abundant throughout Wales, Scotland, Ireland, England, and the United States and may generally be found in damp, grassy places and along the edges of pathways. A common plant, it has attracted a large variety of folk names, more than seventy, in fact, and most of these relate to its resemblance to so many everyday things: "God Almighty's thumb and finger," for example, "crows-toes," and "lady's shoes and stockings," and when the red flushes appear on the bright yellow flowers it may also be known as bacon and eggs. In Wales the bird's-foot is commonly called *traed yr oen,* or "lamb's foot"; in Ireland it is known by the name *cr'ibin éan,* or "bird's claw."

In the Welsh Druidic tradition the bird's-foot trefoil is *cala Duw,* or "God's penis." This is taken from the appearance of the flower's jointed petals and explains why it is used extensively in Celtic sex magic rituals. It is a flower often overlooked by other traditions, mainly because its active ingredients are not remarkable on their own. This is a typical example of how the Druidic tradition, by retaining its spiritual and magical elements, is able to empower the simpler gifts of nature to beneficial effect.

We have seen previously how these flowers are harvested and brought to the workshop, so our work here begins with the first stage of refinement, the separation of the cardinals of the flower. But first a brief word on the workshop ledger.

The Workshop Ledger

As with every other type of workshop procedure, it is imperative that you maintain a detailed and accurate record of your processes, methods, dates and times, observations, and results in a daily ledger. You will find this invaluable both as a means of ensuring the successful repetition of your accomplishments and as a way of identifying the sources of your failures.

Every Druidic practitioner will be constantly maintaining his or her book of spells and incantations, the workshop ledger (recording workings and ritual workings), and a diary of the general activities in which he or she becomes involved. Together, these three books become part of the Druid's cache and a very useful source of reference.

Until recently, the recording of this information has been forbidden by Druidic tradition, but like many others, I feel it is now time to set the tradition to paper. So record your activities and use them daily, but always remember the value of the precious information your ledgers contain.

The Separation of the Two Cardinals of the Flower

The separation of the cardinals is a ritual working, usually carried out by a priest or priestess on his or her own in the workshop. The process has two main elements, the physical crafting of the separation and the spiritual invocation of the four elements and the collective energy to empower the working. Before we can begin this work, however, it is essential that we have a detailed understanding of the structure of the flower itself.

The bright yellow bird's-foot trefoil flower belongs to the group of pea-type flowers. Its five bright yellow petals sit in the light green calyx/sepal cup. The first and largest of these petals forms the *standard,* or broad petal at the rear of the group. The next two petals, the *wings,* form a loose cup shape, inside which may be found the final two petals. These are jointed to form the *keel,* the beaklike or phallic-shaped envelope that gives the flower its Druidic name. Inside this envelope is found the flower's reproductive elements, the *pistil* and *stamen.*

In the process of separation we shall be removing all five petals from the flower, leaving the pistil and stamen still attached to the calyx/sepals. The petals will form

The bird's Foot Trefoil plant
Fused keel petals
Two wing petals
The standard petal
The bird's Foot Trefoil
The separation of the two cardinals
Switzer

the male cardinal; the remaining parts of the flower, the *flower head,* will form the female cardinal.

The bird's-foot trefoil is not the easiest of flowers to work with; in fact, all of the pea-type group are equally difficult because of the formation of their petals. The simpler, rosette-type flowers are much more straightforward. Having said that, the bird's-foot trefoil and its relatives comprise one of the largest groups of flowers used in the Druidic tradition, so it is worthwhile mastering the more difficult technique of separating the male and female cardinals of the pea-type group from the outset.

Separation: The Ritual Working

Like the harvesting of the flower, the separation is a ritual working, meaning it includes a spiritual/magical element within the practical work. The separation is the moment in which the two cardinals of the flower are divided. The male and the female essences will then remain separate until they are united at the Amalgamation during the final ritual for which they are being crafted. This, then, is an extremely significant part of the refinement process, a moment when the flower temporarily loses its unity and natural balance, which will later be restored.

For this reason we ensure that the separated cardinals maintain their energies and potency by invoking the power of the four elemental essences (earth, fire, air, and water) and the fifth elemental essence, or quintessence (the collective energy), to aid our efforts.

For this ritual working we will need:

- **The candle triangle.** See page 133.
- **A vessel of moon-cleansed water.** See page 235.
- **An incense burner** with a suitable incense.
- **The stave and dagger** to cast and seal the Protective Circle. If you are using a permanent working stone within your workshop, you may well have cast the Circle previously, in which case you will need just the dagger to seal its entrance.
- **Two small bowls.** One will contain the separated petals, the other will hold the separated flower heads.

- **The vessel containing the harvested flowers.** Before beginning the ritual working, remove the flowers from their container and make sure that all the stalks have been removed from the base of the flower: if not, nip them off so that only the flower remains. Replace the flowers in their container in readiness for the ritual working.

The working stone should be laid out as shown below in preparation for the ritual working:

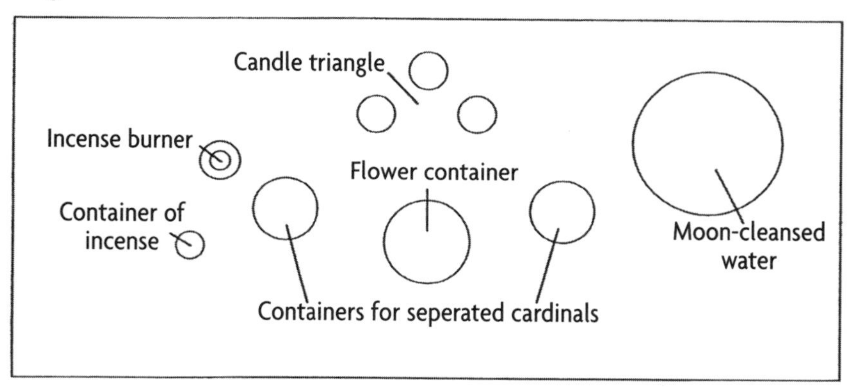

Working stone layout for the separation ritual working.

The working stone is now ready to begin the ritual working, so we must look to the preparation of our body, mind, and spirit before we undertake our work.

The process of personal preparation, by which we mean the cleansing of the body, the purification of the internal energy, the mental preparation, and the raising of awareness, is necessary before every ritual or ritual working. Because of this, the processes are described in detail in part 4, along with the other basic procedures such as casting and sealing the Protective Circle and crafting moon-cleansed water.

Having completed our personal preparation, we are ready to proceed with the ritual working.

If you are working outside your workshop, the first step is to cast the Protective Circle using the stave as described in part 4. If you are within your workshop, you may have already done this for previous activities. With the Circle cast around the working area, the entrance is sealed with the dagger. Again this procedure is explained in part 4.

The ritual working begins during the Circle-sealing process, when the dagger tip is dipped into the vessel of moon-cleansed water and the following words are spoken:

"And so it begins."

As this is the defining point of the beginning of the ritual working, some priest and priestesses also choose to mark the moment by ringing a small bell, beating a small gong, or in some cases blowing a traditional Druidic horn. The charcoal in the incense burner is now lit in preparation for the ritual working.

The next step is the lighting of the candles. We have seen that the arrangement of the candles and the order in which they are lit depends on whether a priest or a priestess is facilitating the ritual. For the sake of this example we shall assume that a priestess is facilitating. (If this needs to be translated for the male facilitator, the sequence of lighting and positioning the flame of the sun candle and the flame of the moon candle should be reversed.)

You will also note that the wording of the invocations provides for more than one person being present at the ritual working. This is because this is often a time when a newly initiated Druidic priest or priestess would be present to learn the ritual working technique.

The priestess stands before the working stone and brings the first of the candles, the flame of the collective energy candle, to the front of the stone. The candle is lit and raised into the air, and the priestess says:

"As this flame burns, so we converge with the collective energy. Our energies mingle, our potential becomes one."

The flame of the collective energy candle is placed at the back and center of the working stone.

The next candle to be lit is the sun, or male, candle (as the ritual is being conducted by a priestess, the moon or female candle is lit last). The sun candle is then held aloft as the priestess says:

"As this flame burns, it binds us with the sun. We invoke the sun's influence upon our workings."

The flame of the sun candle is placed to the left and slightly forward of the flame of the collective energy candle.

The final moon or female candle is then lit and held aloft as the priestess says:

"As this flame burns, I bind myself with the moon. I invoke the moon's influence upon all I do."

The flame of the moon candle is placed to the right and slightly in front of the flame of the collective energy candle to form the candle triangle.

You will see that this second invocation is a personal one. If the ritual is facilitated by the male, then this same personal invocation relates to the flame of the sun candle, which, in this case, is lit last.

With all three candle flames lit, the priestess stands before them at the front and center of the working stone and extends her arms so that each of her palms is directly above each of the sun and moon flames—close enough to feel the heat of the flame without burning her palms. She then brings both hands together above the central collective energy flame to form a cup shape above the flame. As she does this, she says:

"I unite all things with the collective energy, as in nature they belong. I offer myself to this union, together with any others present here. Unite us in your common bond."

This opening part of the ritual, called the *uniting of the flames,* is now complete.

The next stage of the ritual working is the invocation of the collective energy's influence in maintaining the energies and potency of the flowers whose cardinals are about to be separated.

The priestess stands before the working stone and lifts the vessel containing the harvested flowers into the air. In doing so, she says:

"I offer these flowers, taken from our earth for the good of humankind. I call upon the four elemental essences to empower their cardinals and maintain them until they are again united."

The vessel of flowers is then placed at the front and center of the working stone. The priestess forms her two hands into an inverted cup shape and places them above the vessel. As she does so, she says:

"I invoke the power of the elemental essence of the earth that yielded up these flowers, to protect their energies and maintain their potency until they are again united as one."

Then, dipping her fingers into the vessel of moon-cleansed water, the priestess sprinkles some water on the harvested flowers in the vessel and says:

"I invoke the power of the elemental energies of the water that nourished these flowers, to protect their energies and maintain their potency until they are again united as one."

The priestess now sprinkles a little incense on the smoldering charcoal in the incense burner. As the smoke of the incense rises, she lifts the vessel of flowers and holds it in the smoke. As she does so, she says:

"I invoke the power of the elemental energies of the air that gave life to these flowers, to protect their energies and maintain their potency until they are again united as one."

The priestess now holds the vessel of flowers above the flames of the candle triangle (about twelve inches above the flames), and as she moves the vessel in a clockwise circle around all three flames, she says:

"I invoke the power of the elemental energies of the fire (the sun) whose heat and light have given strength to these flowers, to protect their energies and maintain their potency until they are again united as one."

Finally, while holding the vessel above the flame of the collective energy candle, the priestess says:

"I now call upon the one, the collective energy that animates all things, to guide my work and to protect the energies of these flowers and maintain their potency until they are again united as one."

The vessel of flowers is now replaced at the front and center of the working stone, the priestess sits in front of the working stone, and the work of separating the flower's cardinals begins.

Assuming the priestess to be right-handed, she holds the base of the flower by the light green calyx/sepal cup, gripping it firmly between the tips of her finger and thumb. Then, one at a time, the two wing petals are pulled from the flower and placed in the container waiting to receive them.

Next the broad standard petal is removed and placed aside with the others. This

Harvesting the Petals
The flower with the standard petal removed
Removing the petals
Switzer

now leaves the two jointed keel petals sitting in the sepal cup. The keel petals must be removed very carefully, by gripping only the tip of the "beak" formation, and set aside with the others. Removing the keel petals reveals the reproductive pistil and stamen, which remain attached to the sepal cup.

This is the female flower head, and it is placed in the other container and set on the working stone to receive it. This process of separating the petals from the flower heads continues until all the harvested flowers have been divided.

The container that held the harvested flowers may now be discarded and the two vessels holding the flower's cardinals (as the separated parts of the flower are now called) are placed next to one another at the front and center of the working stone.

The two cardinals of the flower are now ready for the next stage of the refinement process, maceration. Maceration, however, is not a ritual working; it is, in fact, one of the many "practical" undertakings of the refinement process, and therefore it need not be done inside the Protective Circle. The ritual working, then, must be brought to a close.

To do this the priestess stands before the working stone and with both hands raised into the air she says:

"And so it ends, as it began."

The Protective Circle is now unsealed and erased as described in part 4 of this book.

The Maceration of the Two Cardinals of the Flower

Maceration is the first step in the crafting of the individual cardinal essences of the plant. This is where the cardinals of the flower are soaked in an alcoholic spirit for a number of days or sometimes even weeks. During this process the cardinals give up the greater part of their physical and magical (spiritual) attributes to the alcohol spirit, and this empowered spirit is the beginning of the cardinal essence that we desire.

Maceration always takes place immediately following the separation of the cardinals, so normally there would be a work table prepared close to the working stone in order to begin without delay.

The Male and Female Cardinals
Flower head
The Female Cardinal
Female flower head containing the moon influences
The male Cardinal
Separated male petals containing the sun influence
Switzer

Maceration: The Working

For this working you will need:

- **The vessels holding the two separated cardinals of the flower.**
- **Two (250 ml) powder jars with screw caps,** to hold the macerating plant material and spirit of alcohol.
- **Spirit of alcohol (40% by volume).** I use proprietary poteen, sufficient to cover the plant material in each of the powder jars.
- **The spatula or stirrer** to stir the macerating plant material.

Begin by putting each of the cardinals into its own powder jar. Cover each with sufficient spirit of alcohol to just cover the plant material in the jar. Stir the contents of each jar well and tightly seal both jars with their screw caps. Label each jar with the name of the flower (the bird's-foot trefoil), the name of the cardinal it contains (either the male petals or the female flower heads), and the date on which the maceration began.

Store the jars in a cool, dark place for the period of maceration. Return to the jars each day and shake them vigorously to ensure that all the plant material is being immersed in the spirit alcohol. If the level of spirit alcohol falls below that of the plant material, top off the jar until all the plant material is submerged.

Macerating cardinals of the flower.

After five days you will begin to notice a difference in the appearance of the plant material. The petals in the first jar will still be bright yellow but they are becoming translucent, and the spirit of alcohol in which they are macerating will take on a light yellow hue. The flower heads in the other jar will be losing their vivid green appearance and taking on a much paler color, and the maceration liquid will be turning a light greenish yellow. Continue to shake each jar every day to ensure even maceration of the plant material. After three weeks the maceration of both cardinal essences will be complete and they will be ready for the leaching process.

The Leaching of the Two Cardinals of the Flower

Leaching is the process of filtration that separates the now partly enhanced liquid cardinal essences from the solid plant material. The separated liquids and solids then go through the further, independent process of sublimation (see page 157).

Leaching: The Working

For this working you will need:

- **The two jars containing the macerating cardinals of the plants.**
- **A glass funnel,** to hold the filter paper through which the liquid will pass.
- **Two filter papers,** of a suitable grade as described previously, one to filter each cardinal.
- **Retort stand with rubber clamp,** to secure the funnel above the receiver flask. Not essential but very useful.
- **Two (100 ml) glass bottles with stoppers,** to receive and store the liquids.
- **Two sheets of 8½ x 11 paper,** on which to dry the solid plant materials.
- **Spatula,** To stir the mixture and help remove the solid plant material from the jar, and to assist the filtering process.

We need to leach both the macerated petal cardinal and the separately macerated flower head cardinal. These two cardinals must remain separate, so for the sake of simplicity I shall describe how to leach each of the cardinals in turn. In practice, of

Filtering cardinals.

course, both may be leached concurrently—assuming, that is, that you have two sets of each piece of equipment necessary.

We will begin by leaching the macerated petal cardinal. Assemble the retort stand and clamp the funnel so that its outlet is about half an inch (1.5 cm) above the open mouth of the glass bottle. This will allow the filtered liquid to drip directly into the bottle without loss.

Fold the circular filter paper in half and then in half again so that it forms a quarter-circle. Now, by separating the edge of the first layer of paper from the remaining three, the paper will form a closed cone. Place this cone inside the funnel and you will see that it fits the funnel shape perfectly. It will come about two-thirds up the funnel wall. This is your filtering funnel.

Gently pour the macerated mixture into the filtering funnel until it reaches within a quarter inch (0.75 cm) of the top of the filter paper. Allow this first quantity of macerated mixture to filter into the glass bottle below before filling the filter funnel with the same amount of liquid again. Repeat this process until all of the macerated mixture has been poured into the filter funnel. Use the spatula to ensure that every last piece of plant material is removed from the jar and goes through the filter funnel. Once the liq-

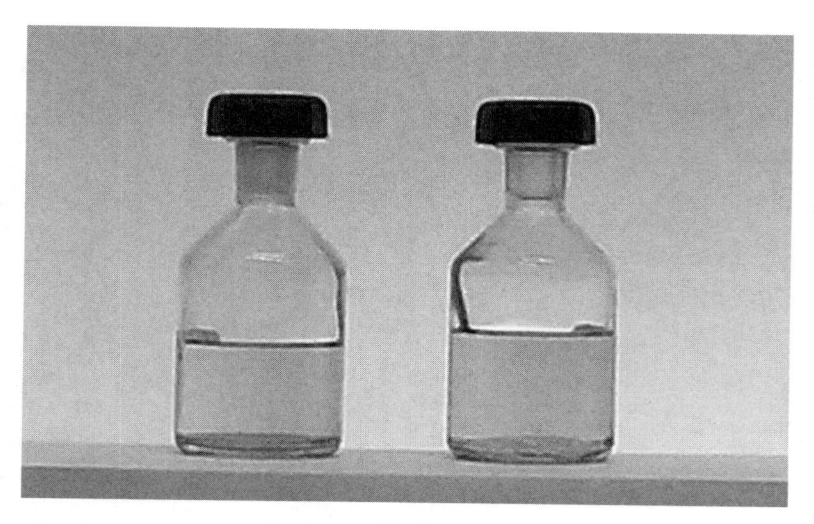

Basic cardinal essences.

uid stops dripping through the filter funnel of its own accord, use the back of the spatula to gently squeeze the remaining liquid from the plant material in the filter funnel. Allow the last of the liquid to pass through the filter paper into the glass bottle below.

Once you are certain that all the liquid has been leached from the solid plant matter, remove the bottle from beneath the funnel and increase the liquid in the bottle to 50 ml by adding more alcoholic spirit. Increasing the volume of liquid by adding more alcohol spirit does not dilute the potency of the essence, as it contains the maximum amount of the plant's energies and attributes yielded up by the plant material. If the bottles already contain this volume of liquid or more, simply seal the glass bottle, label it "Leached Cardinal Essence of the Petal," and set it aside.

Remove the filter paper from the funnel, place it on the work surface, and open it out to reveal the plant material that was left inside the filter cone. Gently remove the plant material from the filter and spread it onto the sheet of 8½ x 11 paper, where it will remain until it dries. Discard the filter paper; do not be tempted to reuse it, as it will contaminate any future workings.

Wash the glass funnel and place it back into the retort stand clamp. Renew the filter paper in the same way as before and repeat the whole process using the macerated flower head cardinal mixture. On this occasion, label the storage bottle "Leached Cardinal Essence of the Flower Head" and set aside with the other bottle.

At the end of this working you should have four products: the leached cardinal essence of the petal, the leached cardinal essence of the flower head, and the two dry solids, one for each of the cardinals mentioned above.

Store the two liquids in a cool, dry place until you need them. Put the completely dry solids into separate powder jars, label them, and seal them to await the next step in the refinement process, the *fermentation*.

Dried solid cardinals.

A Pause for Reflection

The work we have undertaken thus far has a great deal in common with many other herbal traditions. We have already looked at the way that Bach Flower Remedies are prepared by steeping the flowers in water to extract their energies and how similar processes are used in the homeopathic school. The ancient alchemists used much the same method to extract their basic essences before they began its repeated distillation. However, there are a number of very significant differences that distinguish the Druidic methodology from other herbal traditions and the alchemical workings we have looked at in so much detail earlier.

To get to this point in our process we have already endowed our work and our developing complex and incense with the energies of two spiritual/magical rituals, one at harvesting and one at separation. These spiritual/magical workings are one factor that raises the potential of Druidic potions above those of other traditions.

We have also seen that it is only the Druidic tradition that separates the plant into its cardinals, its male and female component parts. All other traditions use the whole of the harvested plant part, whether it is the flower, root, or leaves, as the one source material, without dividing its cardinals. Once the plant material has been macerated, many traditions would consider their work complete and their remedies and elixirs ready for use. Not so with the Druidic tradition: this is only the beginning of our workings.

The liquid cardinal essences we have crafted thus far are just the fundamental essences, containing the basic, unrefined potential attributes of the plant we are using. They therefore need to be further refined and purified before use. The solid cardinals retain the subtler attributes that we still need to extract and add to our refined liquid in order to realize the full potential of the plant's attributes, both physical and magical.

Below we shall explain these unique procedures, called the *sublimation of the cardinals,* and go on to show just how these processes empower the potions we eventually employ.

Sublimation

The *Oxford English Dictionary* defines the verb *to sublimate* as "to divert the energy of primitive impulses into culturally higher activity. To refine, to purify, to make sublime." *Sublime* is defined as "of the highest or most exalted sort." We will now continue the refinement of our cardinal essences, both liquid and solid, into the highest and most exalted sort of essences possible, the creation of the sublime complex, the sublimation.

The two solid cardinals next undergo a fermentation to extract their remaining attributes. The resulting fermented liquids will be added to the leached cardinal essences produced earlier. The remaining solid plant material will be dried once again to form the plant's incense. This is the sublimation of the solid cardinals and we shall look at this process next.

The Fermentation of the Two Solid Cardinals of the Flower

The Druids and the Celts, in general, discovered that certain fruits and vegetables are more suitable for fermentation than others. These discoveries were not only the result of the taste of the resulting drink but also from an understanding that some material actually fermented better than others. Nowadays we understand the need for certain chemicals and compounds to be present in the fruit or vegetable in order for it to ferment successfully.

But for the ancient Druids, fermentation was very much a hit-or-miss process.

Little of the science of fermentation was understood, and for a long time the actual process was seen as a magical one, induced by the Druidic priest (or priestess using his or her fermentation wand.

In order to extract the remaining attributed from the two Cardinal solids left following maceration we must process them in a fermenting liquid as the solids themselves do not hold the necessary sugars that enable fermentation.

The traditional way of doing this is to create a fermenting liquid mixture, or *must,* and then place each of the cardinal solids into its own fermenting must in order for the residual attributes to leach out. The active must was made from fermenting apples and honey, in the same way as cider and mead were brewed. The Druidic name for this active must translates quite simply as "apple must." These processes were well understood by the ancient Druids; ciders, beers, and mead were the mainstay of their alcoholic drinks. Grape wine was introduced much later and was never really popular within Welsh, Scottish, or Irish Celtic society—in fact, wine drinking is still a relatively new thing for the modern-day Welsh/Scottish/Irish person, who would still be much more accustomed to beer or stout as a social beverage.

In planning our schedule for fermentation, we must remember that the solid cardinals need to be introduced to the apple must during its active fermentation period, so the correct timing is imperative. Fermentation is a two-part process. The first stage takes place in an open vessel and therefore in the presence of air. The second stage happens in a vessel sealed with an air lock to prevent air from being present.

It is not necessary to have a detailed understanding of the science of fermentation in order to create an apple must, but further research on the subject will add to the reader's knowledge and reduce the likelihood of making mistakes.

The first step, then, is to create the apple must, which will receive each of the solid cardinals. We will need to create two vessels of active apple must simultaneously, one for the male (petal) solid cardinal and the other for the female (flower head) solid cardinal. It is best if these two active apple musts begin their fermentation separately. Once again, let me underline the need for strict hygiene at every stage of this process, as unwanted bacteria will ruin your work.

Preparation of the Active Apple Must (First Stage): The Working

For this working you will need:

- **Three 400 ml beakers** in which the fermentation will take place.
- **A medium-size saucepan,** to cook the apple and honey mixture.
- **A suitable low heat source,** to cook the apple and honey mixture.

Ingredients

1 teaspoon brewer's yeast

3 teaspoons natural, organic honey

1 medium-size apple or the same volume of whole crab apples

500 ml tepid moon-cleansed water

We start by activating the yeast so that it begins working before it is introduced to the fruit. To do this, we put the brewer's yeast into one of the beakers, add 2 teaspoons of the honey, and add enough tepid moon-cleansed water to make 100 ml. Stir the mixture well and set aside in a warm place to begin its work.

Brewer's yeast is a living organism, and it exists and multiplies best at a constant warm temperature. Ideally a temperature of 70°F (21°C) suits most yeasts and this temperature should not vary by more than five degrees Fahrenheit (2.5 degrees Centigrade) at any time during the fermentation process.

While we wait for the yeast to start working we can prepare the apple for our must. Chop up the apple—seeds, core, and skin included—into small chunks of about 1 inch (2.5 cm) in size. Place the chunks in the saucepan along with the remaining 1 teaspoon of honey and enough moon-cleansed water to cover the base of the pan. Let simmer slowly, stirring constantly, until the chunks have reduced to a lumpy pulp. This should not take more than a few minutes, but you must watch carefully to be sure the mixture does not burn. Once reduced, place the apple mixture to one side to cool.

Remember to use the entire apple, pips, core, and skin included. This reduction should not take more than a few minutes, and it is a good idea to stir the apple mixture constantly as it simmers to prevent sticking and to help it reduce to pulp.

After about 1 hour, the apple mixture should be cool and the yeast mixture should be showing signs of energetic activity. It is now time to combine the mixtures and begin the first stage of the apple must fermentation.

First fermentation of apple must.

Add the active yeast mixture to the apple pulp in the saucepan and mix thoroughly. Pour half of the mixture in one of the remaining 400 ml beakers and the other half into the other beaker. Now add enough tepid moon-cleansed water to the liquid must in each beaker to make 150 ml and stir well.

Place both beakers in a stable, warm environment to encourage fermentation. Do not cover the beakers; this first stage of fermentation must take place in the presence of air. After a few hours, a vigorous fermentation should be taking place and you will see a lively, foamy froth working at the top of each mixture.

This active fermentation will continue for three to four days, or even longer if the temperature varies. When the first stage of fermentation is complete, the foamy froth on the top of the mixture begins to die away. We are now ready to introduce the solid cardinals and begin the second stage of fermentation.

Fermentation of the Solid Cardinals (Second Stage): The Working

This is the true fermentation stage of the refinement process, as the first stage is done merely to prepare the apple must. This process will leach the residual attributes of the petals and flower heads into the fermentation liquid. For this working you will need:

- **Two 500 ml conical flasks** for the fermentation of each solid cardinal.
- **Two airlocks,** to seal each conical flask.
- **Two 6-inch (15 cm) squares of muslin or fine linen,** to hold the solid cardinals during fermentation.

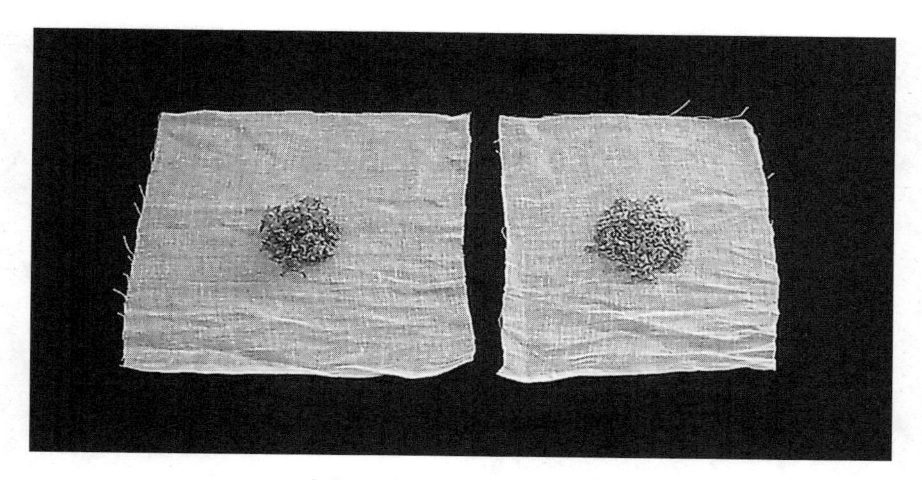

Solid cardinals on linen square.

- **A length of natural cord or twine** sufficient to tie the two muslin squares into bundles.
- **Sealing tape or duct tape,** to seal the air locks into place.
- **Two sheets of 8$^1/_2$ x 11 paper,** to dry the solid cardinals once the fermentation is complete.
- **A mortar and pestle,** to grind the solid cardinals.
- **The active apple must.**
- **The jar containing the solid cardinal of the petals.**
- **The jar containing the solid cardinal of the flower heads.**

Before we introduce each of the solid cardinals to the apple must ferment, we must secure them in muslin or linen bundles so we may retrieve them once the process is complete and so the solid cardinals are not polluted by the apple pulp in the fermenting must.

First place the two muslin squares on the work surface. Carefully pour one of the solid cardinals onto one square and the other solid cardinal onto the second square.

Next, bundle up each muslin square to form a loose package and tie securely with a length of twine, making sure that the loose end of the twine is long enough to reach out of the conical flask, so that you may retrieve the bundle later.

Pour the apple must from the first beaker into the first conical flask, then do the same for the second beaker. You now have a conical flask of active apple must ready to receive each of the solid cardinals.

Before placing the bundled cardinals in the apple must, immerse each in a beaker of moon-cleansed water and allow the bundle to become saturated before removing

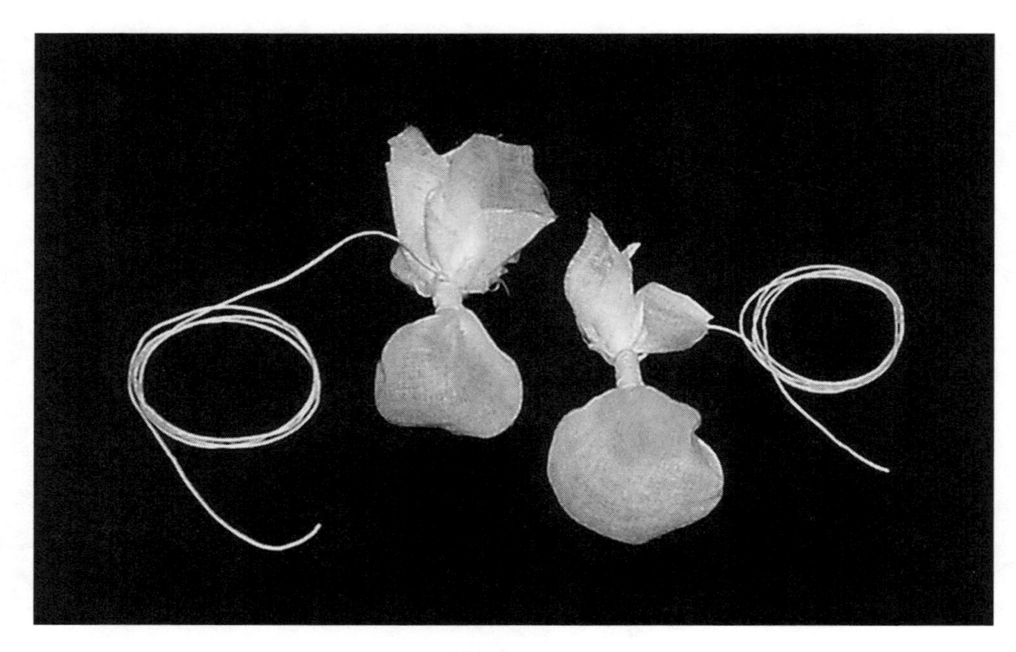

Bagged solid cardinals.

it and squeezing it to remove the excess water. This prevents the loss of fermentation liquid by the initial absorption into the solid cardinal.

Now place one of the bundles of solid cardinal into each of the conical flasks, ensuring that the trailing end of the twine remains outside the flask. Make sure that each bundle is covered by the apple must ferment—if necessary, push the bundle below the surface of the ferment with your spatula.

Second fermentation of apple must.

Both conical flasks are now sealed with the air locks, using the sealing tape to secure each and to ensure an airtight fit.

Label the flasks and return them to their warm environment; now the second, gentler fermentation may begin.

Return to the flasks regularly, at least once a day, and give them a gentle shake to agitate the ferment. After about one month, the fermentation slows down and eventually stops. The fermentation period will vary somewhat, depending on any variation in temperature.

Once the fermentation is complete, unseal both flasks and remove the bundles containing the solid cardinals. Wash each bundle thoroughly under running water, then open the bundles and spread each solid cardinal on a separate sheet of 8½ x 11paper to dry. When dry, put each solid cardinal into the mortar and with the pestle grind the solid into a medium-fine aggregate. Once ground, place each cardinal in a powder jar and seal securely. Later, these two solid cardinals will be amalgamated to form the incense.

Label both jars "Solid Cardinal of the Petals" and "Solid Cardinal of the Flower Head," respectively, and store in a cool, dark place until they are needed.

We are now left with two flasks, one containing a fermented essence of the petals and the other the fermented essence of the flower heads. The next step is to remove the apple must residue from the essence. To do this, filter each fermented essence separately, using the filter-funnel technique just as we did in the leaching process.

The resulting liquids are the fermented essences of the petals and the flower heads, respectively. The storage bottles containing each essence are then made up to 50 ml with moon-cleansed water (if necessary), labeled "Fermented Essence of the Petals" and "Fermented Essence of the Flower Heads," respectively, and stored until they are needed. The solids remaining in the filter papers are the apple must residue, which may be discarded.

This completes the fermentation stage of the refinement process. We now have a total of six products:

> The *leached essence of the petals* and the *leached essence of the flower head,* both produced at the leaching stage and stored until ready for use.

The *fermented essence of the petals* and the *fermented essence of the flower head,* both produced at the fermentation stage and stored until ready for use.

The *solid cardinal of the petal* and the *solid cardinal of the flower head,* produced in the early stages of the fermentation process and stored until ready for use.

We may now begin combining the leached essences with the fermented essences in order to create the two cardinal essences that will eventually make up the complex, the sublime elixir of the Druidic tradition. This is the process of *unification.* At the same time, we shall amalgamate the two solid cardinals in order to create the incense of the flower during the same ritual working.

The Unification of the Essences and of the Solid Cardinals of the Flower

Because this is the first stage of the uniting of the flower's cardinal essences and its incense, the unification is undertaken as a ritual working. There must be a spiritual/magical bonding of the two parts of the cardinal essences and incense along with their physical unification. We must therefore return to our working stone and prepare it and ourselves for the ritual working ahead.

Unification: The Working

For this ritual working we will need:

- **The candle triangle.** See page 133.
- **A vessel of moon-cleansed water.** See page 235.
- **An incense burner** with a suitable incense.
- **The stave and dagger,** to cast and seal the Protective Circle. If you are using a permanent working stone within your workshop, you may well have cast the Circle previously, in which case you will need just the dagger to seal its entrance.

- **Three small bowls,** in which we will reunite the essences and the flower's solid cardinals.
- **The bottles containing the two leached cardinal essences.**
- **The bottles containing the two fermented cardinal essences.**
- **The jars containing the two solid cardinals of the flower.**
- **Two 100 ml storage bottles** in which to store the united cardinal essences.
- **A 250 ml storage jar** to store the flower's incense.

The working stone should be laid out as shown below in preparation for the ritual working.

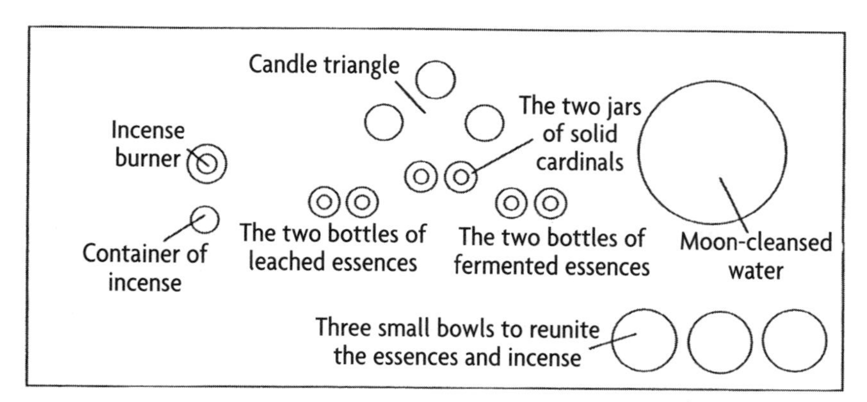

Working stone layout for the ritual working of unification.

The working stone is now ready to begin the ritual working, so we must once again look to the preparation of our body, mind, and spirit before we undertake our work. The process of personal preparation has been discussed earlier and is explained in detail in part 4 of this book.

Having completed our personal preparation, we are ready to proceed with the ritual working of unification. For the purpose of this example, we will again assume that a priestess is facilitating the ritual working.

If you are working outside your workshop, the first step is to cast the Protective Circle using the stave as described in part 4. If you are within your workshop, you may have already done this for previous activities. With the Circle cast around the working area, the entrance is sealed with the dagger. Again, this procedure is explained in part 4.

The charcoal in the incense burner is now lit in preparation for the ritual working. The next step is the lighting of the candles. This part of the ritual has already been described on page 146. Having lit all three candle flames in the required manner, the priestess then facilitates the *uniting of the flames.* This too is described earlier on page 147.

The next stage of the ritual working is the invocation of the collective energy's influence in the reuniting of the energies and potency of the flower's cardinals. The priestess stands before the working stone and raises both hands high into the air. While doing so she says:

"I invoke the power of the collective energy and call upon it to guide my work. I call upon the four elemental essences to empower these cardinals and maintain them as they are again united."

The four bottles containing the plant's essences are then placed at the front and centre of the working stone. The priestess forms her two hands into an inverted cup shape and places them above the four bottles. As she does, so she says:

"I invoke the power of the elemental essence of the earth that yielded up these flowers, to protect their energies and maintain their potency as they are again united as one."

Then, dipping her fingers into the vessel of moon-cleansed water, the priestess sprinkles some water on each of the four bottles and says:

"I invoke the power of the elemental energies of the water that nourished these flowers, to protect their energies and maintain their potency as they are again united as one."

The priestess now sprinkles a little incense on the smoldering charcoal in the incense burner. As the smoke rises, she lifts each of the bottles in turn and holds it in the smoke. As she does, so she says:

"I invoke the power of the elemental energies of the air that gave life to these

flowers, to protect their energies and maintain their potency as they are again united as one." (Repeat in turn for each bottle.)

The priestess now holds each of the bottles in turn above the flames of the candle triangle (about twelves inches above the flames), and as she moves each bottle in a clockwise circle around all three flames she says:

"I invoke the power of the elemental energies of the fire (the sun), whose heat and light have given strength to these flowers, to protect their energies and maintain their potency as they are again united as one." (Repeat in turn for each bottle.)

Finally, while holding each of the bottles in turn above the flame of the collective energy candle, the priestess says:

"I now call upon the one, the collective energy that animates all things, to guide my work and to protect the energies of these essences and maintain their potency as they are again united as one."

The four bottles are now placed in their original positions on the working stone and their stoppers are removed. The priestess stands in front of the working stone, ready to begin the actual unification. Bringing one of the three small bowls to the front and center of the working stone, the priestess takes the bottle of leached cardinal essence of the petals in her left hand and the bottle containing the fermented cardinal essence of the petals in her right hand. Lifting both bottles high in the air, she says:

"Conceived as one, grown as one. I reunite the essences of this flower's cardinals. I create the male essence of the sun."

Having said this, she simultaneously pours the contents of each bottle into the bowl. Then, lifting the bowl carefully into the air so as not to spill any of the contents, she says:

"By my work and with the will of the collective energy, I have created the male cardinal essence of this flower. And so it shall remain until it is again reunited and amalgamated with its equal."

She then places the bowl at the base of the male candle of the flame of the sun as she turns her attention to the remaining female essences. Bringing the second of the three small bowls to the front and center of the working stone, the priestess takes the bottle of leached cardinal essence of the flower head in her left hand and the bottle containing the fermented cardinal essence of the flower head in her right hand. Lifting both bottles high in the air, she says:

"Conceived as one, grown as one. I reunite the essences of this flower's cardinals. I create the female essence of the moon."

Having said this, she simultaneously pours the contents of each bottle into the bowl. Then, lifting the second bowl carefully in the air so as not to spill any of the contents, she says:

"By my work and with the will of the collective energy, I have created the female cardinal essence of this flower. And so it shall remain until it is again reunited and amalgamated with its equal."

She then places the bowl at the base of the female candle of the flame of the moon.

This completes the unification of the leached and fermented essences, so the priestess now turns her attention to the two solid cardinals that will make up the flower's incense. The two jars containing the plant's solid cardinals are then placed at the front and center of the working stone. The priestess forms her two hands into an inverted cup shape and places them above the two jars. As she does so, she says:

"I invoke the power of the elemental essence of the earth that yielded up these flowers, to protect their energies and maintain their potency as they are again united as one."

Then, dipping her fingers into the vessel of moon-cleansed water, the priestess sprinkles a little of the water on each of the two jars and says:

"I invoke the power of the elemental energies of the water that nourished these flowers, to protect their energies and maintain their potency as they are again united as one."

The priestess now sprinkles a little incense on the smoldering charcoal in the incense burner. As the smoke rises, she lifts both jars, one in each hand, and holds them in the smoke. As she does so, she says:

"I invoke the power of the elemental energies of the air that gave life to these flowers, to protect their energies and maintain their potency as they are again united as one."

The priestess now holds both jars above the flames of the candle triangle (about twelve inches above the flames), and as she moves them in a clockwise circle around all three flames she says:

"I invoke the power of the elemental energies of the fire (the sun) whose heat and light have given strength to these flowers, to protect their energies and maintain their potency as they are again united as one."

Finally, while holding both jars above the flame of the collective energy candle, the priestess says:

"I now call upon the one, the collective energy that animates all things, to guide my work and to protect the energies of these cardinals and maintain their potency as they are again united as one."

The two jars are now placed in their original positions on the working stone and their screw caps are removed. The priestess stands in front of the working stone ready to begin the actual unification.

Bringing the last of the three small bowls to the front and center of the working stone, the priestess takes the jar of the solid cardinal of the petals in her left hand and the jar containing the solid cardinal of the flower head in her right hand. Lifting both jars high in the air, she says:

"Conceived as one, grown as one. I reunite the solid cardinals of this flower and create the incense, the energy of fire and air."

Having said that, she simultaneously pours the contents of both jars into the bowl and sets aside the two jars. Then, lifting the bowl with her left hand, she gently stirs the contents with the fingers of her right hand to amalgamate both cardinals. As she does this, she says:

"By my work and with the will of the collective energy, I have created the incense of this flower, bringing together the elemental energies of fire and air."

She then places the bowl at the base of the candle of the flame of the collective energy.

This completes the ritual working of the unification of the essences and of the amalgamation of the solid cardinals of the flower. Each of the two cardinal essences is now poured into a clean storage bottle and sealed. The incense is poured into a clean powder jar and sealed. The Protective Circle is unsealed and erased. Both cardinal essence bottles and the incense jar are labeled and then stored in a cool, dark place until they are needed.

In order to give a complete overview and to aid the reader's understanding of this complicated sequence the entire refinement process may be seen in a schematic form in the diagram on the facing page.

Generally, newly crafted cardinal essences and incenses, are not used immediately, but rather are left to mature for at least one month. This period of rest allows the newly combined energies and attributes of the flower to mingle and increase in potency. Often the color and perfume of the essences will change as a result of the maturation, so try not to disturb this process, as it is a vital part of the empowerment of the potions.

It is best to store the bottles and jar containing all three components together, as they jointly contain the entire energies and the physical and spiritual/magical attributes of the harvested plant. When the time comes to use them in your ritual, they must be used together. You cannot mix the male essence of one plant harvest with the female essence of another, as they will conflict. Nor can you use the incense from one plant harvest with the essences of another. It is *essential* that all the components used are from the same plant harvest; the physical and spiritual/magical workings of their crafting speak of the division and reuniting of the plant's latent energies and attributes. Do not be tempted to mix essences or incenses even if they are from the same genus and species.

The combining of the complexes crafted from the reuniting of the cardinal essences may take place only under very specific circumstances and for very specific reasons. We will look at these *combined complexes* in the last section of this book.

Complex Refinement Schematic for Flowers

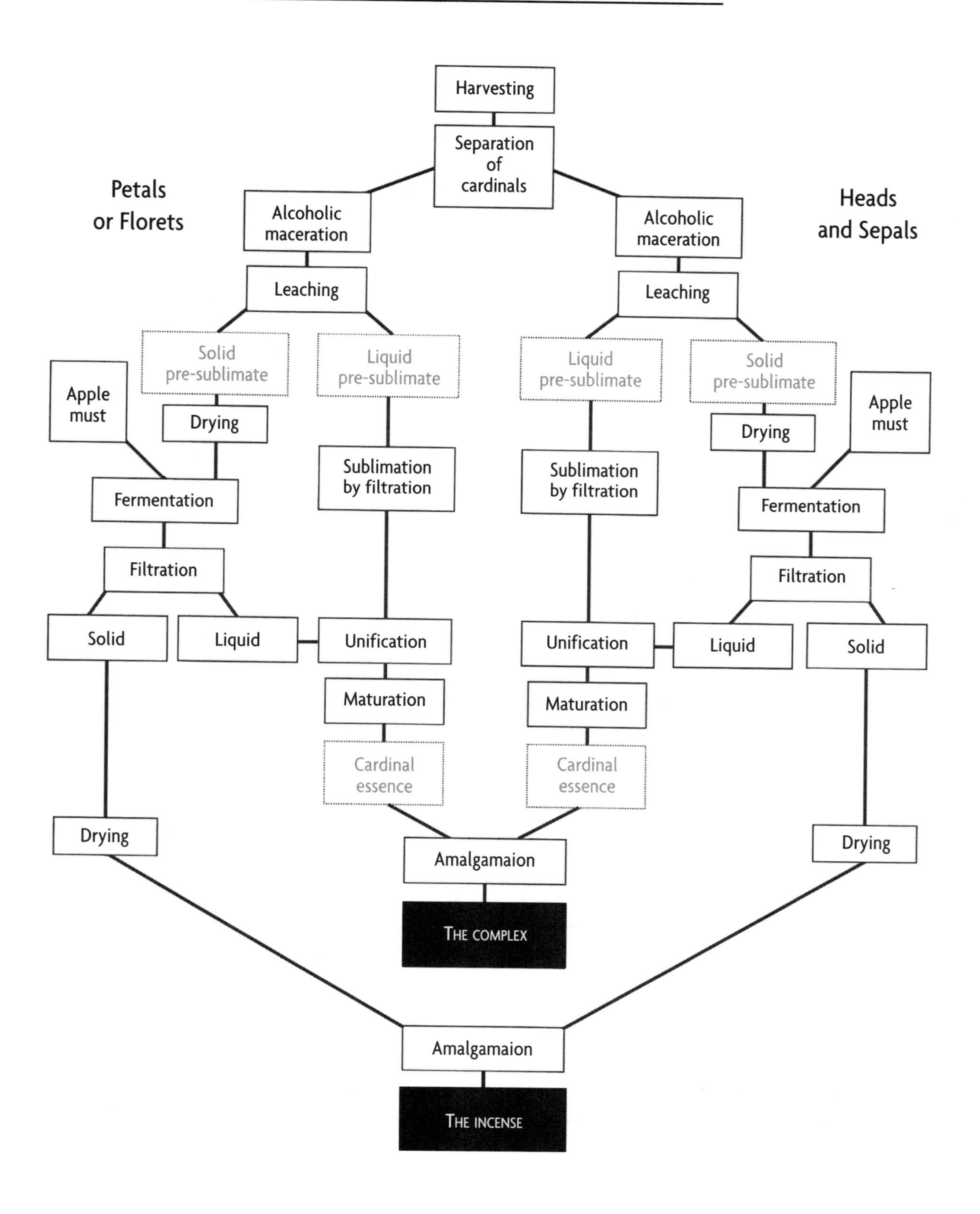

The Amalgamation of the Cardinal Essences to Form the Complex of the Flower

Some three months will have elapsed since the initial harvesting of your flowers before the resulting cardinal essences are mature and ready for use. It is always worth bearing this time span in mind when planning your year's harvest of flowers. When we look at the refinement process of the complex of the tree later, you will see that tree complexes are crafted in a shorter time, six to eight weeks, as there is no fermentation process involved.

The bulk of this three months is taken up with patiently waiting for the various stages to take their course, and because all the processes are natural ones, there is nothing to be done that will accelerate the crafting. While we are waiting, we can busy ourselves with other work as the processes progress. We can harvest another plant, or as one harvest matures we could be macerating another. In this way we may maintain a continuous, overlapping work cycle that fits in with the seasonal availability of the plants and trees whose complexes we require. Before long you will accumulate a cupboard full of the various cardinal essences and incenses that you will be able to draw on for your rituals.

The two cardinal essences of the flower are brought together during the ritual for which they are being used. As they amalgamate, they form the complex (*cymhleth,* in Welsh). The complex, just like a glass of freshly poured effervescent soda, has a limited period during which it can maintain its optimum energy before it goes "flat." As we shall see later, the complex is at its most potent and energetic immediately after it is passed through the rising smoke of the burning incense of the same flower. It is therefore important that we understand the reasons for this before we attempt to use our complexes and incenses in rituals.

To create and energize the complex, we need the three components we crafted earlier: the cardinal essence of the petal (male), the cardinal essence of the flower head (female), and the incense (already combined male and female components). As we combine the two cardinal essences, we reunite not only the empowered energies and attributes of the flower, but also the male and female attributes, restoring the balance of nature in our crafted complex.

The complex thus becomes hermaphrodite, male and female in one, embracing the characteristics of both. It embodies the attributes of the sun and the moon (male and female), but the elemental energies only of earth and water. So in itself the complex lacks the potency of all four elements. The two missing elemental energies, those of fire and earth, are found in the incense. The incense is already hermaphrodite before it is brought to the ritual. (You will remember that we joined the male and female solid cardinals during its crafting.)

So as we pass the hermaphrodite complex through the smoke of the hermaphrodite incense (the *moment of congress*), we are, for the first time, also combining all four elemental energies. At the very moment of congress the complex is empowered with the combined energies and attributes of the specific flower we have selected, plus the combined energies of the four elements, all maintained within the newly restored perfect male/female balance as nature prescribes.

At this moment (and for a short time afterward) the complex is at the peak of its potency. It is the sublime elixir, and becomes the quintessence. This is when we channel its energies and attributes to our needs.

There are some exceptions to this immediate use, and most of those may be found in the use of the complex in remedies and potions after the ritual is over. In these cases it is accepted that the complex is not at its most powerful, and when mixed with carrying agents to form, for example, ointments, balms, and tinctures, there may be a need for repeated applications before the beneficial effects make themselves evident. We shall look at this method of use in detail in part 4.

Let us now move on and look at the crafting of the cardinal essences and incense of the tree.

The Refinement Process: The Complex of the Tree

The tree I have chosen for this example is the pedunculate oak *(Quercus robur)*. Common throughout Wales, Scotland, Ireland, England, and in certain areas of the United States, the oak is renowned not only as a symbol of durability and longevity but also for its association with the Druidic tradition. The oak can survive for thousands of years, and along with the yew and the ash it has become the most sacred tree of the Celtic culture.

There are more than four hundred species of oak, the largest of which may grow to a height of 120 feet (36 meters) with a girth of up to 45 feet (13.5 meters). The oak may take up to sixty-five years to reach reproductive maturity and bear its first crop of catkins.

The oak finds its place in the myths and legends of many cultures. The Greeks, the Romans, the Scandinavians, the Germanic and Baltic cultures, among others, join with the Celts in making the oak the most widely revered of all trees.

Most people's image of a Druidic priest would place him in an oak grove, and indeed this would be an accurate picture. Druids held the oak to be the most knowing and sacred tree and "major oaks" were often the focus of much Druidic activity. Some were even carved with the pagan symbol of the earth (see page 76) in order to protect them, increase their power, and extend their lives. The upper branches of these massive trees are said to hold the most potent energies, and legend has it that Merlin's stave was fashioned from one of these very branches.

Whether or not you subscribe to the Merlin legend, the oak has always played a

major role in all Druidic rituals. In Wales the oak is commonly called *derwen, deri,* or *derw.* In Ireland it is known by the name of *dair* in the modern tongue or *duir* in old Irish. Neither name has an alternative translation. It has been suggested that the title Druid, referring to the wise men of the oak, is derived from one or both of these ancient Celtic names.

We have seen previously how the tree's branches are harvested and brought to the workshop, so our work now begins with the first stage of refinement, the separation of the three cardinals of the tree.

The Separation of the Three Cardinals of the Tree

The *separation* of the tree's cardinals is a ritual working. It is usually carried out by the priest or priestess on his or her own in the workshop. The process has two main elements: the physical crafting of the separation and the spiritual invocation of the four elements and the collective energy to empower the working. Before we can begin, it is essential that we have a detailed understanding of the structure of the tree.

We have looked at the structure and growing processes of the whole tree in part 2. We will now focus on the structure of the branch that we have already harvested. The oak branch will provide us with the three cardinals we need for our work. It consists of the leaves, the wood, and the bark in the proportions that nature defines. We must then use the entire harvested branch, leaving none to waste.

Oak leaves and branches.

In the process of separation, we shall be removing the leaves from the branch and paring the bark from the wood, thereby giving us the three unrefined cardinals of the tree.

As we saw in part 2, the leaves provide us with the male cardinal, the wood with the female cardinal, and the bark with the hermaphroditic, binding cardinal that makes the tree's complex so different from that of the flower.

Separation: The Ritual Working

Like the harvesting of the tree, the separation is a ritual working, meaning it includes a spiritual/magical element within the practical work. The separation is the moment in which the three cardinals of the tree are divided. The male, female, and hermaphrodite essences will then remain separate until they are reunited at the amalgamation during the final ritual for which they are being crafted. This, then, is an extremely significant part of the refinement process, a moment when the tree temporarily loses its unity and natural balance, which will later be restored.

For this reason we ensure that the separated cardinals maintain their energies and potency by invoking the power of the four elemental essences (earth, fire, air, and water) and the fifth elemental essence, or quintessence (the collective energy), to aid our efforts. For this ritual working we will need:

- **The candle triangle.** See page 133.
- **A vessel of moon-cleansed water.** See page 235.
- **An incense burner,** with a suitable incense.
- **The stave and dagger,** to cast and seal the Protective Circle. If you are using a permanent working stone within your workshop, you may well have cast the Circle previously, in which case you will need just the dagger to seal its entrance.
- **Three small bowls,** one to contain the separated leaves, one to hold the separated wood, and one to hold the separated bark.
- **A suitable knife and/or scalpel,** to separate the cardinals.
- **The harvested oak branch.**

The working stone should be laid out as shown below in preparation for the ritual working.

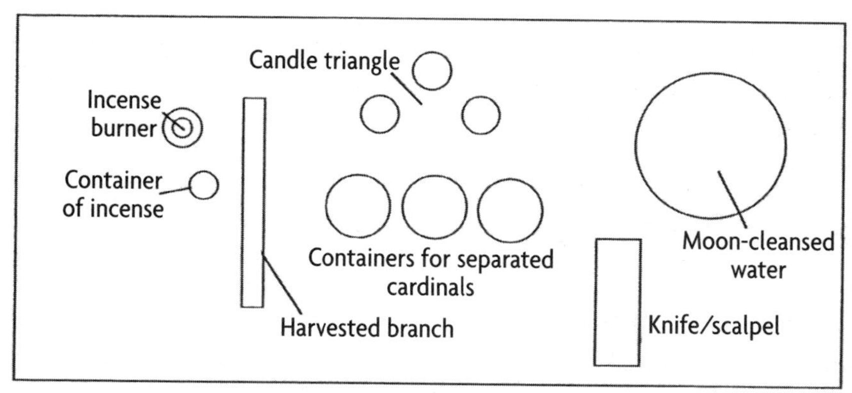

Working stone layout for the separation ritual working (tree).

The working stone is now ready to begin the ritual working, so we must again look to the preparation of our body, mind, and spirit before we undertake our work. The process of personal preparation has been discussed earlier and is explained in detail in part 4.

Having completed our personal preparation, we are ready to proceed with the ritual working of separation. For the purpose of this example, we will again assume that a priestess is facilitating the ritual working.

If you are working outside your workshop, the first step is to cast the Protective Circle using the stave as described in part 4. If you are within your workshop, you may have already done this for previous activities. With the Circle cast around the working area, the entrance is sealed with the dagger. (This procedure is explained in part 4.) The charcoal in the incense burner is now lit in preparation for the ritual working.

The next step is the lighting of the candles. This part of the ritual has been described in detail earlier (see page 146). Having lit all three candle flames in the required manner, the priestess then facilitates the uniting of the flames. This too is described earlier (see page 147).

The next stage of the ritual working is the invocation of the collective energy's influence in maintaining the energies and potency of the branch whose cardinals are about to be separated. The priestess stands before the working stone and lifts the branch high in the air. In doing so, she says:

"I offer this branch, taken from our earth for the good of mankind. I call upon the four elemental essences to empower its cardinals and maintain them until they are again united."

The branch is then placed at the front and center of the working stone. The priestess forms her two hands into an inverted cup shape and places them above the branch. As she does so, she says:

"I invoke the power of the elemental essence of the earth that yielded up this tree and its branch, to protect its energies and maintain its potency until it is again united as one."

Then, dipping her fingers into the vessel of moon-cleansed water, the priestess sprinkles a little of the water on the harvested branch and says:

"I invoke the power of the elemental energies of the water that nourished this tree and its branch, to protect its energies and maintain its potency until it is again united as one."

The priestess now sprinkles a little incense on the smoldering charcoal in the incense burner. As the smoke rises, she lifts the branch and holds it in the smoke. As she does so, she says:

"I invoke the power of the elemental energies of the air that gave life to this tree and its branch, to protect its energies and maintain its potency until it is again united as one."

The priestess now holds the branch above the flames of the candle triangle (about twelve inches above the flames), and as she moves the branch in a clockwise circle around all three flames she says:

"I invoke the power of the elemental energies of the fire (the sun) whose heat and light have given strength to this tree and its branch, to protect its energies and maintain its potency until it is again united as one."

Finally, while holding the branch above the flame of the collective energy candle, the priestess says:

"I now call upon the one, the collective energy that animates all things, to guide my work and to protect the energies of this tree and its branch, maintaining its potency until it is again united as one."

The branch is now replaced at the front and center of the working stone, the priestess sits in front of the working stone, and the work of separating the tree's cardinals begins.

The priestess first removes all the branch's leaves and places them in the first of the three bowls, making sure that none is lost, for the natural proportion of the branch's cardinals must be maintained. Next the branch's bark is carefully stripped away from the inner wood using the knife and/or scalpel. The strips of bark are broken up and placed in the second bowl. The remaining wood is roughly cut up or broken so it will fit into the third bowl. The three bowls holding the tree's cardinals (as the separated parts of the branch are now called) are placed next to one another at the front and center of the working stone.

The three cardinals of the trees are now ready for the next stage of the refinement process, the maceration. Maceration is not a ritual working, however; it is, in fact, one of the many "practical" undertakings of the refinement process. Therefore, it need not be done inside the Protective Circle, so the ritual working must be brought to a close.

To do this, the priestess stands before the working stone and with both hands raised in the air she says:

"And so it ends, as it began."

The Protective Circle is now unsealed and erased in the way described in part 4.

The Maceration of the Three Cardinals of the Tree

Maceration is the first step in the crafting of the individual cardinal essences of the tree. This is where the cardinals of the tree are soaked in alcohol spirits for a number of days or sometimes even weeks. During this process the cardinals give up the greater part of their physical and magical (spiritual) attributes to the alcohol spirit, and this empowered spirit is the beginning of the cardinal essence we desire.

Maceration always takes place immediately following the separation of the cardinals, so normally there would be a work table prepared close to the working stone in order to begin without delay.

Maceration: The Working

For this working you will need:

- **The bowls holding the three separated cardinals of the tree.**
- **A suitable heavy cutting knife,** to cut the bark of the tree into small pieces.
- **A grater,** used along with the heavy knife to grate the wood of the tree into a fine, powderlike consistency.
- **A cutting board,** upon which the cutting and grating will take place.
- **Three (250 ml) powder jars with screw caps,** to hold the macerating plant material and spirit of alcohol.
- **Spirit of alcohol (40% by volume).** I use proprietary poteen, sufficient to cover the plant material in each of the powder jars.
- **The spatula or stirrer,** to stir the macerating plant material.

Begin by preparing each of the cardinals for maceration. The leaves need no additional work, as they are ready to place into the spirit alcohol just as they are, so let them stay in their bowl until they are required. The bark is chopped into a fine, powderlike consistency using the heavy knife on the cutting board. The bark powder is placed back in its bowl. The wood is the most difficult cardinal to prepare, particularly as in this case it is the wood of an oak. First cut it into manageable lengths, then grate each length into the consistency of powder. This may take some time, but remember, as with the other two cardinals, all of the wood must be included. Once it is grated, return the wood powder to its bowl. All three cardinals are now ready for maceration.

Place each of the cardinals into its own powder jar. Cover each with sufficient spirit of alcohol just to cover the plant material in the jar. Stir the contents of each jar well and push down the plant material to ensure that it is submerged in the alcohol. Tightly seal all three jars with their screw caps.

Label each jar with the name of the tree (the oak), the name of the cardinal it con-

Macerating cardinals of the tree.

tains (the male leaves, the female wood, or the hermaphrodite bark), and the date on which the maceration began. The three jars are then stored in a cool, dark place for the period of maceration. Return to the jars each day and shake them vigorously to make sure all the plant material is being immersed in the alcohol. If the level of spirit alcohol falls below that of the plant material, top off the jar until all the plant material is submerged.

After five days you will begin to notice a difference in the appearance of the plant material. The leaves in the first jar will be darker in color, and the spirit alcohol in which they are macerating will take on a light green hue that will become darker as the maceration continues. The wood in the second jar will take on a transparent appearance and the maceration liquid will look slightly milky. The bark in the third jar will also become darker and the alcohol will become the darkest liquid of the three. Continue to shake each jar daily to ensure even maceration of the plant material.

After four weeks, the maceration of the three cardinal essences will be complete, and they will be ready for the leaching process.

The Leaching of the Three Cardinals of the Tree

Leaching is the process of filtration that separates the now partly enhanced liquid cardinal essences from the solid plant material (the solid cardinals). The separated

liquids and solids then go through the further, independent process of sublimation, as we shall see later.

Leaching: The Working

For this working you will need:

- **The three jars containing the macerating cardinals of the tree.**
- **Glass funnel,** to hold the filter paper through which the liquid will pass.
- **Three filter papers,** of a suitable grade (see page 136), one to filter each cardinal.
- **Retort stand with rubber clamp,** to secure the funnel above the receiver flask. Not essential but very useful.
- **Three (100 ml) glass bottles with stoppers,** to receive and store the liquids.
- **Three sheets of 8½ x 11 paper,** on which to dry the solid plant materials.
- **Spatula,** to stir the mixture, to help remove the solid plant material from the jar, and to assist the filtering process.

We need to leach all three cardinals separately. For the sake of simplicity I shall describe how to leach each of the cardinals in turn. In practice, of course, all three may be leached concurrently—assuming, of course, that you have three sets of each piece of equipment that is used. We will begin by leaching the macerated leaf cardinal.

Assemble the retort stand and clamp the funnel so that its outlet is about half an inch (1.5 cm) above the open mouth of the glass bottle. This will allow the filtered liquid to drip directly into the bottle without loss.

Fold the circular filter paper in half and then in half again so that it forms a quarter-circle. Now, by separating the edge of the first layer of paper from the remaining three, the paper will form a closed cone. Place this cone inside the funnel. It will fit the funnel shape perfectly and come about two-thirds up the funnel wall. This is your filtering funnel (see photograph on page 154).

Gently pour the macerated mixture into the filtering funnel until it reaches within a quarter inch (0.75 cm) of the top of the filter paper. Allow this first quantity of macerated mixture to filter into the glass bottle below before filling the filter funnel with the same amount of liquid again. Continue this process until all of the macerated mixture has been poured into the filter funnel. Use the spatula to ensure that every last piece of plant material is removed from the jar and placed into the filter funnel. Once the liquid stops dripping through the filter funnel of its own accord, use the back of the spatula to gently squeeze the remaining liquid from the plant material in the filter funnel. Allow the last of the liquid to pass through the filter paper into the glass bottle below.

Once you are certain that all the liquid has been leached from the solid leaf matter, remove the bottle from beneath the funnel and make the liquid in the bottle up to (50 ml) by adding more alcoholic spirit. Increasing the volume of liquid by adding more alcohol does not dilute the potency of the essence, as it contains the maximum amount of the plant's energies and attributes yielded up by the plant material. If the bottles already contain this volume of liquid or more, simply seal the glass bottle, label it "Leached Cardinal Essence of the Leaf," and place it to one side.

Remove the filter paper from the funnel, place it on the work surface, and open it out to reveal the remaining leaf material that was left inside the filter cone. Gently remove the leaf material from the filter paper and spread it onto the sheet of $8^1/_2$ x 11 paper, where it will remain until it dries. Discard the filter paper; do not be tempted to reuse it, as it will contaminate any future workings.

Wash the glass funnel and replace it in the retort stand clamp. Renew the filter paper in the same way as before and repeat the whole process using the macerated wood cardinal mixture. On this occasion, label the storage bottle "Leached Cardinal Essence of the Wood" and set it aside with the other bottle.

Wash the glass funnel once more and replace it in the retort stand clamp. Renew the filter paper in the same way as before and repeat the whole process, this time using the macerated bark cardinal mixture. On this occasion label the storage bottle "Leached Cardinal Essence of the Bark" and set it aside with the other bottle.

At the end of this working you should have six products: the leached cardinal essence of the leaf, the leached cardinal essence of the wood, the leached cardinal essence of the bark, and the three dry solids, one for each of the cardinals mentioned above.

Three basic cardinal essences of the tree.

Three dried solid cardinals of the tree.

Store the three liquids in a cool, dark place until they are needed. Put the three completely dry solids into separate powder jars, label them, and seal them to await the next step in the refinement process, the sublimation by drying.

Sublimation

We will now continue the refinement of our cardinal essences, both liquid and solid, into the highest and most exalted sort of essences possible—the creation of the sublime complex, the sublimation.

The three liquid cardinal essences will undergo a further filtering process to ensure their purity, while the three solid cardinals will be dried once again to form the plant's incense. Let's look at the sublimation of the liquid cardinal essences first.

Sublimation by Filtration of the Three Liquid Cardinal Essences of the Tree

In order to ensure that all of the liquid cardinal essences are in the purest state possible before they begin their maturation, each is filtered once again, in exactly the same manner as they were during the leaching process.

Some Druidic priests and priestesses actually filter each essence twice during the leaching. This serves exactly the same purpose and also obviates the need to reassemble all the filtering apparatus for a second time. As this working does not contain any spiritual/magical dimension, this shortcut is perfectly acceptable.

I shall not take up space here by reviewing the filtration technique, as it is described in great detail above. It is important, however, to point out that if you intend to use the short method (filtering the essences twice during the leaching), then it is imperative that you change the filter paper and wash the funnel between each of the two filtrations. This is the only way to guarantee the purity of the filtered essences.

Once filtered for the second time (by whichever method you choose), each of the three cardinal essences is poured into a separate glass bottle, labeled, and set in a cool, dark place to undergo a period of maturation.

Sublimation by Drying of the Three Solid Cardinals of the Tree

The three solid cardinals also undergo further refinement before they are amalgamated to form the tree's incense. This is done by an additional drying process, whereby the solids are placed in a warm, dry place, away from any drafts, to allow them to be purified by the sun's light and fresh air.

A sunny windowsill is ideal for this purpose. Spread out each of the solid cardinals on the base of a plate in order to prevent them from being blown away. Set the plate on the windowsill and allow the sun's heat to dry the solids completely. Stir each of the solids once or twice a day and after a period of five to seven days (depending on the weather), return each solid cardinal to its individual jar. Seal tightly to prevent any moisture from entering, and store all three jars in a cool, dark place until needed.

At this stage of the refinement process we now have a total of six products: the leached essence of the leaves, the leached essence of the wood, and the leached essence of the bark, each produced at the leaching stage and stored in order to mature before use, along with the solid cardinal of the leaves, the solid cardinal of the wood, and the solid cardinal of the bark, also produced at the leaching stage and further refined before being stored until ready for use.

We may now begin to amalgamate the three solid cardinals in order to create the incense of the tree during the same ritual working.

The Amalgamation of the Three Solid Cardinals of the Tree

Because this is the reuniting of the tree's three solid cardinals to create its incense, the amalgamation is undertaken as a ritual working. There is a need for the spiritual/magical bonding of the three solid cardinals along with their physical unification. We must therefore return to our working stone and prepare it and ourselves for the ritual working ahead.

Amalgamation: The Working

For this ritual working we will need:

- **The candle triangle.** See page 133.
- **A vessel of moon-cleansed water.** See page 235.
- **An incense burner,** with a suitable incense.
- **The stave and dagger.** To cast and seal the Protective Circle. If you are using a permanent working stone within your workshop, you may well have cast the Circle previously, in which case you will need just the dagger to seal its entrance.

- **A small bowl** in which we will reunite the solid cardinals of the tree.
- **The jars containing the three solid cardinals of the flower.**
- **A (250 ml) storage jar,** to store the flower's incense.

The working stone should be laid out as shown below in preparation for the ritual working.

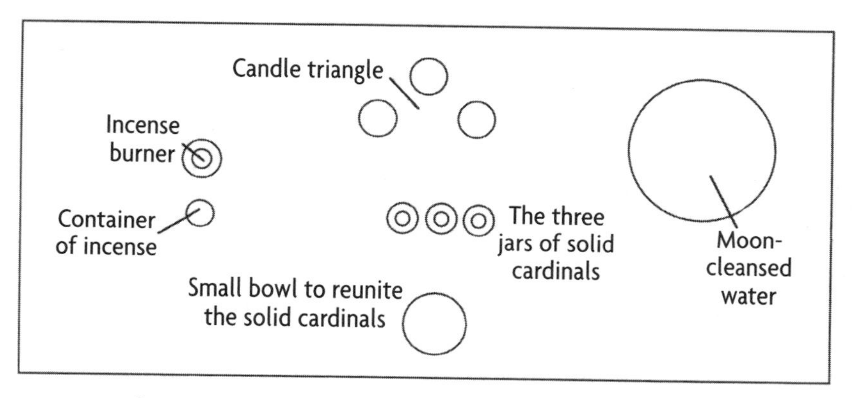

Working stone layout for the ritual working of unification.

The working stone is now ready to begin the ritual working, so we must once again look to the preparation of our body, mind, and spirit before we undertake our work. The process of personal preparation has been discussed earlier and is explained in detail in part 4.

Having completed our personal preparation, we are ready to proceed with the ritual working of amalgamation. For the purpose of this example, we will again assume that a priestess is facilitating the ritual working.

If you are working outside your workshop, the first step is to cast the Protective Circle using the stave as described in part 4. If you are within your workshop, you may have already done this for previous activities.

With the Circle cast around the working area, the entrance is sealed with the dagger. This procedure is explained in part 4. The charcoal in the incense burner is now lit in preparation for the ritual working.

The next step is the lighting of the candles. This part of the ritual has been described earlier (see page 146). Having lit all three candles in the required manner, the priestess then facilitates the uniting of the flames. This too is described in detail earlier (see page 147).

The next stage of the ritual working is the invocation of the collective energy's influence in the reuniting of the energies and potency of the flower's cardinals. The priestess stands before the working stone with both hands high in the air. She says:

"I invoke the power of the collective energy and call upon it to guide my work. I call upon the four elemental essences to empower these cardinals and maintain them as they are again united."

The three jars containing the plant's solid cardinals are then placed at the front and center of the working stone. The priestess forms her two hands into an inverted cup shape and places them above the two jars. As she does so, she says:

"I invoke the power of the elemental essence of the earth that yielded up this tree and its branch, to protect its energies and maintain its potency as it is again united as one."

Then, dipping her fingers into the vessel of moon-cleansed water, the priestess sprinkles a little of the water on each of the three jars and says:

"I invoke the power of the elemental energies of the water that nourished this tree and its branch, to protect its energies and maintain its potency as it is again united as one."

The priestess now sprinkles a little incense on the smoldering charcoal in the incense burner. As the smoke rises, she lifts each of the three jars in turn and holds them in the smoke. As she does so, she says:

"I invoke the power of the elemental energies of the air that gave life to this tree and its branch, to protect its energies and maintain its potency as it is again united as one." (Repeat for each of the three jars.)

The priestess now holds each of the three jars in turn above the flames of the candle triangle (about twelve inches above the flames), and as she moves each in a clockwise circle around all three flames she says:

"I invoke the power of the elemental energies of the fire (the sun) whose heat and light have given strength to this tree and its branch, to protect its energies

and maintain its potency as it is again united as one." (Repeat for each of the three jars.)

Finally, while holding each of the three jars in turn above the flame of the collective energy candle, the priestess says:

"I now call upon the one, the collective energy that animates all things, to guide my work and to protect the energies of this cardinal and maintain its potency as it is again united as one." (Repeat for each of the three jars.)

The three jars are now replaced in their original positions on the working stone and their screw caps are removed. The priestess stands in front of the working stone ready to begin the actual amalgamation. Bringing the small bowl to the front and center of the working stone, she picks up the jar of the solid cardinal of the leaves and, holding it in both hands, she lifts it high in the air and says:

"Conceived as one, grown as one. I reunite the solid cardinals of this tree and create the incense, the energy of fire and air."

Having said that, she pours the contents of the jar into the bowl and sets the jar aside. She then repeats this for the two other solid cardinals until the contents of all three jars are in the bowl. Then, lifting the bowl with her left hand, she gently stirs the contents with the fingers of her right hand to amalgamate all three cardinals. As she does this, she says:

"By my work and with the will of the collective energy, I have created the incense of this flower, bringing together the elemental energies of fire and air."

She then places the bowl at the base of the candle of the flame of the collective energy, and this completes the ritual working of amalgamation of the three solid cardinals of the tree.

The incense (as the combined solid cardinals are now called) is poured into a clean powder jar and sealed.

As the ritual working is now accomplished, the Protective Circle is unsealed and erased. The incense jar is labeled and then stored in a cool, dark place, next to the three cardinal essences of the same harvested branch, until they are needed.

In order to present an overview and to aid the reader's understanding of this

complicated sequence, the entire refinement process may be seen in a schematic form in the following diagram.

Generally, newly crafted cardinal essences and incense are not used immediately, but rather are left to mature for at least one month. This period of rest allows the newly combined energies and attributes of the flower to mingle and increase in potency. Often the color and perfume of the essences will change as a result of the maturation, so try not to disturb this process, as it is a vital part of the empowerment of the potions.

It is best to store together the bottles and jar containing all four components, as they jointly contain the entire energies and the physical and spiritual/magical attributes of the harvested tree branch.

When using these cardinal essences and incense, remember that it is essential that all the components are from the same plant harvest, as the physical and spiritual/magical workings of their crafting speak of the division and reuniting of the plant's latent energies and attributes. Do not be tempted to mix essences or incenses even if they are from the same genus and species.

The Amalgamation of the Cardinal Essences to Form the Complex of the Tree

We have seen that the refinement process of the complex of the tree is shorter than that of the flower. Even so, it takes between six and eight weeks from start to finish.

The resulting three cardinal essences of the tree are brought together during the ritual for which they are being used. As they amalgamate, they form the complex (*cymhleth,* in Welsh). The complex, as we have seen, is most potent at the moment of congress—so, as with the complex of the flower—we need to look at the timing and balance of the combining of these components to fully understand their power.

To create and energize the complex we need all four components that we crafted earlier: the cardinal essence of the leaves (male), the cardinal essence of the wood (female), the cardinal essence of the bark (hermaphrodite), and the incense (already combined male, female, and hermaphrodite components).

As we combine the three cardinal essences, we reunite not only the empowered

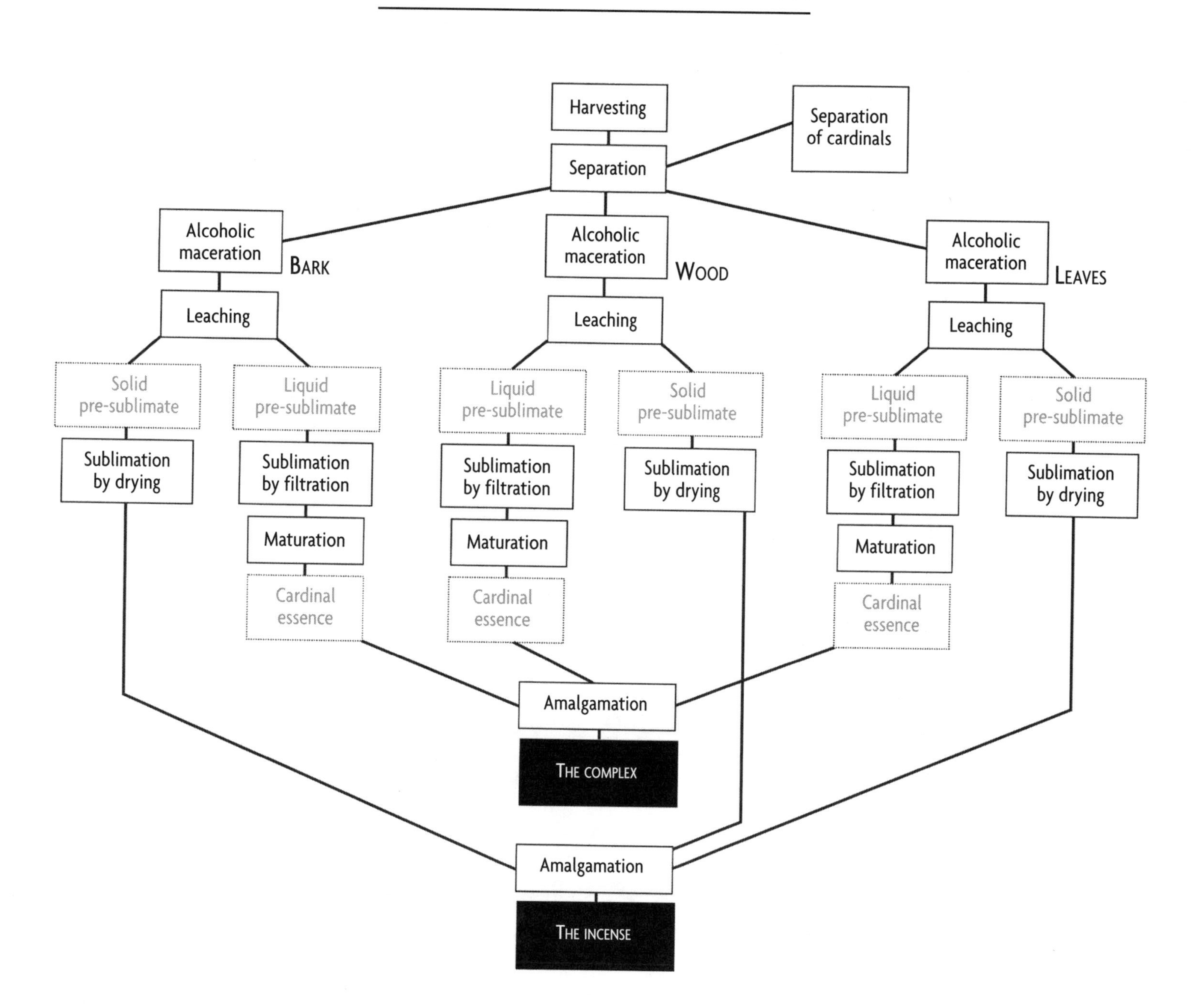
Complex Refinement Schematic for Trees
Harvesting
Separation
Separation of cardinals
Alcoholic maceration
Bark
Leaching
Solid pre-sublimate
Sublimation by drying
Liquid pre-sublimate
Sublimation by filtration
Maturation
Cardinal essence
Alcoholic maceration
Wood
Leaching
Liquid pre-sublimate
Sublimation by filtration
Maturation
Cardinal essence
Solid pre-sublimate
Sublimation by drying
Alcoholic maceration
Leaves
Leaching
Liquid pre-sublimate
Sublimation by filtration
Maturation
Cardinal essence
Solid pre-sublimate
Sublimation by drying
Amalgamation
The complex
Amalgamation
The incense

energies and attributes of the tree, but also the male and female attributes, restoring the balance of nature in our crafted complex. The complex, therefore, becomes hermaphrodite, both male and female in one, embracing the characteristics of both. It embodies the attributes of the sun and the moon (male and female), but only the elemental energies of earth and water. Thus, in itself the complex lacks the potency of all four elements.

The two missing elemental energies, fire and earth, may be found in the incense. The incense is already hermaphrodite before it is brought to the ritual (you will remember that we joined the male, female, and hermaphrodite solid cardinals during its crafting). Thus, as we pass the hermaphrodite complex through the smoke of the hermaphrodite incense (the moment of congress) we are, for the first time, combining all four elemental energies.

At the very moment of congress the complex is empowered with the combined energies and attributes of the specific tree we have selected, plus the combined elemental energies of all four elements, all maintained within the newly restored perfect male/female balance as nature prescribes.

At this moment (and for a short time afterward) the complex is at the peak of its potency. It is the sublime elixir, the quintessence. This is when we channel its energies and attributes to our needs.

As with the complex of the flower, there are some exceptions to this immediate use, and most of those are to be found in the use of the complex in remedies and potions after the ritual is over. In these cases it is accepted that the tree complex is not at its most powerful, and when mixed with carrying agents to form ointments, balms, and tinctures, there may be a need for repeated applications before the beneficial effects make themselves evident. We shall look at this method of use in detail in part 4.

Summary

At this point it should be easier for the reader to fully appreciate the power and potency of the complexes we have crafted and to understand why the Druidic tradition stands apart from other herbal and alchemical traditions in this regard.

The research into the alchemical tradition that began our journey may well have explained some of the principles behind a few of the Druidic techniques, explanations that have been lost to the Celtic world throughout the millennia. It is difficult to believe that Druidic plant lore has not been influenced in some way or another by the wealth of knowledge that has been so accurately recorded by the ancient alchemists. The traditions seem to resemble each other so closely, to have so much in common, that it is almost inconceivable that each grew and developed in isolation. Even though no one can offer a plausible explanation as to how the two traditions could have exchanged knowledge and experience, there is without doubt a common thread.

They have, as we have seen, progressed in different directions, each with its own torch to bear. The alchemist's quest to elevate metals and the search for the philosopher's stone have no equivalent in Druidic lore; alchemy stands alone in this endeavor. The Lesser Circulation of the alchemists and the work of the spagyric adept, however, offer much to the Druidic priest and priestess. Later, in the final section of this book, we shall explore this in greater detail, but before we can do this we must gain an understanding of how the various complexes and elixirs are employed and what benefits may be expected from them.

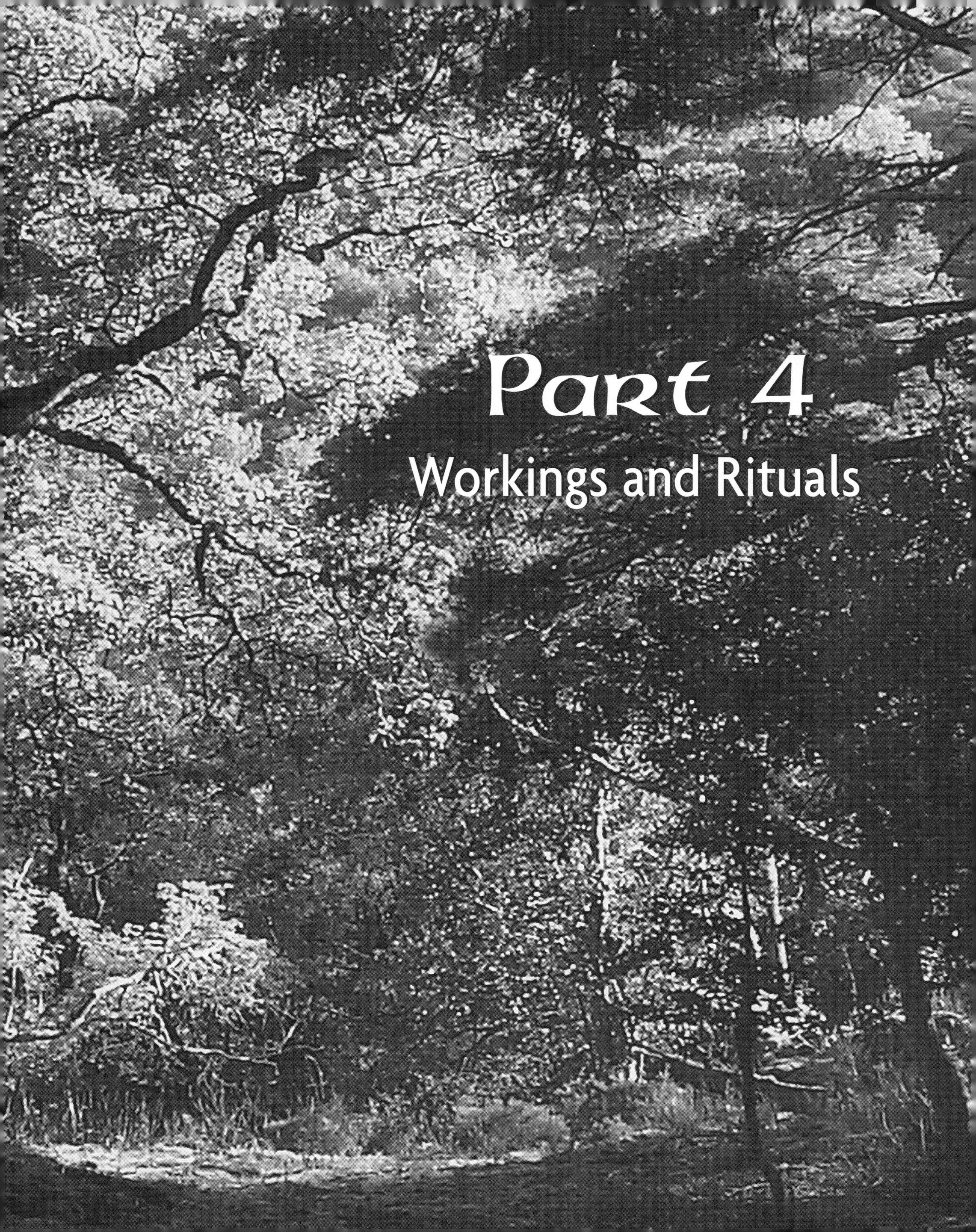

Part 4
Workings and Rituals

The Nature of the Complex

Before you start harvesting your first plants and crafting your first complex and incense, there are a number of considerations you will need to address.

Why do I need to craft a complex?

What will I use it for?

When should I begin crafting a complex?

What results or benefits may I expect from employing the complex?

In order to answer these and the other questions that may be concerning you, first visit your own motives and beliefs. Without a strong belief in what you are creating, it will be impossible for you to focus your own energies and attention on the crafting of any complex. It takes a long time to craft the final complex, together with a fair amount of arduous work, and it is unlikely that you will be able to maintain your enthusiasm for the work if you have doubts about its outcome.

I have quite deliberately used the word *benefits* many times when referring to the outcome of employing complexes. From this you will gather that there is always the intention of good in the work the Druidic practitioner does. Complexes, like all the other tools and techniques of Druidism, are intended for positive ends only.

There is, of course, a darker side to Druidic practice, one that focuses its activities on negative energies and attributes. This darker practice also extends itself into

the crafting of complexes, and, as we have already observed, the plant kingdom is capable of providing these dark practitioners with all the raw material they need.

There is one piece of reassurance that I may offer those wishing to avoid this darker practice at all costs. It is not possible to craft a dark potion by error or misfortune. There are very definite rituals and workings that must be undertaken in order to direct one's work to that darker side, and it is impossible to do these accidentally. It is possible, however, to create poisonous cardinals by error, so you must be constantly vigilant regarding the plants you use and never use any plant or other material about which you are not thoroughly knowledgeable.

I have not, and will not, include any information regarding the negative side of Druidic practices; it has always been a part of my work to counteract and eradicate these elements. Too much time and energy is used up by most Druids and practitioners of other natural magic traditions in working to put right the ills created by dark-magic practitioners for any of us to want to promote the use of such techniques. It is my sincere wish that no reader ever come into contact with this negative area of practice.

We have seen that if you are embarking on the path of crafting a complex, you must first cleanse and purify your body, mind, and spirit. Spirit, in the context of Druidism, may be defined as the part of the universal collective energy that temporarily inhabits your corporeal body. It may also be defined as "personal" or "Internal" energy, and it is the channeling of this internal energy that allows us to influence the collective energy.

Energizing the channeling of your personal, internal energy with the attributes and latent energies that are inherent in the various plant species we harvest is why we craft a plant's complex and incense. Other herbal traditions would have it that the physical effect of each plant's active ingredients—by which they mean their chemical composition—is the only benefit that may be gleaned from any particular species. This is not the case within Druidic plant lore.

It has always been apparent within the Druidic tradition that the physical benefits of the plant extracts we use can and will manifest themselves in both physical and mental improvements when used to address ailments for which they are suited. But because of their energizing and refinement, Druidic plant complexes and incenses have properties that extend their influence far beyond the purely physical realm. It is because of these powerful, far-reaching influences that we must consider very carefully how and why we opt to craft and use Druidic plant complexes and incenses.

The intensity of the power of these complexes and incenses and the immense potency of the combination of complex and incense at the moment of congress is the very reason that we choose to use plant complexes in our work. The unique combination of their physical and spiritual/magical properties means they may address a problem at all levels simultaneously, providing physical and spiritual/magical effects in the perfect balance that nature intends.

Why, then, do we need to use plant complexes and incenses? Quite simply, it is because they are by far the best tool to deal with complicated physical and/or magical disturbances.

As with all powerful remedial treatments, other, less potent remedies should always be tried first. Uncomplicated problems respond to uncomplicated treatments. Only when we are convinced that the sole way to proceed is by the use of a complex should we begin to plan its use.

Bearing in mind always the responsibility we are taking upon ourselves when we use these potent agents, we must remember that we employ them only in the correct circumstances. When dealing with any spiritual/magical agents, we must be sure of all of the circumstances surrounding the episode and also consider the ramifications of the success (or failure) of the working or ritual we intend to undertake. We must be careful not to create a new problem when solving the old and that we are not beginning a sequence of events we may lose control of and regret later.

Generally, complexes are used in one of two ways. They are either taken internally or applied to the skin. When taken internally, they may be used in a physical or practical sense, to address physical, mental, or spiritual disturbances. In these circumstances they would be included in a tincture, syrup, or mulled beverage such as wine or cider. Or they may be used in a magical sense, as when included in a ritual libation or in a particular magical draft prescribed to affect the individual's internal energy in some predetermined way.

Similarly, they may be applied to the skin in a physical or practical method, as a salve, poultice, or hot fomentation (hot compress), or as a magical unguent to energize and increase the internal energy, as in the sex magic ritual we'll be looking at later.

The crafting of these various salves, unguents, and fomentations is described in the section below, Mediums to Carry the Complex, where the relevant dosages and quantities are also discussed.

Once you are certain that the solution to the particular problem you face lies in the use of a plant complex, you may begin to consider its crafting in detail. In doing this, the first thing is to decide on the plant species that has the energies and attributes you seek. In most circumstances, there is more than one plant that harbors the features you will be looking for, so the next consideration is the plant's availability. This will be influenced by such things as geographic location, the plant's life cycle, and the time of year. Usually, the consideration of all these aspects points us toward a suitable species, so now we must go out and find our donor plant in order to plan our harvesting. We have spent a good deal of time exploring the factors influencing our choice of donor plant in the previous parts of this book, so I will not retrace those footsteps here.

Once a suitable plant has been selected, the sequence of harvesting and crafting may begin. We have seen that the harvesting and crafting processes may take between two and four months to complete, and it would not be unreasonable to add another month to that period to allow sufficient time for the original functions of deciding which plant species you need and targeting the specific plant to harvest. Thus, from initial research to finished complex may well take as long as five months.

We can see from this that the process does not lend itself to immediate needs or rapid response. For these circumstances it will be necessary to build up a store of the most commonly used complexes in their cardinal essence and incense form, in *anticipation* of needs.

The response, then, to the question, "When should I begin crafting a complex?" is—as with all things—Follow nature. At the beginning of each year consider the plans of your Gathering(s) and identify any complexes you may want to use. Spend time meditating on your needs and try to anticipate which complexes you will require. Consider those around you and those people you serve within your community. Are there any recurring needs for long-term treatments? Can you see any approaching illnesses (physical, mental, or spiritual) on the horizon? Are you planning to enter into any new areas of practice in the forthcoming year? If so, will you require additional complexes to help your work? Look back at the previous year and consider whether you had sufficient complexes for your needs. Should you increase the quantities you craft or broaden the range of the complexes you use? Did you have the necessary complexes when you needed them (remembering that some complexes may be crafted only at certain times of the year)?

By considering these questions and any others that are relevant, you'll be able to plan your year's harvesting and crafting in a structured way. Even if this only meets 50 percent of your needs, the following year you may again learn from the experience and amend your plans accordingly.

As your stock of cardinal essences and incenses grows, you will find yourself in a stronger position to deal with the wide variety of challenges that you will inevitably come up against. If your cardinal essences and incenses have been crafted and stored in the proper manner, they will last for eighteen to twenty-four months, and even at this age, when they are reunited they will produce the most potent of complexes.

My experience tells me that by using these complexes in the correct circumstances and for legitimate needs, the results will be exactly what you wish them to be. If the correct energies and attributes are channeled toward and focused on the right challenge, the outcome will be certain. Most of the failures I have witnessed were the result of either misreading the portents and indicators, not matching the right energies and attributes to the problem at hand, or improper crafting techniques and storage. Re-crafting the appropriate complex and then empowering it in the correct fashion rectifies nearly all of these failures.

Corresponding the appropriate energies and attributes of the plant to the needs of the challenge is by far the most difficult task that faces the Druidic practitioner. Only research, safe experimentation, and experience will arm him or her with the knowledge needed to identify the most suitable plant for the occasion.

Single and Combined Complexes

In the majority of cases, a well-crafted complex will provide all the benefits intended for your working. In some rare circumstances, however, it may be necessary to combine the energies and attributes of two or more complexes in order to address the whole spectrum of benefits you are seeking.

Combined complexes, as these mixtures are called, incorporate the energies and attributes of each of the complexes that make them up. The most important thing to remember here is that the combined complex includes all of the energies and attributes of the complexes it is made up of, not just the ones that you may particularly need.

The area of crafting combined complexes is one frought with difficulties, and it needs a great amount of knowledge and experience to begin this work. As I have suggested, the main challenge is to fully understand the effects of combining the energies and attributes you are working with. Most of us have the capability to focus on the things we want and to overlook the unwanted, more negative aspects. This is also the tendency with practitioners new to this area of work. It is easy to forget or to push aside the unsuitable aspects of complexes' attributes and just focus on the ones we are looking for. The results of this approach will be the inevitable inclusion of certain energies and attributes that will not help—and may even contradict—the effects we intend.

This work is complicated further by the fact that it is, of course, possible to combine as many complexes as we may feel necessary to achieve the results we desire. The amount of contributory complexes is limited only by those you will have available to you, so the experienced practitioner, with a well-stocked cupboard, may have tens, if not hundreds, of complexes to choose from. Thus, it is imperative to have a detailed understanding of each complex we craft and also the importance of maintaining our workshop ledger with as much information as possible about every stage of every complex's crafting.

There remains one other prime aspect of crafting combined complexes to consider, that of *proportions.* The varying proportions of the constituent parts of a combined complex affect the overall balance and effectiveness of the mixture. A greater amount of any one particular component gives its energies and attributes dominance over the others.

The crafting of combined complexes is one of the most skilled activities in the Druid's repertoire. It offers an infinite choice of variables in both the complexes used and the proportions they are used in. This means that the experienced Druidic practitioner may "tune" the combined complex to suit exactly the needs of the challenge facing him or her.

The other side of this coin is that this very same infinite choice demands that the practitioner know and understand the complexes he or she is working with.

Remember, though, that it is not possible to make a dark potion accidentally, by ignorance. The worst that will happen by combining complexes with incompatible energies and attributes is that the combined complex will be neutral—that is, the energies and attributes of one compound will counteract the energies and attributes of another, thereby rendering the complex ineffective. No harm is done, but a lot of work, time, and valuable compounds may be wasted.

My simple recommendation is to avoid compound complexes until you have mastered the crafting of simple complexes and have given yourself enough time to fully understand their effects. To some extent, this is inevitable, as the individual complexes will have to be crafted first before any combined complexes may be mixed. But let me repeat the maxim I was taught as an initiate: "Never extend yourself beyond your own certain knowledge. Learning, safe experimentation, and understanding must always come first."

Once you are confident that you are ready to craft your first compound complex, I suggest you begin with a two-part compound—one made up of two individual complexes. Because there is a very strong spiritual/magical component to this crafting, it is facilitated as a ritual working or even sometimes within a ritual Gathering in order to strengthen the work with the combined energies of all those present.

The Crafting of a Two-Part Compound Complex: The Ritual Working

This working has two distinct parts. The first is the bringing together of the cardinal essences and their empowerment by their incense and the second is the mixing of the combined complex. Both parts are normally facilitated in immediate succession, as the potency of the individual complexes begins to decline from their moment of congress.

For the sake of this example, we shall look at the combining of two flower complexes, the bird's-foot trefoil and the dog rose. One of the more common combined complexes, this is used in love potions and in sex magic rituals. It is also a very attractive-looking complex, combining the bright energetic yellow complex of the trefoil with the vivid red of the dog rose.

For this ritual working you will need:

- **The candle triangle.** See page 133.
- **A vessel of moon-cleansed water.** See page 235.
- **An incense burner,** to incinerate initially the purifying incense (lavender, for example) and then the incense of the flower with which we are working.
- **The stave and dagger,** to cast and seal the Protective Circle. If you are using a permanent working stone within your workshop, you may well have cast the Circle previously, in which case you will need just the dagger to seal its entrance.

For part 1, the combining of the cardinal essences to craft the individual complexes:

- **A small bowl,** in which we will reunite the cardinal essences to form the complex.
- **The two bottles containing the cardinal essences of the first flower** (the cardinal essence of the petal and the cardinal essence of the flower head). The contents of each of these bottles should be premeasured so that their volumes are perfectly equal and they contain no more of the precious cardinal essences than are needed to serve the purpose intended.
- **The jar containing the incense of the first flower.**

Note: This section will be repeated for the second flower and in other cases for as many complexes as we desire.

For part 2, the combining of the two complexes to craft the combined complex:

- **A small bowl,** in which we will combine the complexes to form the combined complex.
- **The two bottles containing the complexes of the two (or more) flowers we are combining** (in this case, the complex of the bird's-foot trefoil and the complex of the dog rose). The contents of each of these bottles should

be pre-measured so that their volumes are in the exact proportion required (not necessarily equal amounts; see page 201).

- **The jars containing the incense of the two (or more) flowers we are combining.**

The working stone should be laid out as shown below in preparation for the ritual working.

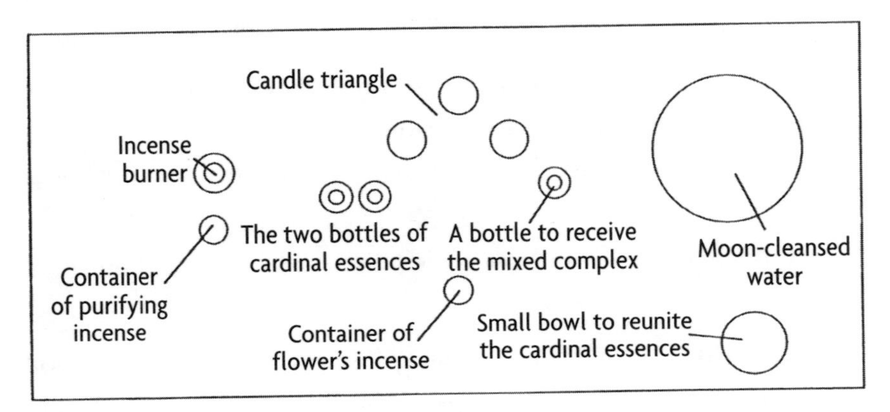

Working stone layout for the ritual working of combining the two cardinal essences to form the complex.

The working stone is now ready to begin the ritual working, so we must once again look to the preparation of our body, mind, and spirit before we undertake our work. The process of personal preparation has been mentioned earlier and is explained in detail in part 4.

Having completed our personal preparation, we are ready to proceed with the ritual working of unification. For the purpose of this example, we will again assume that a priestess is facilitating the ritual working.

If you are working outside your workshop, the first step is to cast the Protective Circle using the stave (see page 237). If you are within your workshop, you may have already done this for previous activities. With the Circle cast around the working area, the entrance is sealed with the dagger (see page 242).

The charcoal in the incense burner is now lit in preparation for the ritual working. The next step is the lighting of the candles. This part of the ritual has been described in detail in the section Ritual Working of the Separation (see page 146).

Having lit all three flames in the required manner, the priestess then facilitates the uniting of the flames. Again, see the section Ritual Working of the Separation.

The next stage of the ritual working is the invocation of the collective energy's influence in reuniting the energies and potency of the flower's cardinals. The priestess stands before the working stone and raises both hands high in the air. In doing so she says:

"I invoke the power of the collective energy and call upon it to guide my work. I call upon the four elemental essences to empower these cardinals and maintain them as they are again united."

The two bottles containing the flower's cardinal essences and the jar containing the flower's incense are then placed at the front and center of the working stone. The priestess forms her two hands into an inverted cup shape and places them above the three vessels. As she does so, she says:

"I invoke the power of the elemental essence of the earth that yielded up these flowers, to protect their energies and maintain their potency as they are again united as one."

Then, dipping her fingers into the bowl of moon-cleansed water, the priestess sprinkles a little of the water on all three vessels and says:

"I invoke the power of the elemental energies of the water that nourished these flowers, to protect their energies and maintain their potency as they are again united as one."

The priestess now sprinkles a little purifying incense on the smoldering charcoal in the incense burner. As the smoke rises, she lifts each of the three vessels in turn and holds it in the smoke. As she does so, she says:

"I invoke the power of the elemental energies of the air that gave life to these flowers, to protect their energies and maintain their potency as they are again united as one." (Repeat in turn for each vessel.)

The priestess now holds each of the three vessels in turn above the flames of the candle triangle (about twelve inches above the flames), and as she moves each vessel in a clockwise circle around all three flames she says:

"I invoke the power of the elemental energies of the fire (the sun) whose heat and light have given strength to these flowers, to protect their energies and maintain their potency as they are again united as one." (Repeat in turn for each vessel.)

Finally, while holding each of the vessels in turn above the flame of the collective energy candle, the priestess says:

"I now call upon the one, the collective energy that animates all things, to guide my work and to protect the energies of these essences and maintain their potency as they are again united as one."

The three vessels are now placed in their original positions on the working stone and their stoppers are removed. The priestess stands in front of the working stone ready to begin the actual unification.

Bringing the small bowl to the front and center of the working stone, the priestess takes the bottle of cardinal essence of the petals in her left hand and the bottle containing the cardinal essence of the flower head in her right hand. Lifting both bottles high in the air, she says:

"Conceived as one, grown as one. I reunite the cardinal essences of this flower and create its one complex, the sublime elixir. Imbue this complex with the power of your energy and maintain its purity until we call upon it once more."

Having said that, she simultaneously pours *equal quantities* of the contents of each bottle into the bowl. Then, lifting the bowl carefully into the air so as not to spill any of the contents, she says:

"Reunited as one, energies and attributes recombined. I bind once more the cardinal of this flower in its purest form."

This said, she places the bowl back on the working stone and, taking a liberal amount of the flower's incense from its container, sprinkles it onto the glowing charcoal in the incense burner. As the smoke rises from the smoldering incense, she again lifts the bowl containing the complex of the flower and holds it within the incense smoke. In doing so, she says:

"By my work and with the will of the collective energy, I have created the com-

plex of this flower. I call upon the four elemental energies to empower this complex, to reunite all again as one in natural balance and harmony. And so shall it remain, conjoined and complete."

She then places the bowl at the base of the candle of the flame of the collective energy. The vessels containing the essences of this first flower are then placed to one side and replaced by the three vessels containing the cardinal essences and incense of the second flower. The process is then repeated to produce the complex of the second flower (and any subsequent flower complexes needed).

This, then, completes the first part of the ritual working and has left us with the two complexes we need for the combined complex.

The working stone now must be rearranged as shown below, to facilitate the second part of the ritual working, the combining of the complexes.

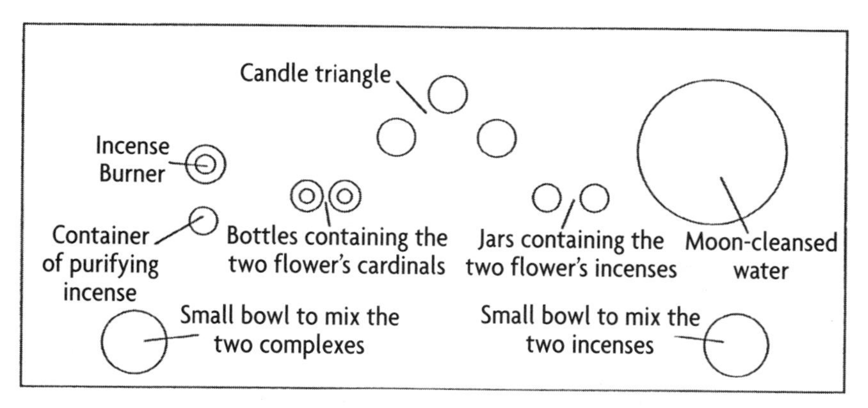

Working stone layout for the ritual working of combining the two complexes to form the combined complex.

As the working stone, Protective Circle, and the priestess's purification remain intact, the second stage of the ritual working begins with the invocation of the collective energy's influence in the forming of the combined cardinal.

The priestess stands before the working stone and raises both hands high in the air. In doing so, she says:

"I invoke the power of the collective energy and call upon it to guide my work. I call upon the four elemental essences to empower these cardinals as they are combined."

The two bottles containing the two flowers' complexes and the two jars containing their incenses are then placed at the front and center of the working stone. The priestess forms her two hands into an inverted cup shape and places them above the four vessels. As she does so, she says:

"I invoke the power of the elemental essence of the earth that yielded up these flowers, to protect their energies and maintain their potency as they are combined as one."

Then, dipping her fingers into the bowl of moon-cleansed water, the priestess sprinkles a little of the water on all four vessels and says:

"I invoke the power of the elemental energies of the water that nourished these flowers, to protect their energies and maintain their potency as they are combined as one."

The priestess now sprinkles a little purifying incense on the smoldering charcoal in the incense burner. As the smoke rises, she lifts each of the four vessels in turn and holds it in the smoke. As she does so, she says:

"I invoke the power of the elemental energies of the air that gave life to these flowers, to protect their energies and maintain their potency as they are combined as one." (Repeat in turn for each vessel.)

The priestess now holds each of the four vessels in turn above the flames of the candle triangle (about twelve inches above the flames), and as she moves each vessel in a clockwise circle around all three flames she says:

"I invoke the power of the elemental energies of the fire (the sun) whose heat and light have given strength to these flowers, to protect their energies and maintain their potency as they are combined as one." (Repeat in turn for each vessel.)

Finally, while holding each of the four vessels in turn above the flame of the collective energy candle, the priestess says:

"I now call upon the one, the collective energy that animates all things, to guide my work and to protect the energies of these essences and maintain their potency as they are combined as one."

The four vessels are now placed in their original positions on the working stone and their stoppers are removed. The priestess stands in front of the working stone ready to begin the actual unification. Bringing the first of the small bowls to the front and center of the working stone, the priestess takes one bottle of complex in her left hand and the other bottle of complex in her right hand. Lifting both bottles high in the air, she says:

"Conceived separately, grown separately, I combine the complexes of these flowers to create one, the sublime elixir. Imbue this combined complex with the power of your energy and maintain its purity until we call upon it once more."

Having said this, she simultaneously pours the desired quantity of each cardinal into the bowl. Then, lifting the bowl carefully into the air so as not to spill any of the contents, she says:

"Combined as one, energies and attributes united. I enjoin the cardinals of these flowers in their purest form."

This said, she replaces the bowl on the working stone. Bringing the second bowl forward, the priestess picks up one of the jars of incense in each hand. Holding them aloft, she says:

"Conceived separately, grown separately, I combine the incenses of these flowers to create one, the sublime elixir. Imbue this incense with the power of your energy and maintain its purity until we call upon it once more."

Having said this, she simultaneously pours the desired quantity of each cardinal into the bowl. These quantities of incense are in the same proportion as their corresponding quantities of cardinals used earlier. Then, lifting the bowl carefully in the air, she says:

"Combined as one, energies and attributes united. I enjoin the incense of these flowers in their purest form."

This said, she replaces the bowl on the working stone. Next, taking a liberal amount of the newly combined incense from its bowl, she sprinkles it onto the glowing charcoal in the incense burner. As the smoke rises from the smoldering incense, she again lifts the bowl containing the combined complex from below the candle of the flame of the collective energy and holds it within the incense smoke. Doing so, she says:

"By my work and with the will of the collective energy, I have created this combined complex. I call upon the four elemental energies to empower this complex, to unite all as one in natural balance and harmony. And so shall it remain, conjoined and complete."

She then places the bowl containing the combined complex at the base of the candle of the flame of the collective energy.

The crafting of the combined complex is now complete. At this point the potent combined complex is usually poured into a decorative ritual vessel of some sort, one that reflects the eminence of the potion it contains. In most cases the combined complex is then used immediately in the continuing ritual that began with its crafting. We shall see this in practice when we explore the way in which complexes are used in sex magic rituals.

Mediums to Carry the Complex

Whether using single or combined complexes, it is common to mix them with a suitable *carrying medium.* The carrying medium used depends on whether the complex is to be applied to the skin or ingested. Let's explore each method.

Mediums for the Application of Complexes to the Skin

Within the Welsh Druidic tradition, applications come in four forms:

Salves (*leddfu* in Welsh)

Unguent (*ennaint* in Welsh)

Evaporations (*ymageru* in Welsh)

Poultices and fomentations (compresses) (*powltis* in Welsh)

Salves are used in the treatment of physical damage or imbalance, such as bruising, cuts, sprains, grazes, irritations, insect and plant stings, and against certain skin ailments. They offer physical comfort, provide relief from pain or irritation, assist healing, and stave off infection.

Unguents are used only in spiritual/magical workings. They are used to energize, strengthen, reinforce, increase potential, and otherwise influence the internal energy of the recipient.

Evaporations are again mainly used in magical workings. The exception is their use to treat sprains and bruising, where they are helpful primarily for their physical benefits.

Poultices and fomentations are used primarily for their physical benefits in easing pain and bringing comfort and for their nurturing properties when used over a longer period.

Crafting and Using Mediums for Skin Application

The work of crafting all of these mediums is usually done in the comfort and convenience of the Druid's workshop. The tasks are simple ones and do not require the facilitation of a ritual working.

Salves are crafted by combining the desired complex with a mixture of vegetable oil and beeswax to create a soft, creamy ointment that may be applied to the skin.

To craft a salve, we will need:

- **A small saucepan,** in which to heat the oil and beeswax.
- **Sufficient sterile, airtight jars to contain the finished salve.**
- **A corresponding number of grease-proof paper disks, cut to fit the jars.** The disks are placed immediately on top of the salve inside the jars to prevent any air from coming into contact with the surface of the salve.
- **200 ml of good-quality vegetable oil.** Any good vegetable oil will work. Do not use nut oils or any essential oils, as these will contaminate the complex.
- **100 ml of organic beeswax,** preferably from a known source. This was a common ingredient in many Druidic potions along with honey, as most Druid priests and priestesses were also beekeepers.
- **25 ml of the selected complex,** to add to the salve.

The most important part of the preparation for this working is the cleaning and sterilizing of all the equipment you intend to use, particularly the storage jars and their caps. Because all the ingredients of the salve are natural, unpasteurized materials, it is imperative that all the equipment be sterilized to prevent bacteria and mold from forming on the surface or the salve and rendering it unusable.

Caution! Raising the temperature of any liquid containing alcohol produces flammable vapors. Do not expose mixtures to unprotected flames or any other heat source likely to ignite such vapors.

Begin by placing the oil and beeswax in the saucepan and gently heating over very low heat. Stir the contents continually. As the beeswax begins to melt, stir the mixture more vigorously. After a short while, the oil and beeswax will combine into a smooth, creamy paste. At this point, remove the saucepan from the heat and allow the mixture to cool to body temperature.

Stir the complex into the salve. Keep stirring until the complex is amalgamated with the mixture. Before the salve becomes too thick, pour or spoon it into the waiting storage jars and seal the surface of the salve in each jar with the grease-proof paper disks.

When the salve is completely cold, screw on the caps and label the jars. The salve is now ready for storage or immediate use.

To use the salve, rub a liberal amount onto the appropriate area. Repeat regularly until the symptoms cease.

Unguents are crafted by combining the desired complex with a mixture of vegetable oil, surgical alcohol (or rubbing alcohol), and beeswax to create a thin, creamy ointment that may be applied to the skin. The surgical or rubbing alcohol that is used is of a very high percent alcohol by volume and creates an evaporating effect that stimulates the area it is applied to and simultaneously concentrates the effect of the cardinal being used.

To craft an unguent, we will need:

- **A small saucepan,** in which to heat the oil and beeswax.
- **Sufficient sterile, airtight jars to contain the finished salve.**
- **A corresponding number of grease-proof paper disks, cut to fit the jars.** The disks are placed immediately on top of the salve inside the jars to prevent any air from coming into contact with the surface of the unguent.
- **200 ml of good-quality vegetable oil.** Any good vegetable oil will work. Do not use nut oils or any essential oils, as these will contaminate the complex.

- **100 ml of organic beeswax,** preferably from a known source. This was a common ingredient in many Druidic potions along with honey, as most Druid priests and priestesses were also beekeepers.
- **50 ml of surgical or rubbing alcohol,** to add to the unguent.
- **25 ml of the selected complex,** to add to the unguent.

Caution! Raising the temperature of any liquid containing alcohol produces flammable vapors. Do not expose mixtures to unprotected flames or any other heat source likely to ignite such vapors.

Begin in the same way as for the salve, by placing the oil and beeswax in the saucepan and gently heating over a very low heat. Stir the contents of the pan continually. As the beeswax begins to melt, stir the mixture more vigorously. After a short while, the oil and beeswax will combine into a smooth, creamy paste. At this point, remove the saucepan from the heat and allow the mixture to cool to body temperature.

Stir the complex into the cool unguent. Keep stirring until the mixture begins to thicken. Before the unguent becomes too thick, add the surgical/rubbing alcohol and stir or whip the mixture to distribute the alcohol and incorporate some air. Spoon the unguent into the waiting storage jars and seal the surface of the salve in each jar with the grease-proof paper disks.

When the unguent is completely cold, screw on the caps and label the jars. The unguent is now ready for storage or immediate use.

The unguent is invariably used only during rituals. The facilitating priest or priestess normally applies liberal amounts of the unguent to the appropriate part of the body. As we shall see later, unguents are used in Celtic sex magic rituals as stimulants and lubricants. In both these forms they imbue the recipient's whole body with the energies and attributes of the complex(es) they contain.

Evaporations are crafted by mixing an amount of the selected complex with surgical or rubbing alcohol. The effect of this method of application is stimulation during the evaporation of the surgical/rubbing alcohol, and the additional penetration of the complex it carries. They are used almost exclusively during rituals to imbue the recipient with the spiritual and magical powers of the complex they contain.

To craft an evaporation we will need:

- **A 300 ml mixing beaker,** in which to mix the evaporation.
- **A long-handled spoon,** to stir the mixture.
- **A suitable storage bottle with an airtight stopper,** to store the evaporation.
- **150 ml of surgical or rubbing alcohol.**
- **50 ml of the desired complex.**

To craft the evaporation, simply pour both the alcohol and the complex into the mixing beaker and stir. The mixture may then be poured into its storage bottle, sealed, and labeled.

To use the evaporation, pour a little onto the palm of the hand and rub into the desired area.

Poultices and fomentations are crafted by mixing the desired complex with oil, beeswax, and the complex's incense. Poultices, in the Druidic context, are applied to the skin cold: fomentations are always warm or hot when applied.

To craft a poultice or fomentation, we will need:

- **A small saucepan,** in which to heat the oil and beeswax.
- **200 ml of good-quality vegetable oil.** Any good vegetable oil will work. Do not use nut oils or any essential oils, as these will contaminate the complex.
- **200 ml of organic beeswax,** preferably from a known source.
- **25 ml of the selected complex,** to add to the salve.
- **One tablespoon of the complex's incense.** Remember that, as in all other cases, the incense used *must* be from the same harvest that the complex was originally refined from.
- **A 9-inch (23 cm) square of muslin or linen,** to hold the solid element of the poultice/fomentation (the incense).
- **A cotton or linen bandage,** to secure the poultice/fomentation to the appropriate part of the body.

All fomentations and most poultices are used immediately following their crafting, so no provision has been made here for their storage.

Caution! Raising the temperature of any liquid containing alcohol produces flammable vapors. Do not expose mixtures to unprotected flames or any other heat source likely to ignite such vapors.

Begin by placing the oil and beeswax into the saucepan and gently heating over very low heat. Stir the contents of the pan continually. As the beeswax begins to melt, stir the mixture more vigorously. After a short while, the oil and beeswax will combine into a smooth, creamy paste. At this point, remove the saucepan from the heat and allow the mixture to cool to body temperature. Stir the complex into the salve. Keep stirring until the complex is amalgamated with the mixture.

Spread the complex's incense over an area of three square inches (7.5 square cm) at the center of the muslin square and fold the square to form a three-inch (7.5 cm) pad. (If a larger square is needed to cover the intended area on the body, increase the amount of incense and the size of the muslin accordingly.)

Place the pad in the warm mixture and allow it to soak up as much of the mixture as it can. If the mixture is to be used as a fomentation, place the warm, saturated pad on the desired area and secure in place with the bandage. If the mixture is to be used as a poultice, remove the saturated pad and place it on a plate to cool. When cold, place it on the desired area of the body, forming it to fit as it warms and softens. Secure in place using the bandage.

Both fomentations and poultices should be left in place for at least two hours. Repeat as often as required to give relief or as part of a healing regimen.

Mediums for the Ingestion of Complexes

Again, within the Welsh Druidic tradition these come in four different forms: syrups (*triagl* in Welsh); tinctures (*lliw* in Welsh); infusions (*hydreiddiad* in Welsh); and libations (*llymaid* in Welsh).

Syrups are used for ingesting the cardinal in order to benefit from its physical and/or spiritual/magical attributes. Usually taken in small quantities, syrups provide a pleasant means of assimilating the cardinal into the body's system.

Tinctures are a means of creating a concentrated solution, and in fact all cardinals are, by definition, tinctures. Usually formed by macerating the desired plant material in alcohol, the tincture is then further diluted before ingestion. Tinctures work entirely on the physical plane, while complexes have the additional benefit of being spiritually and magically energized and may work on both the physical and spiritual/magical aspects of the particular challenge.

Infusions are basically teas. Herbs or other plant materials are infused in hot water to extract their physical benefits. Again, like tinctures, infusions act only on the physical plane.

Libations are intended to work on the spiritual/magical plane only. They are always drunk during rituals and provide a means both of involving the participant in the social activity of the Gathering and of ingesting any cardinals or other potions that may be beneficial to the ritual. Libations are never used for their physical benefits only.

Crafting and Using Mediums for Ingestion

Once again, the work of crafting all of these mediums is usually done in the comfort and convenience of the Druid's workshop. All the tasks are simple and do not require the facilitation of a ritual working.

Syrups are crafted by dissolving the desired complex in honey. They provide a pleasant means of ingesting the complex, especially suitable for children or those people who find it off-putting to take medicines in any other forms. Some complexes have a bitter, unpleasant taste, which may be disguised by taking them as a syrup. For the greater part, syrups are used when we are intending to employ the physical benefits of a complex.

To craft a syrup, we will need:

- **A small saucepan,** in which to heat the honey.
- **A wooden mixing spoon,** to stir the syrup.
- **A storage bottle with an airtight screw top,** to store the crafted syrup.
- **200 ml of organic honey,** preferably from a known source.
- **100 ml of the desired complex.**

Caution! Raising the temperature of any liquid containing alcohol produces flammable vapors. Do not expose mixtures to unprotected flames or any other heat source likely to ignite such vapors.

Begin by gently heating the honey in the saucepan over very low heat. As the honey becomes warm, about body temperature, add the complex a little at a time, stirring constantly to combine the mixture. Do not allow the honey to become too hot, as the complex will evaporate and lose its potency. Once the entire complex has been absorbed into the honey, remove the saucepan from the heat and allow it to cool.

Once cold, pour into the storage bottle and label it. The syrup is now ready for immediate use or may be stored for up to two weeks. To use the syrup, take one teaspoon as required.

Tinctures are very similar to complexes, inasmuch as both are alcohols that have been infused with the desired herbal or plant matter. Complexes are never mixed again with alcohol to produce a tincture; however, complexes may be used as tinctures, but to much greater effect.

To use a complex as a tincture, simply add two or three drops to a cup of springwater and drink as required.

Infusions are created by steeping herbs or other plant material in hot water. Their properties then become infused into the water, which is then ingested. The role of the complex in infusions is to fortify and complement the already created herbal potion. This is necessary because infusions work only on the physical plane, so if the infusion's physical properties need to be reinforced through a spiritual/magical dimension, a suitable complex is added to the infusion just before it is drunk.

To add a complementary complex to an infusion, simply place a single teaspoon of the complex in the hot infusion before drinking it. If the infusion is to be taken cold, add the same amount of complex to the cold infusion just before it is consumed.

Libations are intended to work on the spiritual/magical plane only. They are therefore drunk only during rituals or at times when a spiritual/magical influence is needed to fulfill an intention. Many libations, such as some mulled beers, mulled cider, and Druidic metheglin (a Welsh Druidic mixture), will already contain herbs, flowers, or other plant material designed to influence those who take it. Any complexes added to these "charged" libations would be superfluous, as they already contain the required energies and attributes; in fact, by adding certain complexes, we could confuse or even negate the effects we intend.

If we are to use a complex in this situation, we must craft a "neutral" libation first and then, just before it is taken, add the complex as the only other ingredient.

In most cases, a simple mulled beer, cider, or wine is created by heating the liquid with a red-hot mulling iron or poker. Once the liquid is warm, the desired complex is added in the proportion of 1 part complex to 10 parts beer, cider, or wine. A typical libation for a small Gathering would consist of one liter (1.75 UK pints) of beer with 100 ml (0.20 UK pints) of the desired complex. Because most of the beers, ciders, and wine we use will have been manufactured through industrial processes, their original energies and attributes will have been lost or diluted to such an extent as to be rendered ineffectual. We can therefore use them as a carrier in the sure knowledge that the only energies and attributes within the libation will be those of the complex we add to it.

As this is a spiritual/magical potion, the liquid is mulled and the complex added during the ritual for which it is to be used. The libation is immediately distributed among the Gathering and drunk while it is still warm.

In general terms, it is best to craft a carrying medium containing a complex only as and when it is needed. Most of the mediums mentioned above will lose their potency after a few weeks or even days. In some cases, they must be used immediately following their crafting or they will become ineffective.

The Role of the Complex in Sexual Potency

One of the main uses for Druidic complexes is in the area of personal sexual potency. In this context, an individual's sexual potency may be looked at as two separate but interconnected capacities. The first element is one's sexual potency in regard to one's personal sexual energy and capacity—one's sexual performance, if you prefer. The second is one's ability to produce generated energy through one's orgasm, the type of energy that is channeled in the practice of sex magic rituals.

It is, of course, impossible to address one of these areas without having some effect on the other, but as we shall be looking at the use of Druidic complexes in the facilitation and empowerment of sex magic rituals later, I shall focus here on their use in enhancing the sexual energy and capacity of the individual in his or her everyday relationships.

One's level of sexual energy and capacity or appetite for sexual activity profoundly affect every individual, both male and female. They influence every aspect of people's lives and will be one of the determining factors in any relationship they may form. Whether practiced within a permanent loving relationship or as a casual, recreational pursuit, sexual energy and appetite will eventually be the defining elements in the success or failure of the association. Few couples find it possible to remove this aspect from their relationship, and few manage to overcome any great discrepancy in appetite for sexual activity.

This is where Druidic complexes may play a part in redressing the balance of the relationship, by harmonizing the sexual appetites and energies of the partners.

221
The Role of the Complex in Sexual Potency

Within the Druidic tradition, ideal sexual relationships—as with all other relationships—are seen to be in a state of natural balance, reflecting the male/female balance of the cosmos as maintained by the collective energy. In any state of balance, its equilibrium depends on its component parts. In the case of a sexual partnership, these component parts are the two individuals involved. It becomes clear, therefore, that the lack of balance may be due to either or to both of the individuals concerned.

It is important in all these cases to explore the unbalance by involving both partners, and in my experience there is no reason to believe that it is predominantly a male or a female problem. It is also fair to say that the use of Druidic complexes is equally effective for both sexes. There are also occasions when it is necessary to treat both individuals simultaneously, but not, perhaps, with the same complex.

This male/female balance suggests that the entire philosophy holds true only within a heterosexual relationship. This is not the case at all. By far the majority of homosexual and lesbian relationships place the partners in clear "male" and "female" roles, and no matter how loosely these metaphorical roles may be, each partner brings with him or her the energies and attributes of the role he or she fulfills. This same male/female balance is evident inside every one of us; homosexuality and lesbianism are seen within the Druidic tradition as just another way of achieving and maintaining this natural balance.

Complexes crafted from the cuckoo flower *(Cardamine pratensis),* the honeysuckle *(Lonicera periclymemum),* the yellow iris *(Iris pseudacorus),* the marigold *(Calendula officinalis)*, the greater periwinkle *(Vinca major),* the sweet violet *(Viola odorata),* and the bird's-foot trefoil *(Lotus corniculatus)*—used in the example in the last section—all have energies and attributes that affect sexual potency and appetite.

The herbs cotton thistle *(Onopordon acanthium),* starwort *(Stelleria media),* coltsfoot *(Tussilago farfara),* common feverfew *(Tanacetum parthenium),* bridewort *(Filipendula ulmaria),* round-leafed mint *(Mentha sauveolens),* and sneezewort *(Achillea ptarmica)* also contain potent sexually related energies and attributes.

The most potent trees for this use are the crab apple *(Malus sylvestris),* silver birch *(Betula pendula),* blackberry *(Rubus fruticosus)*, hawthorn *(Crataegus monogyna),* common heather *(Calluna vulgaris),* ivy *(Hedera helix),* mistletoe *(Viscum album),* oak *(Quercus robur),* and rowan *(Sorbus aucuparia).*

Complexes refined from any of the above will have the capacity to influence sexual potency and appetite; however, each addresses the problem in a slightly different way and brings a wide range of subtleties to the therapy. It is for each practitioner to determine which is the most appropriate complex to use in individual cases.

For guidance, study the tables of physical and magical attributes for flowers/herbs and trees (see pages 81 and 105). As a starting point, the flower bird's-foot trefoil *(Lotus corniculatus*), the herb coltsfoot *(Tussilago farfara),* and the tree oak *(Quercus robur)* are considered the most potent and are often the first to be employed.

The complex is used in fundamentally the same way for both males and females. Having decided which complex to employ, the method of application will be determined by circumstances under which the complex is used.

The first decision the practitioner must make once the appropriate complex has been chosen is whether there is a need for the complex to be used in a ritual involving the individual or whether it may be used by the individual and his or her partner within the privacy of his or her own home.

This again is a matter for the practitioner's judgment. If the case is extreme, it is often best to employ the power of a ritual Gathering to reinforce the work of the complex even further. If the case is one that needs long-term treatment, it is best for this to be done at home. This decision will also be influenced by the practitioner's knowledge of the individual's personality. There is little to be gained by bringing a shy, introverted person into a ritual environment and focusing the attention of the entire Gathering on him. It is much better to adopt a slow, progressive response to his problem. There are exceptions to this rule of course, and where it becomes necessary to invoke powerful energies to address the problem, this is best done within a ritual Gathering, and it may be necessary to expose the individual to this group work despite his shyness.

If the complex is to be employed during a ritual, it must be crafted during the ritual in which it is to be used and then may be employed in any, or all, of the following ways:

- Include the complex in a libation, given to the individual and shared by the rest of the Gathering.

- Include the complex in an unguent and, with the individual lying on the convocation stone, massage the unguent into the solar plexus, inner thighs, soles of the feet, and inner arms. In the case of a male, the unguent should also be massaged into the scrotum, anus, and penis. For a female, the unguent is massaged into the anus and vagina, particularly the area around the clitoris. As we will see later, if this activity is to be a part of a wider sex magic ritual, the unguent may also be used as a lubricant during masturbation or penetration.
- Include the complex in an evaporation, which is then poured into the center of the priest or priestess's hand and gently applied to the same areas as described for the unguent. This may be particularly effective for arousal and just prior to masturbation or penetration.

If the complex is to be used during a longer course of treatment at home, it must be crafted by the priest or priestess during a ritual working and given to the individual with precise instructions to use it in any, or all, of the following ways:

- As a concentrated libation—1 part complex to 4 parts wine, beer, cider, or springwater. This to be taken four times a day.
- As an unguent, to be used in the same way as above, only this time applied by the individual's partner, at least once a day or prior to sexual activity.
- As an evaporation, again applied as explained above, only by the individual's partner, at least once a day or prior to sexual activity.

All of these treatments may continue for up to two weeks, or less if the benefits become apparent sooner. Very often these home programs are part of a wider course of treatment that may include sexual stimulation exercises, relationship development, and some level of awareness raising.

The Role of the Complex in Sex Magic Rituals

The enactment of Celtic sex magic in the Welsh Druidic tradition is wholly dependent on the power of the energy generated through the sexual orgasms of the people involved in projecting the spell or intention.

The greater part of the ritual is spent in amplifying the potential of this climactic burst of primeval energy, which acts as a vehicle for the projection and binding of the spell being invoked. Any safe means of enhancing the potential of this energy must be considered a benefit. The use of complexes is one of the best of these means.

Sex magic channels the projected energy of the orgasm, one of the strongest concentrations of energy that a human being is able to produce, and focuses it such that it may be used to benefit both individuals and society as a whole.

The exploration of the Celtic tradition of sex magic is far beyond the scope of this book, but the reader may find a detailed explanation of the theories and practices involved in my previous book, *Celtic Sex Magic*. We shall take a detailed look at one particular sex magic ritual later in this book, and it is with this in mind that we need to gain some understanding of the role of the complex before we embark on the ritual itself.

As we have seen during their crafting, the energies and attributes of any particular plant may be refined, empowered, and held in perfect natural balance within the plant's complex. It is the complex's intense power, maintained in this harmonious balance, that we seek in order to magnify the already awesome power of the sexual climax.

225
The Role of the Complex in Sex Magic Rituals

When facilitated for more than one participant, the sex magic ritual focuses the attention of the Gathering on one particular individual, the *Principal Conduit.* It is the power of this person's orgasm that propels the Gathering's communal spell or intention to its recipient and then binds it to him or her. This is done through a visualized journey undertaken by the Principal Conduit, when he or she accompanies the vision of the projected energy carrying the spell from its point of projection within their bodies to its destination within the recipient.

The role of the other participants at the Gathering is to support and fuel this projected energy and its journey to its recipient by entwining their combined energies with that of the Principal Conduit's. It is by a similar entwinement of the energies and attributes of the complex with that of the Principal Conduit's that the complex is able to amplify and reinforce the power and journey of the spell or intention.

This is achieved in two ways: first, by introducing the complex to all the participants in the Gathering so their energies may be enhanced; and second, by introducing the complex to the Principal Conduit through various methods, in order that he or she may benefit from its inherent potency. There follows an explanation of the ways in which a complex may be used during a typical sex magic ritual.

The complex may be used in the Gathering's libations. This ensures that everyone present (including the Principal Conduit) shares the energies and attributes preserved within the complex. There are usually three libations taken during the ritual, and each libation may if necessary carry a different complex.

The complex may be taken by the Principal Conduit as a tincture during the ritual. This has sometimes been partly misinterpreted as "the taking of magic potions" by those outside the tradition, for the tincture is often a small amount of carrier (wine or moon-cleansed water) with equal amounts of complex, the total amount of liquid being no more than 50 ml. Although some may call this a magic potion, it serves a very different function, as we have already seen.

When the complex is applied as an unguent, it acts as a stimulant and as a lubricant during sexual activity. It may be used during the pre-orgasm period of the ritual to help in arousal, during the orgasm itself as a means of lubrication and empowerment, and after to maintain the *continuance* or continued state of arousal following the orgasm when the visualized journey of the projected energy takes place.

The same complex (or a different one) may also be included in an evaporation and, like the unguent, it may be used during the three phases mentioned above. The immediate effects of the evaporation, however, do not last as long as those of the unguent, so the application of the evaporation must be timed more precisely.

You will see from this brief insight that using one or more complexes within one or more carrier agents may complicate the ritual considerably, and careful planning is important in order to maximize the effects of their use. It is also necessary to plan the ritual in a way that allows for the crafting of some of the complexes and all of the carrier/complex mixtures during the course of the Gathering.

A ritual Gathering that incorporates one or more of these sex magic activities can last a number of hours, and may end up with your working stone looking more like a science bench than the focal point of ritual activity. The more complicated the ritual, the more likely you are to make mistakes, so plan your rituals to be as simple and concise as possible, particularly when you are new to the work. Stick to one main activity per Gathering, and you and the other participants will gain experience and knowledge as you develop as a working group.

Personal Preparation

The first step in every Druidic activity is personal preparation: preparing your body, internal energy, and mind for the task ahead. This is a three-stage task. The first step, cleansing the body, is usually carried out at home prior to the working or ritual. The second step, cleansing the internal energy, can be carried out either at home or at the place of the working or ritual, depending on the extent of cleansing the individual feels is required. The third step, preparing the mind, must be carried out in the moments just before the working or ritual begins, therefore it is inevitably undertaken at the site of the working or ritual.

Cleansing the Body

As a matter of hygiene, your body must be physically clean before a working or ritual, as you will most likely be coming into direct bodily contact with others. How you clean your body is determined by:

- the level of internal energy you feel in your body,
- whether you are cleansing yourself or another person is undertaking the task, and
- the amount of time you can dedicate to the task.

If you feel your internal energy is at low ebb or if you feel listless, take this opportunity to regenerate some of that energy. One quick and effective rejuvenative cleansing technique is the cool shower. Most people will find this invigorating and stimulating.

A less shocking method is to take an herbal bath. There is a range of herbal bath products available commercially. Alternatively, you can place a few drops of an appropriate essential oil in your bath water or, as I prefer, allow a few sprigs of fresh herbs to infuse the bath water. This is a centuries-old, worldwide practice, only recently made popular in the West by the development of aromatherapy.

Herbs to choose from for an energizing herbal bath are:

Cinnamon

Marigold

Peppermint

Myrrh

Primrose

Thyme

If, on the other hand, you feel your internal energy is overactive and you are overly stressed, you will need to relax in a stress-relieving herbal bath. The best herbs for this purpose are:

Bay

Clove

Lavender

Juniper

Rosemary

If you are using fresh herbs, tie them together into a bundle, bruise them a little to encourage the release of their natural oils, and place them in the warm bath water at least ten minutes before you bathe to give them the opportunity to release their fragrance and attributes.

Use a gentle, natural soap for your cleansing, and once you have cleansed your entire body, lie back and enjoy the aromatic water. You will feel the stress flow from your body and your energy increase as it absorbs the attributes of the herbs.

It's also a good idea to burn a little incense in the room as you bathe. Try cinnamon for energizing or cedarwood for relaxation. Turn off the lights, light a few candles, and play some ambient music to create an even more relaxing environment.

Whichever atmosphere you decide to create, you will emerge from your bath with a clean and fragrant body, a new sense of purpose, and a stabilized internal energy.

Some fundamentalist Druids will cleanse only in rainwater, ideally only as it falls from the sky. This a wonderful experience but can be hard to arrange. Few things lend such a sense of communion with nature and the collective energy as standing naked in the rain and cleansing yourself with natural soap and bunches of fragrant herbs.

Having someone cleanse your body for you can be a most exhilarating experience too. Mutual cleansing is yet another option.

Try to dedicate as much time as is feasible to your bodily cleansing session. It can be a time of great creativity, and I often experience it as a time when I find solutions to many of the problems that confront me. The modern world does not present us with too many opportunities to lie back and contemplate our circumstances, so don't allow the opportunities to slip through your fingers on the few occasions that they occur.

When proceeding immediately from the cleansing to the working or ritual, some people choose to dress in a simple form of ceremonial garb. The choice is yours, but bear in mind that if you are traveling across town to the site of your ritual, it may be embarrassing if you are stopped for a traffic violation or have to leave your car for some other reason when you are dressed in some form of extravagant regalia. Actually, it would be even more embarrassing if you were stopped in the traditional Druidic ritual garb of absolutely no clothes at all! As a compromise, I suggest wearing loose-fitting, sensible clothing until you are at the site and ready to begin your ritual.

Purifying Internal Energy

You have already attended to some of the needs of your internal energy as you bathed and cleansed your body. The efforts you have made so far have served to stabilize your internal energy in preparation for the more concentrated cleansing you are about to undertake. At this stage your internal energy is neutral—not torpid, overenergized, or erratic.

Purifying your internal energy frees it from any extraneous or intrusive influences. This may be achieved through the same tranquil meditation process described in part 1. The effect of your meditative purification may be enhanced by the use of sympathetic essential oils, incense, and herbs. These may be burned or evaporated, allowing their attributes to permeate your consciousness. I recommend the following:

Bay
Bladderwrack
Borage
Cinnamon
Camphor
Cloves
Dandelion
Lavender
Mace
Marigold
Rose
Sage
Thyme

All of these will benefit your psychic powers and focus your concentration on the purification.

If the purification is taking place immediately prior to the sex magic ritual, make sure your selection contains cinnamon or lavender, as they contain particularly potent sex magic attributes.

To begin the purification, seat yourself comfortably in your usual meditation environment. You may now choose either to make the visualized journey to one of the special places you have reserved within the collective energy especially for meditation or to begin your purification exactly where you are.

The first step is to focus on your awareness of your own internal energy. Again, this takes practice. Being able to turn your consciousness inward and explore what is happening within your "self" is a difficult concept. I was taught a visualization technique to help me understand this exceptionally valuable ability.

Once you are settled and tranquil, visualize your "mind" or "self" as a glade of trees, a forest clearing with many paths and tracks radiating from it. For a moment, travel outside your body and see yourself sitting in that clearing. Make yourself familiar with the trees that enclose it and the paths that radiate from it. Look for a particularly wide path that distinguishes itself from the others by its width and the high trees that border it. Stand before this path and look down along it. It appears to be endless, stretching off into infinity. Remember where this path is within the clearing; you will soon be using it.

Behind these trees and down along these paths are all the prospective disruptive and intrusive energies that are likely to inhibit your internal energy's effective workings. Return to your body and sit quietly, waiting for the first of them to appear.

As your consciousness presents each of these energies to you, confront it, deal with it in the best way possible, and send it down the wide path to infinity.

Once a particular disruptive energy has been dispatched, it may never trouble you again, but it also may return time and time again to confront you. Whichever is the case, it has, for the time being, been dispatched from your consciousness at least for the next few hours while you participate in your ritual.

As each successive disruptive energy is removed from your internal energy, you will begin to feel lighter and less troubled, and a sense of well-being will begin to settle over your consciousness. Eventually the procession of disruptive energies will slow down and finally stop. When it seems that there are no more to deal with, make a visualized journey to each of the paths and tracks, call down them, and search them for any remaining disruptive energies, no matter how small.

Once you are confident that all have been dealt with, visualize yourself sealing the entrance to the wide path with a dagger or triple-knotted rope in the same manner that you seal your cast Circle. This prevents the disruptive energies from reentering your consciousness or interfering with your internal energy.

As you return to worldly awareness from your meditative state, you will be bathed in a confident glow of well-being.

By definition, a disruptive energy is any form of energy that interferes with or disrupts your personal internal energy. If it is an external energy, such as a magnetic force, a ley line, a noise, a light, or something else in your environment, it can be dealt with in the physical world.

If you are being disturbed by a magnetic force or disrupted by any other external energy, find it, eliminate it, or move location.

On the other hand, disruptive energies may also be internal. These internal disruptive forces include stress, worry, preoccupations, memories, plans, and so on; they are any part of your conscious awareness that interferes with or intrudes upon your internal energy and disrupts its ability to focus. It is these worries, memories, and preoccupations that are dealt with in the course of your purification.

If your purification is carried out well before your ritual or working, be prepared to have to maintain your purified state until your ritual begins. It may be very difficult to remove yourself from any internal or external influences that negate your purification if in the meantime you have to function in the everyday world for any length of time. My advice is not to begin the purification until you are preparing for your ritual. I find that the best time for purification is immediately after the cleansing and just before I leave for the site of the ritual.

Mental Preparation and Awareness

This is the final stage of preparation prior to the ritual or working itself, and it must be carried out in the moments just before you cast the Circle.

When your body has been cleansed, your internal energy has been purified, and your ritual space has been laid out in preparation for your working, then is the time to begin your mental preparation. You find yourself standing before the ritual space, possibly clad in your ceremonial garb, with your Gathering milling around you. You now need to prepare yourself mentally for the task ahead and raise your awareness of what is going on around and within you to a higher level. You should have your stave with you.

To begin your mental preparation, place your feet together and the base of your stave on the ground between them, with its tip pointing skyward. Holding the shaft of your stave with both hands at shoulder height, push the stave away from your body until your arms are fully extended, so that your body and the stave form an inverted pyramid. The point of the pyramid is formed by the conjunction of your two feet and the base of the stave; the triangular base of the pyramid is described by the lines formed between your first shoulder and the stave, between the stave and your second shoulder, and between your two shoulders.

The focus of power in all pyramids is the central point of the base. The converging sides serve to focus and concentrate this energy before it is projected from the point or tip. The purpose of your inverted triangular pyramid is to focus your internal energy downward, toward the earth from where the matter of which you are formed originates.

Now you want to position the core of your mental preparation and awareness (your mind) at the center point of power within the pyramid (the center of the triangular base). To do this, simply drop your head forward and look at the convergent point at your feet. You will find that your head is in exactly the place you want.

This stance is used frequently in a range of ritual acts because it focuses, concentrates, and projects your energies and thoughts toward the earth, one of the principal recipients of spells and intentions.

In this position you will instantly feel the power of your internal energy. Systematically banish all unwanted and unnecessary thoughts from your consciousness and replace them with positive thoughts related to the ritual you are about to facilitate. Briefly go through the planned successions of the ritual, placing them in order and organizing your intended actions accordingly.

Once you have mentally mapped out your plan for the ritual, focus your concentration on raising your mental and physical awareness. I use five simultaneous actions to do this. If you plan to emulate my method, you will have to remember to place a few leaves of peppermint or spearmint in your mouth before you take up the inverted pyramid stance. Keep them at the side of your mouth, and do not chew them until the appropriate moment.

You will introduce each action in turn, maintaining the previous ones as you go so that as you arrive at the fifth, all five actions will be working concurrently.

Focus first on the sense of feeling in your hands. Rub your hands slightly against the shaft of the stave that you are holding. Concentrate on feeling the sensory stimulation of touch. Now squeeze the stave shaft in a pulsating fashion, feeling the pressure on your hands. Continue this rubbing and pulsing as you proceed.

Now focus on your sense of sight. Examine the ground upon which you are standing. Do not turn your head, but look intensively at the small area surrounding your feet. Try and take in as much detail as you can. Look at every speck of dust, every grain of dirt; try to absorb the infinite details of the area you are scrutinizing. Add this to the previous action and maintain them both.

Next focus on the sense of taste. Begin rhythmically chewing the mint leaves you have in your mouth. Focus on the release of the flavors from the leaves. Experience the taste in all areas of your mouth—the whole surface of your tongue, underneath your tongue, at the roof of your mouth, at the back of your mouth. Let the experience fill your mouth as you chew. Add this sensory experience to your vision and touch actions and keep all three going at the same time.

By now you should begin to feel a sense of heightened awareness throughout your whole body and mind, a feeling of increased energy and amplified sensory activity.

Next focus on the sense of smell. As you chew the mint leaves they release both flavor and fragrance. Focus now on their fragrance. You will be able to smell their perfume as you breathe out through your mouth and in through your nose. You will also sense their fragrance migrating through the areas that connect your mouth with your nasal passages. Feel the aroma acting on all of your nasal sensors, filling your head with their perfume. You are now stimulating four of your senses simultaneously.

Finally, focus on your sense of hearing. As you chew your mint leaves, begin to hum or chant softly and quietly. Listen to the sound of your voice, hearing it resonate through your body as well as the air.

Now try and make yourself aware of all five senses at once. You know that each is being stimulated by a source under your control, so if you are "missing" one from the group, amplify its source a little: squeeze harder, chew faster, or hum louder. Think of each sense as a channel on your stereo that can be amplified or reduced to bring the overall experience into balance.

Once you have balanced your sensory perception, experience it for a few moments, feeling the excitement and letting it build to a crescendo before returning to the conscious world again. Your senses will now be raised and tuned and your awareness heightened; you will have an acute sensory awareness of the world around you. In this uniquely lucid state you are now fully prepared for the ritual or working you are about to undertake.

Moon-Cleansed Water: The Working

Moon-cleansed water forms the core of many workings and is involved in one way or another with nearly every activity the Druidic priest or priestess undertakes. It is not difficult to make, although its creation may disrupt your sleeping pattern a little.

For this working you will need:

- **A supply of fresh springwater.** Draw it yourself from a freshwater spring or purchase natural springwater (still, not sparkling) at a store.
- **A clear glass bottle or container,** used to hold the springwater during the moon cleansing. Should be cleansed, purified, and sterilized before the working.
- **Blue glass bottles or containers.** Have enough to hold the amount of springwater you are cleansing. Should be cleansed, purified, and sterilized before the working.

Begin with good-quality bottled springwater. If you have a source of fresh springwater close to you, consider using it, particularly if it is drawn from a place that you have an affinity for. Remember, though, that you and the other participants in your rituals will sometimes consume this water. So unless you are absolutely sure that your source is pure, unpolluted, and safe to drink, stick to the bottled springwater.

You will need to plan your cleansing working to coincide with a "fat" moon. A fat moon is apparent a few days before, during, and after the full moon, when the visible

moon is at its largest and emits the maximum amount of moonlight. This is generally a very good time to facilitate your sex magic rituals, particularly those held outdoors and those involving predominantly female participants. Every Druidic priestess is most active in her workings and rituals during the fat moon phase. It is also an excellent time for group sex magic rituals with a female Principal Conduit. If a priestess also facilitates the ritual, the generated energy can be extremely potent indeed.

The moon-cleansing working begins at dusk, or, more accurately, as soon as the moonlight is visible. The cleansing process is very simple. If you have drawn your water from a local source, just seal it in a sterilized, clear glass bottle and place it outside in a location where it is exposed to the maximum amount of moonlight. I place mine on top of two standing stones that I have in my garden. In the morning, before the sun rises, decant the cleansed water into a sterilized blue glass bottle and seal it.

If you are using store-bought springwater, simply remove the label from the bottle by soaking it in water for a few minutes and then peeling. This gives the moonlight access to more of the water in the bottle. Then place the bottle outside as explained above. There is no need to break the seal on the bottle until you decant it just before dawn. Store the moon-cleansed water in its blue glass bottle or container until you are ready to use it. It becomes part of your cache and will be cleansed and purified regularly along with your other tools.

Casting the Circle

Every Druidic ritual is conducted within a protective Circle, and the drawing or casting of this Circle is one of the most significant responsibilities of the Druidic priest or priestess. The purpose of the Circle is to protect those participants within it from any potentially intrusive or harmful energies on the outside, to focus the energies of the participants on the ritual, and to contain the Gathering's generated energy until the time of projection, preventing it from dispersing. It also denotes the boundaries of the ritual activities; those within are included, and those outside are not.

There are a number of ways to cast a Circle. We shall concentrate on just one of these, the triple-cast Circle, as it best suits the sex magic ritual. It is also the strongest form of the cast Circles and offers the greatest protection to those inside it.

As the name suggests, the triple-cast Circle is cast three times, each time using the attributes of one of the basic elements, air, water, and fire. The fourth basic element is the earth upon which the Circle is cast, so once the Circle is complete, its occupants have the attributes of all four basic elements for their protection.

The word *circle* is slightly misleading. Druidic lore, being fundamentally based in nature, is not very keen on symmetry. The Circle is never really a perfect one. More often it is a line connecting the bases of a ring of trees or a crudely drawn approximation of a circle. It would never be drawn in a perfect geometric fashion as achieved when using a central peg and a length of string to describe the circumference.

The principles governing the casting of a Circle are as follows:

- It is always cast from the inside.
- Although never a precise circle, it must not have any sharp curves or corners.

- The Circle must always present a visible boundary for the participants of the Gathering to respect.
- The Circle will always have a center point marker and a marker indicating the cardinal points of the compass.
- The working stone will always be located at the northern cardinal point of the Circle and lie in the west/east orientation.
- The convocation stone will always be in a south/north orientation, with the center point of the Circle falling on the surface of the convocation stone just where the head of the Principal Conduit will lie.
- The Circle will always have an entrance portal in its circumference, with candles or small fires at each side of the portal. The portal will always be in the southern side of the circumference so that as the participants enter they are facing north, toward the working stone.
- The Circle will be of a size to accommodate the number of the Gathering.
- Other than these basic factors the Circle may take whatever form the person casting it wishes.

A typical cast Circle with its relative working spaces is shown below.

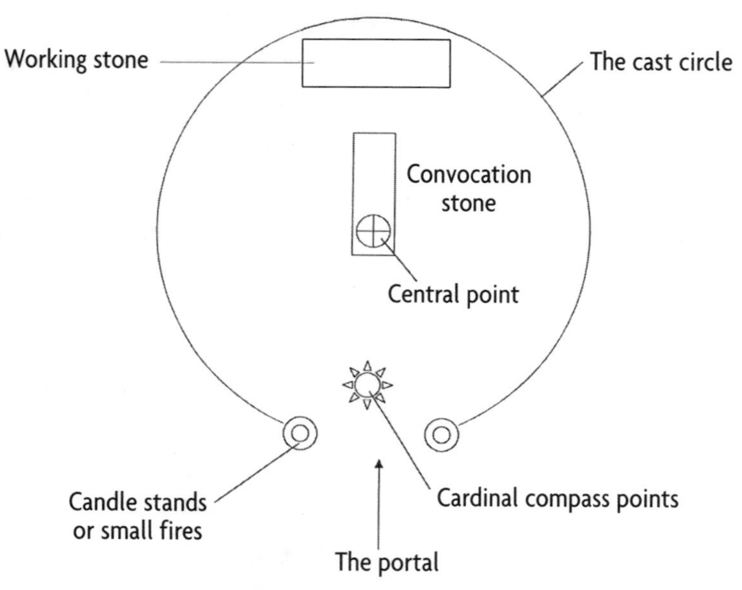

A schematic illustration of the layout of the Circle.

The Triple-Cast Circle: The Ritual

In order to choose the site for your ritual you will need to define first the purpose of the ritual, then exactly how the ritual is to be facilitated.

Some of the factors that affect the choice of site will be:

- The number of participants at the Gathering
- The site's accessibility
- Whether the site needs to be indoors or outside
- The weather
- Whether the ritual will be held at night or during the day
- What ritual tools and accessories will be required and how they will be transported and placed within the site

There are other factors to take into account, of course. The response of your internal energy to the location you are contemplating is immensely important. The influences of local ley lines and other external influences will also have to be considered.

Many ancient pre-Christian gathering sites have particularly potent intrinsic energies that have been amplified by the resonance of the rituals conducted on them for millennia. If you are not able to use one of these energized locations, the next best choice should be a neutral location, a site that is free from negative influences. This is often the case if you are intending to facilitate an indoor ritual. There will be very few positively energized indoor sites. Most represent a neutral environment, unless you are unfortunate enough to select an indoor location that has at some time been contaminated by previous workings of a negative influence.

It will be necessary for you to cleanse and purify the site as explained earlier to safeguard against any lingering unwanted influences. Cleansing a ritual site is the physical cleaning of the site prior to use—sweeping, dusting, washing, whatever is required to make the site usable. Once your site is selected and you have gathered together the tools and accessories for your working, you may begin to arrange your ritual site.

The first step in casting any Circle is to identify the orientation of your ritual site. This is normally done by using an ordinary compass. There are, however, some people who have the gift of being able to dowse the cardinal points; others choose to use the traditional Druid's stone or a magnetized needle.

Whatever method you choose, once you have oriented your site, mark the cardinal points on the ground. This can be done with a simple cross somewhere near the proposed entry portal of the Circle showing the four cardinal points of the compass. Then walk to the "notional" center of the Circle and mark the center point with a similar cross, again oriented to the cardinal points.

Depending on your chosen location, you may now need to erect your portable working stone and convocation stone, if that is what you are using, and set out your ritual tools and candles before casting the Circle. Remember that the head of the person lying on the convocation stone must be located at the center point of the Circle. The person will be lying in the north/south orientation, feet pointing toward the working stone and head at the center. Once the stones are erected and your ritual tools are in place, you may begin the working for casting a triple-cast Circle.

For this working you will need:

- **Your stave,** to cast the first Circle.
- **Your salt canister,** should contain enough salt to cast the second Circle.
- **A flask of moon-cleansed water,** to anoint the Circle.
- **Two floor-standing candleholders plus two natural wax candles,** or enough material to set two small fires. These will be set on each side of the entry portal of the Circle and will be used to cast the third Circle.

To begin the working, stand at the southern extremity of the proposed Circle, at the center point of the proposed entry portal, facing the north and the center mark of your intended Circle. Place a candleholder at your left and right sides, arms' width apart. This marks the entry portal.

Like most other rituals and workings, the Circle-casting working begins with the Druidic priest or priestess focusing their sensory awareness using the power position of the inverted triangular pyramid. Standing between the entry portal candles, assume the inverted pyramid stance and focus your awareness as explained earlier. Once you are confident that you have achieved your desired level of sensory awareness, lift your stave in both hands as high into the air as possible and say:

"I begin the casting and call upon the energy of the elements to protect all those within."

Place the base of your stave at the base of the candleholder on your left. Step inward into the inside of the circumference and begin to draw or cast the Circle on the ground, encompassing the area you plan to use in your ritual. You will end at the base of the second candleholder, thereby completing an unbroken circle from one candleholder to the other, leaving only the space between them as the portal.

Set aside your stave by leaning it against your working stone. (As a point of etiquette you should never lay your stave flat on the ground.) Pick up your salt canister from the working stone, open it, and, holding it high in the air with both hands, say:

"I continue the casting and call upon the energy of the elements to protect all those within."

Beginning at the same point at the base of the candleholder on your left, walk around the inner circumference of your Circle sprinkling salt on the ground at the Circle's perimeter until you again reach the second candleholder, thereby casting an unbroken salt Circle from one candleholder to the other.

Replace the salt canister upon the working stone and pick up your matches or flint or whatever you intend to ignite your candle with. Walk to the first candleholder and light its candle. Remove the second candle (from the candleholder on the right) from its holder and light it from the flame of the first candle. Holding the second candle high in the air with both hands, say:

"I complete the casting and call upon the energy of the elements to protect all those within."

Place the wick of the second candleholder back into the flame of the first candleholder, and from that point walk the perimeter of the cast Circle with the flame of the second candle directly over the previously cast circumference. When you arrive at the second candleholder, place the lit candle in it, thereby having cast an unbroken flame Circle from the first candleholder to the second. As you place the candle into the candleholder, say:

"The casting is complete, the Circle is closed. Once sealed, let none defile its protection."

This then completes the Circle casting. The Circle should now be entered and exited only through the portal left between the two candleholders.

Sealing the Circle: The Ritual

The triple-cast Circle is the most powerful protective Circle you can cast. There is little point in casting such a powerful protective Circle, however, if you leave its portal vulnerable. You must then triple-seal your Circle to maintain its integrity.

The Circle is sealed only once all the participants are inside its boundaries and the ritual or working is about to proceed.

Circles may be sealed with a dagger or, less often, with a triple-knotted rope. The triple-knotted rope is usually used only if the dagger is required for some other purpose during the ritual. In the case of the triple-cast Circle, some people feel that the affinity of the triple casting and the triple knot gives the Circle a stronger protective quality. I understand this argument but feel that as the dagger sealing is a triple-action sealing, with the dagger being opened and closed three times, it has just as strong an affinity as the triple-knotted rope.

The triple-cast Circle is sealed as follows. You will need:

- **Your dagger,** used to seal the Circle.
- **A cauldron containing moon-cleansed water,** to anoint your dagger.
- **Your salt canister,** should contain enough salt to seal the portal.
- **A natural wax candle.** Its flame will seal the portal.

Having cast the triple-cast Circle, pick up the dagger.

Stand before your working stone. Holding the dagger above your head with the handle in the right hand and its scabbard in your left (reverse these instructions if you are left-handed), draw the dagger from its scabbard. Dip the tip of the dagger into the cauldron of moon-cleansed water, at the same time saying:

"And so it begins."

Standing before the working stone (thereby facing north), place the dagger approximately halfway into its scabbard. Hold the partly sheathed dagger high in the air and say:

"I am part of the collective energy, I hold its power within me, as does every other creation. I use my being to empower this dagger and awaken the potential energy within it."

Slam the dagger fully into its scabbard with enough force to let the participants in the Gathering know that you have done it.

Turn ninety degrees to the right (so that you are now facing the east). Holding the dagger high in the air as before, half-draw the dagger from its scabbard and say:

"With this dagger I begin the seal, and I call upon all unsympathetic energies to leave this Circle."

Slam the dagger closed again.

Turn one hundred and eighty degrees (so that you are now facing west). Holding the dagger high in the air as before, half-draw the dagger from its scabbard and say:

"With this dagger I strengthen the seal and ask a second time for all unsympathetic energies to leave this Circle."

Slam the dagger closed again.

Turn ninety degrees to your left (so that you are now facing south). Holding the dagger high in the air as before, half-draw the dagger from its scabbard and say:

"With this dagger I make the seal and ask a third time for all unsympathetic energies to leave this Circle."

Slam the dagger closed again.

Facing the south (as you now stand), you are also facing the entrance portal to the Circle. Walk to the entrance portal and place the fully sheathed dagger on the floor between the entry pillars. As you do this say:

"With this dagger I seal this Circle. I invoke its protection. I focus my energy within it. Let all those without stay without."

This ends the first sealing.

Pick up your salt canister, walk back to the portal, and sprinkle a line of salt from the base of the left candleholder to the base of the right candleholder as you say:

"With this salt I double-seal this Circle. I invoke its protection. I focus my energy within it. Let all those without stay without."

This ends the second sealing.

Replace the salt canister on the working stone and pick up the natural wax candle. Walk back to the portal and light the candle from the flame of the left-hand portal candle. Move the hand-held candle slowly from the left-hand side of the portal to the right. As you do this say:

"With this flame I triple-seal this Circle. I invoke its protection. I focus my energy within it. Let all those without stay without."

Blow out the candle and place it next to the dagger on the ground between the portal candles.

This ends the third and final sealing.

Your Circle is now sealed. You will feel its protective power around you and experience the focus and concentration it affords you.

If you choose to use the triple-knotted rope seal, you will need a length of rope about two meters long. Mark the center point of the rope and place it on the working stone before you begin the ritual.

The Circle is sealed as follows.

Having cast the circle, pick up the rope.

Holding the rope stretched between your outstretched hands, dip one of the hanging ends into the cauldron of purifying water. At the same time speak the opening statement:

"And so it begins."

Standing before the working stone (thereby facing north), hold the stretched rope high in the air and say:

"I am part of the collective energy, I hold its power within me, as does every other creation. I use my being to empower this rope and awaken the potential energy within it."

Turn ninety degrees to the right (so that you are now facing east). Lower the rope and tie the first knot about 8 inches to the right of the center point as you say:

"With this first knot I begin the seal, and I call upon all unsympathetic energies to leave this Circle."

When you have tied the first knot, turn one hundred and eighty degrees (so that you are now facing west). Tie the second knot at the center mark on the rope. As you do this, say:

"With this second knot I strengthen the seal and ask a second time for all unsympathetic energies to leave this Circle."

Having tied the second knot, turn ninety degrees to your left (so that you are now facing south). Tie the third knot about 8 inches to the left of the center point of the rope as you say:

"With this third knot I make the seal and ask a third time for all unsympathetic energies to leave this Circle."

By facing south, you are also facing the entrance portal to the Circle. Walk to the entrance portal and place the extended rope on the floor between the entry pillars. As you do this, say:

"I seal this Circle. I invoke its protection. I focus my energy within it. Let all those without stay without."

Sealing the Circle is an imperative part of every ritual or working. It should be done with the utmost care and consideration. It is the final act leading up to the ritual and also the last solitary act by the priest or priestess prior to the group activity of the ritual. If it is done correctly and with power, it imbues a sense of security and intensifies the focus of the Gathering. If it is done lethargically, it will not have the same effect.

Unsealing and Erasing the Circle: The Ritual

At the end of each ritual or working the protective Circle is unsealed, and once all the participants of the Gathering have left the Circle it is erased. Never leave a cast Circle standing until the next ritual; this simply does not work. Even if you are using a permanent site such as a standing stone Circle, as I often do, it is essential that the protective Circle be cast and erased for every individual ritual or working.

Make it your habit to unseal the protective Circle as soon as the ritual is over.

Do not stand around talking to the other participants, and do not allow them to stand around talking to each other inside the sealed Circle. Make the unsealing of the Circle a part of the ritual; until the Circle is unsealed, the ritual is not over. Educate your Gathering to stay focused and involved until the final words, "It is ended," are spoken.

To unseal a triple-sealed Circle, first pick up the hand-held candle from its place on the ground between the portal candles. Relight the candle from the flame of the right-hand candle, then move the flame of the hand-held candle slowly across the portal to the flame of the left-hand candle. Hold the lit candle high in the air and say:

"I remove the flame seal."

Blow out the hand-held candle and return it to the working stone.

Return to the portal. With your right hand disperse the salt line on the ground between the portal candles, saying:

"I remove the salt seal."

Next pick up the dagger from the ground. Holding it high in the air, remove the dagger from its scabbard and say:

"The seal is broken, the Circle is open."

Walk to the cauldron on the working stone; dip the tip of the dagger into the moon-cleansed water within it, saying:

"And so it ends."

Replace the dagger in its scabbard and place it on the working stone.

Turn to face the Gathering. Lift your hands high in the air for all to see and say in a loud voice:

"It is ended!"

This ends the ritual and indicates to the Gathering that they may now disperse, leaving the Circle to collect their clothing and dress.

The Sex Magic Ritual: The Pair

Probably the sex magic ritual practiced most often, the paired ritual both is an opportunity to develop your awareness and skills and, when conducted correctly, is capable of generating enormous energy.

It is usually the case that practiced pairs are the most effective, committed, and valuable participants in a Gathering. They form the basis of most regular groups, and if you were to conduct a detailed census I am sure that the bulk of existing binding vessels contain earth compounds donated by practiced pairs.

Having practiced pairs in a Gathering is ideal for all concerned. It alleviates the task of the priest or priestess to institute gender balance, it ensures a high level of participation at Gatherings, and, as these pairs often become regular participants, it allows the priest or priestess to develop the Gathering as a group with common goals and well-understood practices.

If, in addition to their enthusiasm for being involved with each other, the paired individuals also share an enthusiasm for becoming involved with other individuals and pairs, then all the better.

You will find that as the Gathering divides into groups during the sex magic ritual, the practiced pairs will be the basis for the formation of larger active groups within the gathering. However, there must always be the opportunity for these pairs to participate between themselves, without including any additional group members.

The Ritual Incorporating the Complex of the Flower

Putting these group advantages to one side, we must look at the sex magic ritual as conducted between two individuals. We shall look at how a paired couple may facilitate a ritual in order to rebalance the diminished sexual appetite of the male partner by using a libation, unguent, and evaporation of the complex of the flower of the bird's-foot trefoil *(lotus corniculatus)*.

The purpose of the ritual is to restore the natural balance of the individual male and to increase his personal sexual appetite and energy. Adjustments must be made as appropriate, as with all the sections of this book, for lesbian and gay couples. If it is the intention to address the ritual at the female of the pair, then simply reverse the roles. If the facilitating partner does not feel confident enough to undertake the ritual, then substitute their role with that of a Druidic priestess, preferably the presiding Druidic priestess from their usual Gathering.

There are basically two formats for paired individuals: one priest or priestess and a participant, or one priest and one priestess. The relationship and commitment of the two individuals involved often determines this. If only one of the individuals is interested and committed enough to develop their knowledge, skills, and attitudes sufficiently to undertake the role of Druidic priest or priestess, but the other is interested enough to be an active participant, then their roles are determined for them. If both have equal commitment and dedication, they may work together as priest and priestess or exchange roles as they see fit.

However, for every ritual there must be a dominant role (that of priest or priestess) and a cooperative role (that of active participant). In the case of the paired ritual there must be a priest or priestess to facilitate the ritual and an active participant, who in this case is a male whose sexual balance has been disrupted.

The priestess will provide the majority of the stimulation, and her orgasm, although secondary to that of the participant, should be synchronized with it. The participant will be stimulated to the peak of his sensory potential, and his orgasm will begin the process of rebalancing the sexual energies.

It is important to remember, however, that both "roles" (and that word is again a poor translation from its Welsh equivalent) are equally important. Neither can function to their full potential without the collaboration of the other.

For this ritual you will need:

- **Your wand(s),** used in all your rituals.
- **Your stave,** to cast your first Circle.
- **Your salt canister,** to cast your second circle, should contain sufficient salt for the purpose.
- **Your hand-held candle,** to cast your third Circle.
- **Your dagger,** to seal the Circle, along with the salt and candle above.
- **Your cauldron,** filled with moon-cleansed water, for the purification activities within the ritual.
- **Two floor-standing candleholders,** to create the portal within your Circle. The flames of these two candles will be at shoulder height.
- **Three working stone candles, in candleholders,** the center focus of your working stone.
- **Your phallus,** for stimulation during the ritual. Use a number of phalluses if you have them, together with the necessary condoms needed to ensure hygiene.
- **The two cardinal essences of the bird's-foot trefoil,** to be combined to create the flower's complex during the ritual.
- **The incense of the bird's-foot trefoil.** The Incense will energize and balance the flower's complex as it is crafted.
- **An incense burner and charcoal or peat as fuel,** to place the flower's incense on.
- **200 ml of moon-cleansed water in a goblet,** to craft the libation.
- **The unguent prepared just prior to the ritual from the flower's same cardinal essences.**
- **The tincture prepared just prior to the ritual from the flower's same cardinal essences.**

(It is sufficient to craft just the libation during the ritual. The unguent and tincture may be prepared just prior to the ritual, as long as they are all crafted from the same cardinal essences and incense.)

- **Cleansing cloths.** As many as you feel are necessary.

The ritual begins with the priestess raising her sensory awareness using the inverted triangular pyramid working. She then casts a triple-cast Circle of a suitable size. All the necessary tools and accessories have already been arranged within the Circle and upon the working stone.

The working stone has already been adorned with the covering cloth and decorated with fresh flowers and herbs with the appropriate attributes, as the season provides. The incense burner has been lit.

As each of the two participants enters the Circle, they extend their arms to each side, level with their shoulders, passing each hand quickly through the flames of the two portal candles, a symbolic final purification of the body. Once both are inside the Circle, the priestess seals the Circle with the triple seal. Both participants are now enclosed within the protective Circle and are ready to begin the sex magic ritual.

The male sits on the ground facing the working stone.

The priestess stands before the working stone and brings the first of the candles, the collective energy candle, to the front of the stone. She lights the candle, raises it into the air, and says:

"As this flame burns, so we converge with the collective energy. Our energies mingle, our potential becomes one."

The "flame of the collective energy" candle is placed at the back, in the center, of the working stone.

The priestess then lights the sun, or male, candle, holds it up, and says:

"As this flame burns it binds us with the sun. We invoke the sun's influence upon our workings."

The "flame of the sun" candle is placed to the left and slightly forward of the "flame of the collective energy" candle.

She then lights the third and final moon or female candle, holds it up, and says:

"As this flame burns I bind myself with the moon. I invoke the moon's influence upon all I do."

The "flame of the moon" candle is placed to the right and slightly in front of the "flame of the collective energy" candle, forming the candle triangle.

You will see that this third invocation is a personal one. If the ritual is facilitated by the male, then the moon candle is lit before the sun candle, and this same personal invocation is given for the sun candle.

With all three candle flames lit, the priestess stands before them at the front and center of the working stone and extends her arms out so that each of her palms is directly above each of the sun and moon flames, close enough to feel the heat of the flames without burning her palms. She then brings both hands together above the central collective energy flame to form a cup shape above the flame, saying:

"I unite all things with the collective energy, as in nature they belong. I offer myself to this union, together with all those present here. Unite us in your common bond."

This opening part of the ritual, called the "uniting of the flames," is now complete.

Picking up her wand in her right hand (or in her left if she is left-handed), the priestess moves to the convocation stone. Extending her wand above the stone, she walks around it three times, saying quietly to herself:

"I invoke only what is good, I intend only what is beneficial, I banish all that is unwelcome."

The priestess then returns to the working stone, picks up the cauldron with the moon-cleansed water, and returns to the convocation stone. Again she walks three times around the stone, but this time she dips the tip of the wand into the water and sprinkles drops of it on the stone as she walks. She again says:

"I invoke only what is good, I intend only what is beneficial, I banish all that is unwelcome."

She returns the cauldron to the working stone and stands with her back to it, facing the center of the Circle. She says, in a loud voice:

"Come forward who wishes to lie here."

The Principal Conduit approaches the priestess and says:

"That is I."

The priestess says:

"And are you named?"

If the Principal Conduit has already been named, then his name is spoken. We shall use the name "David" for the sake of this example.

The Principal Conduit (David) says:

"Yes, my name is David. I wish to lie here."

The priestess says:

"Then as I know your name to be David, take your place as it is offered."

David then takes his place on the convocation stone, with his head at the center point of the Circle and his feet facing the working stone. This means that he is lying in the south/north orientation, so the energies will flow through him from his head to his feet, aiding the projection of generated energy from his body.

The priestess now stands between the two stones, facing the center of the Circle, and says:

"I welcome all those that wish us well. We are gathered with the intention of creating change. Change that offers benefit and goodwill. Our spell is crafted and I offer it to you."

She then speaks the spell for the first time. The Gathering, in this case just her partner, already knows the spell and will have committed it to memory. For the sake of simplicity we shall just call it "the spell."

A typical spell for these circumstances would be as follows.

"We call upon the collective energy and the four elemental energies to assist us in our work. David seeks a balance in his internal order, one that reflects the balance present in nature. Restore to him what was once his, restore the harmony of his being and the natural potency of his internal energy."

The priestess says:

"The spell."

The Principal Conduit repeats the spell three times:

"The spell; the spell; the spell."

The priestess, picking up her wand and cauldron, walks to the convocation stone where the Principal Conduit now lies and says:

"Our Principal Conduit is David. Through him we shall cast and bind our spell."

She sprinkles the Principal Conduit with the moon-cleansed water, using her wand to do so. As she does this, she says:

"I anoint you, David, and commit my efforts to your internal energy."

The cauldron and the wand are placed back on the working stone and the crafting of the complex and the libation begins.

The complex is crafted by uniting the flower's two cardinal essences in the same method as described on page 164. This ritual working must be carried out in its entirety, including the initial purification processes, for the complex to be properly empowered. Pour 100 ml of the empowered complex into a small ritual vessel.

The vessel containing the flower's complex is now placed at the front, center of the working stone and the goblet containing the moon-cleansed water for the libation is placed next to it.

The priestess lifts the goblet in her left hand and the complex in her right, and as she pours the complex into the goblet of moon-cleansed water, she says:

"I craft this libation with the complex of the flower, whose energies and attributes I imbue upon all who take of it."

The priestess turns to face the Principal Conduit and pours a very small amount of the libation onto the ground at her feet. She does this three times, saying:

"I return a part of what has been given in good faith, may it always be so."

She lifts the goblet high into the air with both hands and says:

"We share the gift; we take its complex within us and about us. We begin the work of restoration."

The priestess then drinks a small amount of the libation and passes the goblet to the Principal Conduit who drinks the remainder.

The seven phases or "successions" of the sex magic ritual now begin.

Each succession of the projection cycle represents a distinct form of activity that combines to form the sex magic ritual. The first succession, the Awakening, is the inital period of the ritual when all of the participants focus upon their sexual awareness and begin the process of arousal, a time for gentle exploration of bodies and for the abandonment of everyday cares and worries. The second succession, the Augmentation, is the time when the Gathering begins to increase their sexual stimulation. Their full connection is now on sexual arousal, and the Gathering, if large enough, will have divided into smaller groups. The next succession, the Intensification, involves more intense physical arousal, which results in the repeated approach and withdrawl from the quickening or commitment to the orgasm. Each withdrawal leaves the participant in a more stimulated state than the previous until eventually he or she enters the quickening succession. The Quickening is the period when the participant has committed to that last, irrevocable journey to the orgasm. A brief period of immensely heightened sensual excitement, but not the actual orgasm itself.

The fifth succession is the orgasm, when the Principal Conduit projects the spell that the Gathering has composed. This is the point of projection of maximum energy and it is upon this stream of intense energy that the spell is carried to its recipient. Following the orgasm or projection succession comes the continuance succession, where the Principal Conduit's state of arousal is maintained in order to fuel his or her visualized journey to bind the spell to its recipient. The final stage of the cycle is the relaxation succession, where the Principal Conduit and the other participants of the Gathering relax and return their consciousness to the mundane world.

As the pair progress through the first three successions—the Awakening, Augmentation, and Intensification—a variety of techniques may be employed to arouse and stimulate both the Principal Conduit and the priestess. The purpose of this stimulation is to bring the Principal Conduit to an orgasm so that he may experience the heightened sensory pleasure this ritual provides. This is his first step toward the restoration of his sexual energy and appetite.

What follows is just an example of a typical progression to use as a guide. There is no set format to this part of the ritual; it is up to the priestess to judge the most appropriate and effective methods. Each priestess will develop her own repertoire of techniques and actions together with a sensibility in relation to what is or is not acceptable.

The Awakening usually involves a gentle and sensuous awakening of the sexual senses. It may involve the use of massage, oils, lotions, creams, and the like, applied to the bodies and genitals of both the Principal Conduit and the priestess. These may be applied by hand and exchanged bodily massage. It can also involve gentle oral stimulation of the sensitive areas and genitalia.

This is always a slow buildup of sexual awareness and a gentle introduction to the pleasures to come, and it should result only in a simple arousal. It is the opportunity to get to know your own body and that of your partner in the ritual. The emphasis is on slow, sensual movement and gentle physical contact with fingertips, tongue, nipples, lips, and so on. It can be enhanced by the use of perfumed oils, incense, and sensual music.

As the ritual progresses to the Augmentation succession, the form of stimulation may change. The slow sensuality may become more physical. At this stage both the Principal Conduit and the priestess will be masturbating themselves and each other. Individuals may now part company in order to provide their partner with more visual stimuli. This can range form watching each other masturbate and stimulate themselves to using the phallus on and in themselves to erotic dance and other forms of exhibitionism.

As the couple passes the threshold into the Intensification succession, the stimulation, both visual and physical, becomes more intimate, involving more intense physical arousal and even greater heights of pleasure requiring even greater self-control. The couple becomes much more physical, their passion becoming much more intense. This is the time for close physical interaction. Both individuals may lie on the convocation stone together as they intensify each other's sexual stimulation.

As the male is the Principal Conduit in this case, the priestess may position herself between the male's legs and, bending over the convocation stone, take his penis in her mouth, using her hands to caress his testicles, stomach, and nipples. She may also insert a phallus into the male's anus. Alternatively, the priestess may gently bite the nipples of the male as she masturbates his penis, or she may sit over the male in opposite direction, with her vagina just above the male's face, while she bends over and takes his penis in her mouth. This is a particularly good position for her to stimulate his anus with fingers or a phallus. At the same time the male may stimulate the priestess's vagina with mouth, fingers, and phallus.

Various methods and combinations of penetration, whether vaginal, anal, or oral, are also used at this stage by both priestess and the Principal Conduit.

These ideas are put forward simply to illustrate the level of intensity of the contact between the priestess and the Principal Conduit. Many other positions are possible, and there is a great variety of source materials from which these imaginative positions may be drawn. The point is that both individuals should be doing their utmost to ensure the maximum stimulation of the other.

There will be innumerable approaches to the threshold of the Quickening and the same amount of retreats until, eventually, the priestess decides to commit to the Quickening. Only the priestess may make the decision to take the Gathering to the next succession of the Projection Cycle.

It is worth remembering that we are focusing here only on the physical and sensual elements of the ritual. You must not forget the duality of the approaching orgasm and the need to recall and invoke your spell.

The priestess and the Principal Conduit have now committed to the Quickening. This is the point at which the approaching orgasm in inevitable and very imminent. Hopefully, their impending orgasms have been synchronized by the cycle of repeatedly approaching and retreating from the threshold of the Quickening, so that when they both commit they may do so in a synchronized state.

As both parties commit to the Quickening, the priestess says:

"The Quickening is here!"

As soon as she has said this, both parties begin to chant the spell repeatedly, increasing in speed and volume as the orgasm approaches. It is possible for both parties to synchronize their orgasm by synchronizing their chanting of the spell.

If the pair is coupled when the priestess acknowledges the Quickening, they separate and lie together on the convocation stone to reach orgasm. They may augment each other's stimulation by continued contact but must never reach orgasm while coupled.

The arrival of the orgasm and the projection of the generated energy are marked by the shouting of the spell as the energy is projected. The vocalization of the spell at high volume assists and magnifies the power of the Projection and the potency of the spell.

Once the Projection is complete and the orgasm subsides, it is the role of the priestess to maintain and fuel the generated energy's journey by further stimulation of the Principal Conduit. In the circumstances described here, that is, the priestess and the male Principal Conduit, the favored position for this continued stimulation is as mentioned above, with the priestess standing between the male's legs, stimulating the penis in her mouth and the testes and anus with her fingers. This is done gently and sympathetically so as not to distract the male during his visualized journey.

Once the Principal Conduit has "returned" from his journey, the parties separate.

Following the Relaxation succession, the male returns to his original place, seated on the ground facing the working stone, and the priestess stands in front of the working stone facing the center of the Circle.

The priestess now begins the group congress. Three times she chants the spell and the male repeats it. Then the priestess says:

"The spell is cast. The spell is bound. Let it run its course, and let no one interfere!"

This is the final part of the Projection Cycle and the confirmation of the spell.

If there are no other matters to be attended to within the protective Circle, the working stone candles are extinguished and the Circle is unsealed and erased. The ritual site is dismantled and the gift left for nature as the participants depart the site.

One of the most common observations brought to me by students reading about or experiencing this ritual for the first time is that it appears that both the priestess and the Principal Conduit receive equal amounts of the flower's complex.

This is an accurate observation, but if you have read and fully understood the previous parts of this book the answer to this dilemma may already be apparent to you. As with the Doctrine of Signatures and the measure of the proportions of the plants we use, nature provides and uses what is required to restore a natural balance. Therefore, in the same way that each branch we harvest from the tree provides us with the correct proportion of leaves, bark, and wood that we need for a perfectly balanced complex, so the amount of the complex's energies and attributes absorbed by each individual using it is proportionate to his or her needs. This tells us that even though the priestess and subject may have consumed and used the same amount of libation, unguent, and evaporation, the subject will have assimilated into himself more of the properties of the complex than the priestess. In fact both would have assimilated sufficient for his or her needs, whatever they may be.

You may also have recognized that there are many opportunities for you to personalize the ritual, make it your own unique working and use your own individual phrases. The only governing factors, which deal with the more "spiritual/magical" aspects of the ritual, have been emphasized both here and in the section. Outside these imperatives, you are free to interpret the Ritual in your own special way.

As a result of the use of the bird's-foot trefoil's complex during this ritual the Principal Conduit's sexual energy and appetite will have been reinforced and will continue to increase for some days without further action. The work may be further empowered by the regular use of the unguent as a home treatment regimen over the following few weeks.

The Sex Magic Ritual: The Group

The group ritual is potentially the most difficult form of sex magic to both organize and facilitate.

One of the more difficult tasks of the priest or priestess is ensuring partner balance at rituals. It is essential that there are adequate males present for those participants who prefer to interact with males and adequate females present for those who prefer to interact with females. Bearing in mind that all sex magic workings and rituals are totally participatory, having surplus males or females either creates a small audience for those involved or puts undue pressure on particular males or females who end up with additional unwanted suitors. Neither is an ideal situation.

Planning this balance can be a very challenging activity, and even the best-laid plans can go astray if someone is taken ill or cannot attend the Gathering.

On a few, very rare occasions, a priestess may appoint herself the Principal Conduit and assemble a small (say two- to six-person) all-male Gathering. In this case all the male participants serve the wishes and desires of the priestess as she progresses through the Projection Cycle. A priest may convene a similar assembly with an all-female cast.

A balanced gender mix ensures a high level of participation at the Gatherings and also offers the most rewarding experience possible for each of the participants. It may well be the case that couples or pairs of individuals will choose to exchange partners or combine into larger groups, but these will always be balanced by the underlying mathematics of the equal gender balance.

Just as in the ritual for the pair, the roles the individuals in the Gathering adopt often reflect their everyday sexual predilections. A sexually dominant individual will undoubtedly be attracted to submissive participants, and in the same way, the submissive participants will be attracted to him or her. The result will be small groups of submissive participants focusing their attention on a dominant male or female.

The Ritual Incorporating the Complex of the Flower

The particular ritual we shall be looking at next is one that is to incorporate the use of a Druidic complex to enhance the power of the Principal Conduit's internal energy and empower his projection and binding of the spell involved. For the sake of simplicity we will again use the complex of the bird's-foot trefoil.

For the purpose of this example we will assume that a priestess is facilitating the ritual, the Principal Conduit is male, and the rest of the Gathering are male and female in equal proportion. You can then superimpose your own circumstances upon the workings as appropriate.

For this ritual you will need:

- **Your wand(s),** used in all your rituals.
- **Your stave,** to cast your first Circle.
- **Your salt canister,** to cast your second Circle, should contain sufficient salt for the purpose.
- **Your hand-held candle,** to cast your third Circle.
- **Your dagger,** to seal the Circle, along with the salt and candle above.
- **Your cauldron, filled with moon-cleansed water,** for the purification activities within the ritual.
- **Your chalice and libations goblets,** to hold and distribute your libations.
- **Your libations**—liquid and baked libations for the Gathering.
- **Two floor-standing candleholders,** to create the portal within your Circle. The flames of these two candles will be at shoulder height.

- **Three working stone candles, in candleholders.** The center focus of your working stone.
- **Your phallus,** for stimulation during the ritual. Use a number of phalluses if you have them, together with the necessary condoms needed to ensure hygiene.
- **Your binding vessel.** Use only if you have created a binding vessel for this particular Gathering and all the participants who contributed donations of compounds earth to the binding vessel are present.
- **The two cardinal essences of the bird's-foot trefoil.** These will be combined to create the flower's complex during the Ritual.
- **Incense burner and charcoal or peat as fuel on which to place the flower essences.**
- **The Incense of the Bird's Foot Trefoil.** The incense will energize and balance the flower's complex as it is crafted.
- **Cleansing cloths.** As many as you feel are necessary.

The ritual begins with the priestess raising her sensory awareness using the inverted triangular pyramid working. She then casts a triple-cast Circle of a suitable size. As each of the participants enters the Circle, they extend their arms to each side, level with their shoulders, passing each hand quickly through the flames of the two portal candles, a symbolic final purification of the body. Once all are inside the Circle, the priestess seals the Circle with the triple seal. The participants are now enclosed within the protective Circle and are ready to begin the sex magic ritual.

The priestess stands in front of the working stone, facing the Gathering, and says:

"You are welcome among friends. May each welcome the other as we gather here together."

As this is said, the participants of the Gathering mingle, greeting each other with a handshake, hug, or whatever gesture feels comfortable at the time. The priestess also walks among the Gathering and greets everyone in the same way. She then returns to the working stone.

The participants of the Gathering (including the Principal Conduit) sit on the ground facing the working stone.

The priestess stands before the working stone and brings the first of the candles, the collective energy candle, to the front of the stone. She lights the candle, raises it into the air, and says:

"As this flame burns, so we converge with the collective energy. Our energies mingle, our potential becomes one."

The "flame of the collective energy" candle is placed at the back, in the center, of the working stone.

The priestess then lights the sun, or male, candle, holds it up, and says:

"As this flame burns it binds us with the sun. We invoke the sun's influence upon our workings."

The "flame of the sun" candle is placed to the left and slightly forward of the "flame of the collective energy" candle.

She then lights the third and final moon or female candle, holds it up, and says:

"As this flame burns I bind myself with the moon. I invoke the moon's influence upon all I do."

The "flame of the moon" candle is placed to the right and slightly in front of the "flame of the collective energy" candle, forming the candle triangle.

You will see that this third invocation is a personal one. If the ritual is facilitated by the male, then the moon candle is lit before the sun candle, and this same personal invocation is given for the sun candle.

Note also that it is the "flame" of the candle that holds the name and is important, not the candle itself.

With all three candle flames lit, the priestess stands before them at the front and center of the working stone and extends her arms out so that each of her palms is directly above each of the sun and moon flames, close enough to feel the heat of the flames without burning her palms. She then brings both hands together above the central collective energy flame to form a cup shape above the flame, saying:

"I unite all things with the collective energy, as in nature they belong. I offer myself to this union, together with all those present here. Unite us in your common bond."

This opening part of the ritual, called the "uniting of the flames," is now complete.

If the Gathering has a previously crafted binding vessel, the priestess now lifts it aloft, saying:

"This binding vessel binds all present to one. I now bind it to the united flames as a symbol of our affinity."

She passes the binding vessel quickly through each of the three flames, then places it in the center of the candle triangle, at the base of the "flame of the collective energy" candle. As we have seen previously, the center point of a triangle is a power point.

The preparation of the working stone is now complete.

The next step of the ritual is the giving and receiving of the first libation. The first libation is a liquid one, usually a mixture of metheglin and poteen. Some Gatherings use mead or a mixture of mead and poteen; others use wine, cider, ale, or whatever is favored by the participants. The advantage of metheglin is that it can be fermented with whatever herbs, spices, and flowers you feel have the appropriate attributes for your working. Whichever libation is chosen, an amount sufficient for all the participants is placed in the chalice before the ritual starts.

The libation may be served cold or warm. To warm the libation, follow the directions in part 1.

The priestess positions the chalice and a number of libation goblets at the front and center of the working stone. With her hands on either side of the chalice, she says:

"To welcome all here I offer this libation."

Taking the chalice ladle, she ladles a small amount of the libation into one of the libations goblets. Raising the goblet into the air with both hands, she says:

"What we have taken from the earth, we share with the earth. Whatever we take to ourselves we return threefold."

Having said this, she pours the contents of the goblet onto the ground in three successive parts.

The priestess then fills sufficient goblets with the libation and they are passed among the participants of the Gathering, each of whom takes his or her fill. There need not be a separate goblet for each participant. If the goblets are of a normal size, one goblet will contain sufficient libation for three participants. If the goblets run dry before all have had their fill, they can be returned to the priestess and refilled.

The priestess retains one goblet for herself and drinks her libation from it.

The goblets are returned to the priestess, who wipes them quickly with a cleansing cloth and returns them to the working stone.

The priestess must now prepare the convocation stone to receive the Principal Conduit.

She then speaks the spell for the first time. The Gathering already knows the spell and will have committed it to memory. For the sake of simplicity we shall just call it "the spell."

The priestess says:

"The spell."

The Principal Conduit repeats the spell three times:

"The spell; the spell; the spell."

The priestess, picking up her wand and cauldron, walks to the convocation stone where the Principal Conduit now lies and says:

"Our Principal Conduit is David. Through him we shall cast and bind our spell."

She sprinkles the Principal Conduit with the moon-cleansed water, using her wand to do so. As she does this, she says:

"I anoint you, David, and commit my efforts to your internal energy."

As the preparation of the working stone is now complete. The priestess must now prepare the convocation stone to receive the Principal Conduit.

Picking up her wand in her right hand (or in her left if she is left-handed), the priestess moves to the convocation stone. Extending her wand above the stone, she walks around it three times, saying quietly to herself:

"I invoke only what is good, I intend only what is beneficial, I banish all that is unwelcome."

The priestess then returns to the working stone, picks up the cauldron with the moon-cleansed water, and returns to the convocation stone. Again she walks three times around the stone, but this time she dips the tip of the wand into the water and sprinkles drops of it on the stone as she walks. She again says:

"I invoke only what is good, I intend only what is beneficial, I banish all that is unwelcome."

She returns the cauldron to the working stone and stands with her back to it, facing the center of the Circle. She says, in a loud voice:

"Come forward who wishes to lie here."

The Principal Conduit approaches the priestess and says:

"That is I."

The priestess says:

"And are you named?"

If the Principal Conduit has already been named, then his name is spoken. We shall use the name "David" for the sake of this example.

The Principal Conduit (David) says:

"Yes, my name is David. I wish to lie here."

The priestess says:

"Then as I know your name to be David, take your place as it is offered."

David then takes his place on the convocation stone, with his head at the center point of the Circle and his feet facing the working stone. This means that he is lying in the south/north orientation, so the energies will flow through him from his head to his feet, aiding the projection of generated energy from his body.

The priestess now stands between the two stones, facing the center of the Circle, and says:

"I welcome all those who wish us well. We are gathered with the intention of creating change. Change that offers benefit and goodwill. Our spell is crafted and I offer it to you."

At this point the priestess speaks the spell for the first time. The Gathering, in this case just her partner, already know the spell and will have committed it to memory. In this case the spell is focused on the male subject, David, whose sexual energies we are intending to rebalance.

A typical spell for these circumstances would be as follows:

"We call upon the collective energy and the four elemental energies to assist us in our work. David seeks a balance in his internal order, one that reflects the balance present in nature. Restore to him what was once his, restore the harmony of his being and the natural potency of his internal energy."

For the sake of simplicity we shall just call it "the spell."

The priestess says:

"The spell."

The Principal Conduit repeats the spell three times.

"The spell; the spell; the spell."

The priestess, picking up her wand and cauldron, walks to the convocation stone where the Principal Conduit is now lying and says:

"Our Principal Conduit is David. Through him we shall together cast this spell and bind it to him."

She then sprinkles the Principal Conduit with the moon-cleansed water using her wand to do so. As she does this, she says:

"I anoint you David and commit my efforts to your internal energy."

The cauldron and the wand are placed back upon the working stone, and the crafting of the complex and the libation begins.

The complex is crafted by uniting the flower's two cardinal essences in the same method as described in the previous section entitled "The Amalgamation of the Two Cardinal Essences of the Flower to Form Its Complex." This ritual working must be carried out in its entirety, including the initial purification processes, in order for the complex to be properly empowered. Sufficient amount of the empowered complex to create a mixture of 1 part complex to 5 parts moon-cleansed water is then placed into a suitable ritual vessel.

The vessel containing the flower's complex is now placed at the front and center of the working stone, and the chalice containing the moon-cleansed water for the libation is placed next to it.

The priestess lifts the vessel containing the complex in both hands and as she pours the complex into the chalice of moon-cleansed water she says:

"I craft this libation with the complex of the flower, whose energies and attributes I imbue upon all who partake of it."

Having mixed the complex and moon-cleansed water she partially fills a goblet with the mixture using the ladle.

The priestess turns to face the Gathering and pours the contents of the Goblet onto the ground in three successive pourings. As she does this, she says:

"I return what has been given threefold and in good faith, may it always be so."

She then replaces the goblet on the working stone, lifts both hands high into the air, and says:

"We share the gift, we take its complex within us and about us. We begin the work of empowerment."

The libation in the chalice is then ladled into the waiting goblets and distributed to the participants in the Gathering, who drink their fill.

The priestess retains one goblet, then drinks a small amount of the libation before passing the goblet to the Principal Conduit David, who drinks the remainder.

As the seven successions of the Projection Cycle have been explained in detail in the previous section of this book, we will concentrate here on the aspects of the ritual involving the use of the flower's complex in its various carriers.

As the Gathering progresses through the first three successions of the Awakening, Augmentation, and Intensification, a variety of techniques may be employed to arouse and stimulate the Principal Conduit, the priestess, and the other participants in the Gathering.

What follows is just an example of a typical progression and is only to be considered as a guide. There is no set format to this part of the ritual and it is for the priestess to judge the most appropriate and effective methods. Each priestess will develop her own repertoire of techniques and actions together with a sensibility in relation to what is or is not acceptable.

Before the Awakening begins, as small, pre-arranged group of participants will join the Priestess and congregate around the Principal Conduit on the convocation stone. The purpose of this small group is to help the priestess in her work and assist in stimulating the Principal Conduit, the priestess, and each other.

The Awakening usually involves a gentle and sensuous awakening of the sexual senses. It may involve entire Gathering moving from one person to another, caressing them, gently stimulating each other, and arousing other members of the Gathering in whatever way they feel is mutually appropriate.

The pre-prepared unguent is applied to the bodies and genitals of both the Principal Conduit and the priestess. These may be applied by hand and/or exchanged bodily massage. It can also involve gentle oral stimulation of the sensitive areas and genitalia. The other participants of the Gathering will also be stimulating each other, though they will not be using the unguent as this is intended for the Principal Conduit and priestess only.

This is always a slow buildup of sexual awareness, a gentle introduction to the pleasures to come, and should result only in a simple arousal. It is the opportunity to get to know your own body and that of the others participating in the ritual. The emphasis is on slow, sensual movement, gentle physical contact, incorporating the use of the fingertips, tongue, nipples, lips, and so on. It can be enhanced by the use of perfumed oils, incense, and sensual music.

As the ritual progresses to the Augmentation Succession, the form of stimulation may change. The slow sensuality may become more physical. At this stage the Principal Conduit and the priestess will be masturbating themselves and/or each other, as will the other participants, who by now will have formed smaller active groups. This is also the time when individuals may part company in order to provide their partner(s) with more visual stimuli. This can range from watching each other masturbate and stimulate themselves, to using a phallus on and in themselves, to erotic dance and other forms of exhibitionism.

Physical behavior may also form an important stimulus. This is where the actions of the priestess play a role. This is also where body decoration and body adornment become important to some. Fetish adornment and accessories may work in a suitable Gathering or, alternatively, submissive, innocent behavior and body language may also stimulate some individuals. On some occasions I have even seen independent, professional erotic dancers employed to provide stimulation during the Augmentation Succession.

As the priestess takes the Gathering past the threshold into the Intensification Succession, the stimulation, both visual and physical, becomes more intimate, involving more close physical contact, more intense physical arousal, and even greater heights of pleasure requiring even greater self-control.

The contact becomes much more physical, the passion becoming much more intense. This is the time for close physical interaction. Both the priestess and Principal Conduit may lay on the convocation stone together as they intensify each other's sexual stimulation and the surrounding participants assist. This is the stage where the unguent is used to greatest effect upon the Principal Conduit.

As the Principal Conduit is in this case male, the priestess may position herself between the male's legs and, bending over the convocation stone, take his penis in her mouth, while using her hands to massage his testicles, stomach, and nipples using the unguent. One of the priestess's hands may also be used to insert a phallus into the male's anus and reciprocate it, again using the unguent as a lubricant. Alternatively the priestess may gently bite the nipples of the male as she masturbates his penis using the unguent as a sensual lubricant.

Another alternative is for the priestess to sit over the male in the opposite direction, with her vagina just above the male's face, while she bends over and takes his penis in her mouth. This is a particularly good position for her to stimulate his anus with her fingers or a phallus, using the unguent as a lubricant. At the same time the male may stimulate the priestess's vagina with mouth, fingers and phallus.

Various methods of penetration are also utilized at this stage, vaginal, anal, and oral, by both priestess and Principal Conduit. Multiple penetration of the priestess is an option using the penis and phallus in any combination. In all these situations the unguent may again be used as a lubricant.

These ideas are just put forward to illustrate the level of intensity of the contact between the priestess and the male. Many other positions are possible, and there are a great variety of source materials from which these imaginative positions may be drawn. The point is that both individuals should be doing their utmost to ensure the maximum stimulation of the other.

There will be innumerable approaches to the threshold of the Quickening and the same amount of retreats, until eventually the priestess, and only the priestess, will decide to commit to the Quickening. Commitment to the Quickening is irreversible and only the priestess may decide to progress to the next succession of the Projection Cycle.

It is worth remembering here that in this case we are focusing only on the physical and sensual elements of the ritual. You must not however forget the duality of the approaching orgasm and the need to recall and invoke your spell. The principle of duality in this context is explained in detail in my previous publication *Celtic Sex Magic.* Duality is, in simple terms, the practiced ability to focus in a balanced way on two functions simultaneously. They may be functions of the body, mind, or spirit, or any combination of the same. In this case the two functions are the physical progression toward the desired orgasm along with the mental/spiritual endeavor of projecting the spell or intention. An example of a physical duality would be the two hands of a pianist, each playing different notes in different formations independent of each other, yet combining to produce a single tune. To the nonplayer, this seems difficult if not impossible, but to the practiced pianist, it becomes second nature. As with the pianist, practice enables the sex magic practitioner to achieve this duality and establish it as second nature.

As the priestess identifies that the Quickening is approaching she begins to massage the Principal Conduit's penis, scrotum, and anus with the Evaporation. This is done by pouring a little of the evaporation liquid into her cupped hand and applying it to the entire genital region. As the evaporation is applied it evaporates (as the name implies) and the cooling, stimulating effect of the evaporation stimulates the Principal Conduit even more. The complex, however, does not evaporate, but becomes absorbed by the skin, allowing its energies and attributes to be assimilated into the Principal Conduit's own internal energy. This final stage of stimulation is usually more than enough to ensure that the Principal Conduit is brought to the point of no return and is committed to the orgasm.

The priestess and the Principal Conduit have now committed to the Quickening. This is the point where the approaching orgasm in inevitable and very imminent. Hopefully, their impending orgasm has been synchronized with each other and the other participants in the Gathering by the cycle of repeatedly approaching and retreating from the threshold of the Quickening.

As all the parties commit to the Quickening, the priestess says:

"The Quickening is here!"

As soon as she has said this all the parties begin to chant the spell repeatedly, increasing in speed and volume as the orgasm approaches.

If any pairs are coupled when the priestess acknowledges the Quickening, the pair separate and lay together to reach orgasm. Individuals, including the priestess, Principal Conduit, and the priestess's assistants, may augment each other's stimulation by continued contact but no one must ever reach orgasm while coupled.

It is possible for all of the parties to synchronize their orgasm by synchronizing their chanting of the spell. Their rhythm increasing in speed and volume as the orgasm arrives.

The arrival of the orgasm and the projection of the generated energy are marked by the shouting of the spell by the entire Gathering as the energy is projected. The vocalization of the spell at high volume assists and magnifies the power of the projection and the potency of the spell.

Once the projection is complete and the orgasm subsides it is the role of the priestess and her assistants to maintain and fuel the generated energy's journey by further, sympathetic stimulation of the male Principal Conduit.

In the circumstances described here, that is, the priestess and the male Principal Conduit, the favored position for this continued stimulation is as mentioned above, with the priestess standing between the male's legs, stimulating his penis in her mouth and the testes and anus with her fingers. This is the time when she returns to the use of the unguent to lubricate and gently stimulate the Principal Conduit. This is done gently and sympathetically so as not to distract the male during his visualized journey.

The other participants in the Gathering are at this point also gently stimulating each other in order to prolong their state of sexual pleasure.

Once the Principal Conduit has "returned" from his journey, all parties separate.

Following the period of relaxation the Principal Conduit and the other participants return to their original place, seated on the ground facing the working stone, and the priestess stands in front of the working stone facing the center of the Circle.

The priestess now begins the group congress. This is where the spell is reinforced by the communal invocation of the entire Gathering. She chants the spell and the Gathering repeats it. This is done three times, then the priestess says:

"The spell is cast. The spell is bound. Let it run its course and let no one interfere!"

This is the final part of the Projection Cycle and the confirmation of the spell.

The priestess and her assistants then distribute the final libation, which usually consists of a liquid libation (as with the opening libation, the drink does not include the complex), together with a baked libation.

Once the libation is assembled and before it is distributed, the priestess stands before the Gathering, lifts her arm into the air, and says:

"Take of food, drink, and hospitality; nature rewards those who help her in her work."

The libation is then distributed. This is a social activity and the priestess and Principal Conduit circulate around the Gathering, discussing the events that have just taken place, or any other appropriate topic.

If there are no other matters to be attended to within the Protective Circle, the ritual may then come to an end. To do this the priestess again stands before the working stone, facing the assembled Gathering. She lifts her arms into the air and says:

"The task is complete; our work has ended. And so we scatter."

The working stone candles are extinguished and the Circle is unsealed and erased.

The ritual site is dismantled and the gift left for nature as the participants depart the site.

This then completes the sex magic ritual for a group or Gathering.

By using the complex of the bird's-foot trefoil flower throughout this ritual we have, by our work, enhanced and reinforced all the activities that we have undertaken. By using different complexes it is possible to emphasise any aspect of the nature of the work of the ritual or the spell that we choose.

You may have recognized that, as with all sex magic rituals, there are many opportunities for you to personalize the facilitation, make it your own unique activity, and use your own individual phrases. The only governing factors have been emphasised both here and in the previous section. Outside of these imperatives, you are free to interpret the ritual in your own special way.

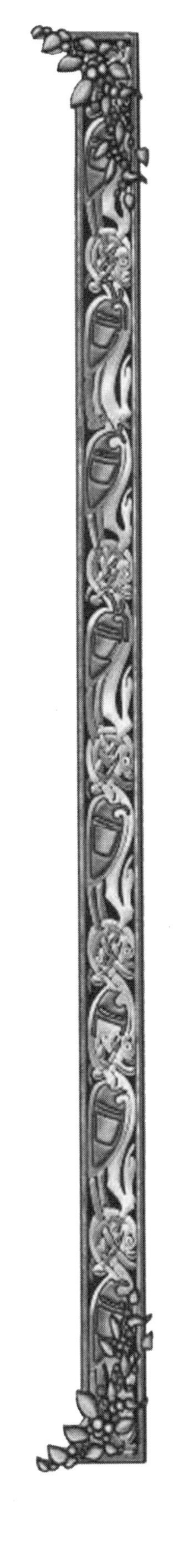

Druid or Alchemist? A Conclusion

From the very first sentence of this book we have undertaken a journey of exploration and discovery. By comparing the ancient and arcane traditions of Druidism and alchemy we have discovered a common, underlying thread. A thread that history tells us could not have developed through mutual discussion or by the sharing of the knowledge of the ancients, as we must acknowledge that there was little, if no contact between the civilizations involved in nurturing the two traditions.

The origins of both traditions are unknown, lost in myth and fable. Druidism evolved within the Celtic nations while the various schools of alchemy developed in Egypt, India, China, and later in Europe. It is fair to say that, due in part to their varying histories, Druidism and alchemy have evolved in different directions, each taking the course determined for it by nature. Alchemy has its inner and outer elixirs; Druidism has its physical and spiritual/magical attributes. The wording is different, but the meaning is very much the same. Druidism works with its complexes while alchemy has its quintessence and philosopher's stone. In both cases we are referring to the same sublime elixir, the ultimate essence of the power and balance of nature.

There are also some remarkable differences. The Druidic tradition, for example, has no equivalent to the alchemist's elevation of materials, the Greater Circulation, the quest to turn base metals into gold. But even this pursuit, which has been ridiculed and reduced to a caricature of the true alchemist, when translated into the

metaphorical elevation of the impure body into the refined spiritual being has its equivalent philosophy within Druidic lore.

The methods of work and the techniques employed by both traditions vary considerably. Druidism has little mention of distillation in its workings, while this is the main technique of the alchemist. Similarly, many of the spiritual/magical elements of alchemy have been understandably abandon, while they are always the fundamental element of all Druidic plant lore.

When we look at the Lesser Circulation of alchemy and the work of the spagyric practitioner in particular, we see so much in common with Druidic plant lore that it is difficult to imagine that both traditions developed totally independent of each other, but this is surely the case. Many of the same plants are used for the same purposes, and both traditions extend the use of plants beyond the sphere of the herbalist and homeopathic practitioner. But once again there are also profound differences. The species of plants used by the spagyric are much more exotic, reflecting no doubt the countries of origin of the various schools of the tradition. The techniques of the Lesser Circulation are much harsher, and again we see the use of repeated distillation. And finally, once again the spiritual/magical aspect has been all but abandoned.

So then, as a lifelong Druidic practitioner, what have I gained from this exploration, how will it help me (and the reader) to become a better Druid?

The answer is not a simple one.

By repeating many of the alchemical experiments I have learned about, I have without doubt gained a greater understanding of the work I undertake day by day in my own workshop. My research and experimentation has also revealed to me a number of "missing links," gaps in Druidic plant lore theory that have grown, generation upon generation, or have been distorted by well-meaning Druidic tutors who, because of the times they lived in, had no scientific understanding of how or why what they were doing worked so well.

By comparing these traditions I have come to understand that they all embrace the true nature of humankind. They each reflect and address the needs of humanity within our natural environment, and they all hold us responsible, not only for our own well-being but also for that of our environment and planet.

For me, the journey has also redefined the legitimacy of my Druidic beliefs and practices. Proving that the Druidic tradition has a fundamental role to play in the life and nature of humankind.

Researching and writing this book has been a watershed in my relationship with my belief system. It has given me moments of despair on the one hand and blinding revelations and insights on the other.

The Druidic tradition has an built-in "self-evaluation" system, taught by Druidic masters and tutors to their new initiates over the millennia. Every seven years all Druids are required to stand outside themselves and look at their relationships with their belief system, their community, and the Gatherings with which they work. It is an opportunity for each individual to revisit all of his or her work, motives, and beliefs in a way that few other belief systems provide.

This undertaking is called *myfi fy hun* in Welsh, which loosely translates as simply "myself" in English, and that is exactly what it is. An opportunity to define what I think and know about myself.

The process is a long one, using a number of self-facilitated rituals, meditation techniques, and complexes. It is a time for what may be called "soul-searching" or the exploration of one's inner energies. The results of this process are intended to inform one's activities and learning for the following seven years, until the tradition demands the process to be undertaken once more.

Over the forty or so years of my involvement as a practicing Druid I have undertaken this process at least five times (if my math is correct), and on most of these occasions it has proven to be a difficult and exhausting task.

It is not my intention to give a detailed account of the process—there is insufficient room to do so, nor is it directly related to the subject matter of this book. I mention it only to underscore the profound effect that researching and writing this book has had upon "myself."

The decision to write this book came from *myfi fy hun,* as part of a larger decision to explore the validity of Druidic plant lore and to expose myself to the knowledge and experience of other traditions.

The decision has led me to more "how's" and "why's" than I ever imagined it would, and the journey has given me a greater insight and understanding of the Druidic tradition. It has been a more revealing and rewarding experience than any *myfi fy hun* I have ever undertaken. It in fact has been a continuous two-year *myfi fy hun,* as the process has continued from the start to the finish of the book-writing period.

As to whether Druids are also alchemists, I believe they are—maybe more so in some areas than others, but we definitely have more in common than that which separates us. Does the combining of the traditions offer any improvement to one or the other? From the Druidic viewpoint, again my answer is yes. Alchemical writings fill in the missing gaps in the Druidic lore. Some alchemical uses of plants expand the Druidic theory and practice. The ancient alchemical relationships with Eastern belief systems provide knowledge and experience that may certainly inform the practices and theories of Celtic sex magic, and I would have to admit that my Druidic imagination, my *byd y breuddwyd,* remains intrigued by the theories of the Greater Circulation.

The concept of elevating, or in the Druidic tradition "refining," the base human to a sublime spiritual being, of stimulating the basic internal energy of a person to the point of spiritual perfection is worthy of further investigation. One of the main areas of Druidic practice that supports and employs this notion is sex magic, and, by now, having read this book, you will see that this is also very close to the Lesser Circulation of alchemy. Maybe further work to integrate the Greater Circulation of Alchemy with the inherent potency of Celtic sex magic will provide us with the sublime spiritual refinement: the Golden Orgasm.

Index

Please note that pages in italics indicate illustrations. Tables are indicated with a *t*.

Index

Index